SPEED DEMONS

STEVE HARMISON

MY AUTOBIOGRAPHY

SPEED*DEMONS*

STEVE HARMISON

MY AUTOBIOGRAPHY

Sport Media S

For Hayley, Emily, Abbie, Isabel and Charlie.
You make my life worthwhile.

HAR

Sport Media

Copyright © Steve Harmison

Written with John Woodhouse.

First published in Great Britain and Ireland in 2017 by Trinity Mirror Sport Media, PO Box 48, Old Hall Street, Liverpool, L69 3EB.

www.tmsportmedia.com
@SportMediaTM

Trinity Mirror Sport Media is a part of Trinity Mirror plc.
One Canada Square, Canary Wharf, London, E15 5AP.

1

Hardback ISBN: 978-1-910335-68-0
eBook ISBN 978-1-911613-00-8

Photographic acknowledgements:
Steve Harmison personal collection, Tony Woolliscroft, Mirrorpix, PA.

Book editing: Chris Brereton
Production: James Cleary
Jacket design: Rick Cooke & Chris Collins

Printed and bound by CPI Group (UK) Ltd, Croydon, CR0 4YY.

CONTENTS

THANKS

More than anything I'd like to thank my wife Hayley, my daughters Emily, Abbie and Isabel, and my son Charlie for being the most amazing family any man could ever wish for.

I would also like to thank my mam and dad Margaret and Jimmy for everything they have done for me. They are two great people and I cannot praise them enough. Hayley's parents, Sue and Mick, have also been incredibly supportive, while in the early years my uncles, Mel and Kevin, took me everywhere and helped me so much – thank you.

Thank you to Steve Williams and Michael Thewliss, invaluable in my early years at Ashington CC, a club that means so much to me and will always have a place in my heart.

Bedlington CC too will also always be special as it was where I played my first game of cricket. Thanks to Durham, the club to which I gave everything, and loved playing for, and in particular Geoff Cook, the man himself, who was always there for me, put up with a lot, and for whom I have absolute respect and trust. I wouldn't have achieved what I did in my career without him. Geoff, I am eternally grateful. Thank you also to all the players and coaches I have played with and for. They made the journey eventful and enjoyable all the way.

For their advice and guidance, Neil Fairbrother and International Sports Management have been an amazing support, as has John Morris. Thank you so much.

Trinity Mirror Sport Media gave me this chance to tell my story, and I would like to thank John Woodhouse, who helped me get my thoughts on paper, and editor Chris Brereton for their diligence and patience.

A special mention also to Opening Up Cricket, an incredibly worthwhile organisation promoting mental wellbeing and suicide prevention through cricket, as well as the PCA, which has been invaluable in spreading the message about mental health. Praise also to the Sir Bobby Robson Foundation which has done sterling work in helping cancer patients in the north-east.

To meet all I've encountered on this rollercoaster ride through life has been a privilege.

Steve Harmison, May 2017

FOREWORD BY
ANDREW FLINTOFF

Playing for England is obviously amazing.

You go to incredible places, meet incredible people, and all while representing your country at a sport you love. But there was one thing that made it extra special for me, and that was to do it with my best mate.

When me and Harmy walked off the pitch at the Oval after the final Ashes Test match in 2009, it was the end of something very special – we had been through so much, on and off the pitch. But that last game epitomised Harmy for me. He came up to me, with the ball in his hand, when he should have been bowling himself, and asked, "Do you want to bowl?" He did that because he recognised what that game meant for me. As it was, my knee had gone – I could barely stand, let alone bowl. But that was Harmy all over, selfless to the last. This was, after all, more than likely his last Test as well.

In this book, Steve talks about the help I've given him down the years, not so much on the pitch, but off it. But what people don't realise is, for all the help I've given him, he's given it back to me 10 times over. Genuinely, I owe him so much. The thing with professional sport is so much of it is about putting on an act, and that's what I did when I was having my own mental health problems. I'd pretend to be something I wasn't so people couldn't see what was happening in my head. The person people saw on the outside wasn't necessarily the person on the inside. Steve understood that. He thanks me for listening to him, being alongside him, when he was suffering, but in my darkest times he was the friend who was always there.

Steve is different to me in that he's never been anything but himself, and I don't think too many people can say that. When he was low you could see he was low. It's the hardest thing to see a friend go through that, to know what they're going through, but not able to do anything about it. Because, that's the truth, there's only so much you can do. No matter how much you'd like to, you can't wave a magic wand and make them better.

What I found doubly hard was that so often Steve was hung out to dry. No-one took the time to get to the bottom of what was happening with him. Instead, if England failed, it was easier to make him the scapegoat. It was easier to talk about what was happening in terms of homesickness rather than spending the time working with him to find out what exactly it was. People called it homesickness when in reality it was much more than that. People chose not to understand him. They looked the other way.

What amazes me is that we're not talking ancient history here – Steve's last Test was in 2009 – and yet so much has changed in the times since. Now, a mental health issue like Steve's would, I hope, be dealt with by patience and understanding. While, in Steve's day, it seemed barely anyone wanted to know, now mental health is a priority. There are people in professional cricket ready to delve deeper. There are people, and Steve is one of them, who will go round the counties and advise today's players on anxiety and depression. Again, he is giving something back.

I've known Steve now for 21 years. We've seen each other's families grow up. All the best points of my life, he's been involved in them. When I had my daughter, Holly, he was there at the birth – well, not quite, that would be taking friendship a bit far – what I mean is, he was the first person I celebrated and went for a drink with. Steve was an early starter on that front, a dad at 19 – "Steve, what are you doing!?" I consider him as family, and he considers me the same.

He's certainly changed a bit since I first clapped eyes on him when we got together for an England under-19 tour of Pakistan. I'd heard a bit about this kid from Durham who could bowl at 90 miles an hour. When up turned this tall gangly lad with long hair, I thought, 'Who the hell's this?' But it didn't take long to see we were two of a kind. Our backgrounds soon brought us close together, although when he then started knocking on my door in the middle of the night, I wasn't quite so sure what I'd let myself in for. Pakistan is a tough tour at any time, but even more so for Steve, who'd barely been out of Ashington at the time. He had a hard time on that trip and eventually came to my room and said he wanted to go home. He was very open and honest about how he felt, in a way that not many people would be, and I could see even then that what was troubling him was beyond homesickness. In the end, I wanted him to go home as well so I could get some sleep!

Pakistan was a difficult start for Steve, but I knew he'd be back. Players like him don't come along very often. I remember fielding at slip to him for the first time. The keeper and the other lads were standing way back. I was thinking, 'What's going on here?' Then he ran in and bowled – and it came through quicker than I'd ever seen. With his height and action, he had something unique.

Sometimes when we talk about mental health it can overshadow a player's achievements, it can become the way they are defined. That shouldn't happen to Steve – he was one of the greatest I, and England, have ever seen.

Harmy was integral in changing England into a successful team. It's my firm belief that it was his slower ball that got Michael Clarke at Edgbaston which won us the Ashes in 2005. I still don't know how he did it – he had a terrible slower ball. I was cringing when I saw him running in and realised he was going to do it.

It was Steve all over that he immediately shook hands with and consoled Brett Lee at the end. It was also him all over that the cameras missed it and captured me doing the same instead!

It's unfair that he then received so much stick for the wide ball he bowled first up at Brisbane in the Ashes of 2006-07. Looking back, I should have bowled that over. I could tell he was nervous and I should have taken the ball out of his hand and bowled myself. Again, it seemed to suit some people's narrative to have a go at Steve about that. It was one ball, it happens to us all. It showed the character of the man that again he came back.

Hand on heart, I can honestly say I wouldn't have been half the player I was if it hadn't have been for Steve, and also Marcus Trescothick, another who has had his difficulties. They were the two best players I turned out with for England by quite some distance. It was their brilliance which allowed me the freedom to be the player I was.

Harmy has done so much for me and my career, but he's helped so many others as well. When people talk about Steve Harmison as a bad tourist it makes me laugh. He was the saviour of so many England tours. His room was the centre of everything. People would stop by and have a handful of his Minstrels, a game of darts, and then he'd have his DVDs, *Auf Wiedersehen, Pet*, anything with a Geordie slant. We saw Jimmy Nail so often, it was like having him as 12th man.

If Steve had a fault, if it can be called a fault, it was that he was too generous. He would do anything to help anyone. He gave everything for coaches, captains, other players, the lot. Even people who treated him like rubbish he would do anything for, in life or in cricket. The shame was that not always in his career did he have that coming back, be it from players or coaches.

It would be true to say me and him have got in some scrapes down the years. I imagine he's come up with a few examples of his own in this book! But for all the glitz and the glamour of being an international sportsman, me and him are cut from the same cloth. We like the simple life, and that's probably the key to our relationship. We've always rather surrounded ourselves with family and friends than do all the other stuff, the nightclubs, the posh restaurants. He's grounded and proud of the area he's from, and I admire him for that.

I'm actually feeling quite emotional writing about Steve, because that's how much he means to me. He's someone I trust implicitly. When he says he's going to do something, you believe him.

I'm just lucky to have seen him in action first hand. For me, to go through my England career with my best mate at my side was what really made it special.

Yes, it wasn't always easy. Steve can be stubborn at times. In fact, when it comes to Harmy, my biggest achievement was to convince him that everything didn't have to come with oven chips. That took me 10 years. When I saw him eating sushi one day, I knew my work was done.

Andrew Flintoff, May 2017

1

AN ASHINGTON LAD ABROAD

"I was the number one bowler in the world. And that was as bad as it got"

St George's Park, Port Elizabeth, Friday, December 17, 2004

I'm stood at the top of my mark. St George's Park is waiting.

In this grand old stadium, sparkling stands of green, the England fans are buzzing, the South Africans less so – my opening partner, Matthew Hoggard, has just whipped out their captain, Graeme Smith, for a duck in the opening over.

All eyes are now on me. I'm the top-ranked bowler in the world. What am I going to do? How am I going to perform? Considering where I was two weeks ago, not collapsing in a heap would be an achievement.

In my mind I can see myself back in my car on the drive of my house in

Ashington, the old north-east mining town, and home to my entire world, everything I hold dear.

Behind the front door are my wife Hayley and our toddler Abbie. I have just said goodbye to them. I've done the same with our five-year-old daughter Emily that morning before she goes to school.

As I get in my car, that's when it really hits me. I don't want to go. I really don't want to go to South Africa.

In my sparkly new Volkswagen Tourag, the official sponsor car of the England team, I am sobbing my eyes out. It could be a battered old Polo for all I care.

For four days, I've been ill just thinking about this moment. The pains in my stomach are so bad I've had to lie on the floor, the lump in my throat so large I can hardly breathe.

At night, I lie there and stare into the dark. I am alone with my thoughts, and for me that's a dangerous place to be. Now, alone in my car, those thoughts are with me again. 'There are plenty of roundabouts on the short drive to Newcastle airport. What if I pull out on somebody at one? If I do it right, I'll buy myself another few days at home.'

I can only think so much. The unavoidable fact is the time has come. Even then, I can't move. It takes me three or four times just to get off the drive. My body won't do what my brain is telling it. 'Here I am,' I think. 'The top-ranked bowler on the planet. If people could see me now.'

Eventually, I manage to get the car into gear, put my foot on the accelerator, and set off. In my rear view mirror I can see our treasured four-bed house, with its pretty garden, overlooking the school, vanishing into the distance. Me and Hayley are both from humble beginnings, we moved here when we had Abbie and it's our everything.

As I drive, my head is whirring. All I can think is, 'How can I get out of this in the next 20 minutes before I pick up my dad?'

It's back to creating deliberate accidents, but somehow I make it to the American Air Filters factory where he works. I'll drive the rest of the way and then he'll take my car home.

The airport is only five minutes away and nothing much is said on the way. It doesn't need to be. Dad knows exactly how I'm feeling.

He knows I don't want to go and my mind is in a bad place. In the car, he does everything he can to make it as normal as possible, fiddles with the radio, turns the heater up and down. We've never really spoken about my issues but it's an unwritten thing that he knows.

He's seen it all before. He's heard me ring home in tears and knows the way I am. He understands this is not a good day for me and doesn't want to make it worse with a great fanfare at the airport.

That's why Hayley and our two girls aren't here. No way am I going to have them come to the airport with me. I've made that mistake before.

One of the first times I ever went away, to the England Cricket Academy, in Australia, Hayley and Emily came to the airport. It was a nightmare. So hard to say goodbye. It just made everything a million times worse. From that point on, that was it. No more. The days I leave have to be like any other. We do it this way every time I go away.

The airport's in front of us all too quick. I take the bags out the boot, and we shake hands. "Good luck," dad says. "See you later," and off he goes. Nothing more to it than that – keeping it as normal as possible.

At the airport, I meet my fellow Durham and England colleague Paul Collingwood. I'm glad for the company. I don't tell him how I'm feeling but having someone else there helps my anxiety drop a little.

The time it's worst is when I'm in my own head, on my own. That's when the other thoughts come. 'What's Hayley doing? What's Abbie doing? Emily? Where would I be now? Would I be doing this? Doing that?' It weighs you down. A mental lead weight.

We take the shuttle down to Heathrow and meet the rest of the tour party at an airport hotel. There we have all our bags checked in so we don't have to do it at the airport. We're pampered us cricketers, we can just get straight on the plane, although on this occasion I'd have welcomed the delay.

I don't know if anybody can see I'm distressed. I've got quite good at hiding it down the years, but, even so, whether people notice or not isn't really a concern.

I'm not bothered what other people are wondering about where I'm at. All I'm bothered about is where I really am at. If I'm bothered about what other people are thinking, it'll only make it a thousand times worse. There's only me who is in the situation, only me who can deal with the situation, only me who can get out of the situation.

Anyway, now I'm with the group I start feeling better. It's when I'm away from the other players that I start to think about things I shouldn't.

At Heathrow, I'm meeting a journalist for a chat about the trip. I'm away from the rest of the team and again it's a chance for unwelcome thoughts to return – where I'd rather be, the simple fact that I'm missing my family. Have you ever tried to tell a five-year-old that daddy's not going to be home for weeks on end?

At that moment I really wish I wasn't a cricketer. I really wish I'd stayed working in the factory with my dad. This feels like the worst day I've ever had.

Walking through Heathrow, I'm in a daze, but it's not far off Christmas and I can tell other people are happy. They're going places they want to go. They're probably going off to see their families.

Occasionally, someone recognises me and wishes me good luck, but none of it really registers. All I'm doing is walking, concentrating on not cracking. 'I'm not giving in,' I tell myself. 'I'm not giving in.'

While I'm still in England, the possibility is always there that I might cave in to these feelings and I will not let them beat me. Once I get on the plane the decision is taken for me. I'm captive. I'm going. There's nothing I can do about it. Planes don't turn round. They don't come back.

I have a quick couple of pints to calm myself, then it's on to the flight. We're in alphabetical order so I'm sat next to Matthew Hoggard.

Sometimes that's good, sometimes it's bad. Once on the way to Australia he sat staring at me for 18 hours with his middle finger in the air. I don't share anything with Hoggy about how I feel. It's not that I don't think he'll understand – there's a lot more to Hoggy than meets the eye – it's more about not wanting to show your weaknesses to the group.

Before you know it, questions are being asked about whether

you should be playing. There can be repercussions, so I try not to let it out too much. Truth is, though, there are tears in my eyes.

I'm really struggling. I'm really finding it hard to control my emotions. As we taxi down the runway and leave the ground I try not to cry, but I can't help it. It feels like everything I love is being left behind. It's all gone.

It's a night flight so the lights are off, it's quiet, there's no entertainment. I never find it easy to sleep, and this is no exception. It seems to go on forever, just me and my mental torment, until finally the sleeping pills I've taken kick in. I'm woken a few hours later with a bump. A horrible bump. We've landed.

It's a big moment. I'm hoping this will be the time when my brain starts telling itself there's no way back but from previous episodes I know mental health problems don't turn around that quick.

As I wait by the baggage carousel, it's soon apparent my bag has gone missing. The way I'm feeling I'll be back in England before it arrives. We're bussed right into the middle of Johannesburg where we're staying at the plush Sandton Hotel, which itself is in a shopping centre. I'm doing anything and everything to divert my mind away from negative thoughts and I walk round the shops for hours with Andrew Flintoff and Rob Key.

I've known these two for years, we've grown up in cricket together. They're beyond friends, they're family. Between us there's an unspoken knowledge of what's going on. Fred and Keysey are trying to stick with me, make sure I don't go on a downward spiral.

They keep suggesting things – going for something to eat, maybe the cinema – anything to stop me retreating into my own head. I leave them in a shop at one point to go outside to phone home.

When I get through, I can hear Abbie shouting, "Daddy! Home! Daddy! Home!" Hayley does her best to reassure me that they're all OK, that I'll be OK, but even so I'm in tears when I come back into the store. Fred and Keysey can sympathise, they can be mates, but there's only so much they can do. I feel worse than ever.

We head back to the hotel. Everything is getting on top of me and I go to my room feeling anxious and depressed. I feel totally overwhelmed by what's going on in my head. I feel panicky and really negative about myself.

I ring home again and this time Emily answers. Then I hear Abbie in the background. She's fallen over and is screaming "Daddy! Daddy!" so Emily rings off. I feel even worse, even further away and even more unable to do anything.

A few minutes later Hayley rings and tells me they thought Abbie had broken her arm, but she's started to move it and it's OK. I'm relieved, but the tears come again. That must be 10 times since we landed and I'm seriously thinking about my future in the game.

Something has to give, and right now I want to go home.

I'll give it until the last practice day in Johannesburg and if I haven't improved I'll leave the tour. That will be the end of my international career. I'll never be seen again. There'll be no understanding, no second chances.

That'll be it, right there, gone.

And with all this whirring around my head, here I am, at St George's Park with thousands watching, attempting to do the day job.

2

GROWING PAINS

"I didn't know what I was doing. It all happened so quickly"

I never set out to be a cricketer.

Bowling in a Test match for England was never even part of a dream when I was a kid.

Harmison was a football name in Ashington, which itself was a football town, having produced not just two World Cup winners in Bobby and Jackie Charlton, but the legendary England and Newcastle United centre-forward Jackie Milburn too.

The Harmisons never quite reached those heights, but my dad Jimmy did play centre-half for Ashington and Blyth Spartans, and had a proper crack at a career in the game with Yeovil Town, whose manager at the time was from the north-east and who he knew well.

He quit his job down Ashington pit and him, my mam Margaret, and their toddler Steve upped sticks to Somerset.

There's a picture of me at Yeovil's Huish Park ground when I'm 18-months-old dressed in their green and white strip. That was in 1979-80, the very first year of the National League, now the Conference, effectively Division 5, and dad got a job down there as a fitter at Westland Helicopters to make it all happen.

In Jimmy's day, Yeovil were a good non-league side and he played against Norwich in the FA Cup third round. There was mention of a couple of clubs coming in for him while he was down there.

Cardiff was talked about, but my mam couldn't settle away from Ashington. The decision was made when Yeovil played Blyth Spartans away in the FA Trophy and we all came back and stayed in Ashington for the weekend. That was it then, mam and dad could see how much they missed the place. Their minds were made up.

As soon as the draw came out, the Yeovil manager said that would happen, and he was right. When the Ashington FC boss found out that Jimmy was going to be available again, he had a removals van down at their house in Yeovil in two days. He also got Jimmy his old job back at the pit. The Harmisons returned and everyone resumed the life they had before. Jimmy wasn't alone in playing for Ashington, his brothers Mel and Kevin played for the club, and I turned out for them as well as my brothers Ben and James.

All the above, and my half-brother Darren, have also played on a Sunday morning for Ashington and District Royal Antediluvian Order of Buffaloes Club – you can see why we call it the Buffs.

The Buffs team has been in existence for more than 40 years and every season they've had at least one Harmison in the side. There were occasions when the team would include Jimmy, his three sons and his two brothers. Six Harmisons on the team sheet. Beat that. I'm surprised my sister Joanne didn't get in on the act.

I didn't know Darren existed until I was 12. Dad had been married before, at a very young age, and had Darren back then. I don't know the full story and have never asked.

I just got told by mum that I'd got a half-brother and he had a different surname. I didn't meet him until I was 17. I was always intrigued to, but I didn't even know if he knew we existed. At home we never broached the subject. Eventually we were introduced.

Darren lived in a little village up the road and once he got to know us all, he changed his name to Harmison. From that point on, whenever he met us, we all had the same attitude, "Let's look forward, not back."

I don't see Darren as much as I do James and Ben, but I still think of him as my brother, a brother who just happened to come into our lives later.

I'm so pleased he has, because he's got a great family and four lovely children. It could have been a problem, where the situation was frosty, but I'm so glad it's not.

You might by now have worked out that mine was a big family and a close family. We were brought up brilliantly. It was a working-class background, we didn't have a great deal, but mam and dad gave us everything they could. Mam's a natural carer, that's why she's a district nurse, and probably always will be.

The way it worked in our house was that mam told us what to do and dad made us do it! The loving of both parents was undoubted, as was the support. Everybody's mam and dad are great, but mine were special.

Ashington was a tough place to grow up, tough because of what was happening. It was once known as the largest pit village in the world, things had been relatively rosy round here, lads had money in their pockets, shoes on their feet, full bellies.

But in the '80s, things were changing. Industry in the north-east was being decimated, and the pit was employing hundreds instead of thousands.

The miners' strike in 1984 was a last-ditch attempt to save it. I was six when the strike happened, I don't remember much about it but I do know it was tough. My dad worked at Ellington pit just up the road, a massive colliery which went right out under the North Sea.

He drove the diesels, and was out on strike for the full year. Overnight, he'd gone from earning a wage to practically nothing. Mam and dad would sometimes sacrifice their own food to make sure their kids had some on their plate. Elsewhere in Ashington, people were relying on food banks. They had virtually nothing at all.

We were lucky because mam still had her job and so there was still one wage coming in, and I was lucky because I had dad at home for a year. The strike ended in 1985 and dad marched proudly back to work, through Ashington and then the four miles on up to Ellington.

It was a time when the family had really pulled together and stayed solid. Others were ripped apart when family members broke the strike and went back to work early. For some, even now, those scars have never healed.

In Ashington, the last coal was mined in 1988. For the town to go from vibrant pit community to nothing was tragic, absolutely tragic, and in some ways it's never really recovered.

I love the place but I still worry about it now. Like a lot of areas in the north-east, Ashington has been forgotten about. My dad would go on to be a shot-blaster at American Air Filters, and now works driving massive JCBs with wheels bigger than me. He knows what it's like to have the frustration of not working though. He had five years where he couldn't when he had both ankles fused, and both knees replaced due to arthritis. He's a proud man and it knocked him not being able to work, which is probably why, even now, in his sixties, he carries on. Make no mistake, he's fit. Not only has he played football and cricket all his life but he used to run miles and miles. We always ask him when he's going to give work up. "Never," he says. "I enjoy it too much."

I had no idea where I'd end up working but it was pretty obvious from a young age that I wasn't going to be academic. I was a very slow learner.

Reading and writing was always the problem. Even now, while I can read, I would never dream of reading something out loud. No way. I just wouldn't feel confident doing it. I'd rather face Brett Lee at 90 miles an hour. That's how uncomfortable I am with that kind of thing.

People have said since that maybe I was – am – dyslexic. I don't know whether I am or not. I've never seen anyone to say for sure. Either way, I struggled to read, still do to some degree. When it came to anything academic, the easy thing was always to run away from it – and that's what I did.

When I moved up to Ashington High School, I pretty much stopped going. I tried to jump out my mam's car once at 10 miles an hour to avoid it. She had to drag me up the street and into school. I hated it, absolutely hated it. When I did turn up, I spent most of my time sat in a corridor.

I'd deliberately get myself sent out of lessons. I saw more of the corridors than the classrooms. I wasn't the greatest at school, I must admit, but I wasn't really disruptive. The only person I was disruptive to was myself. I've always had a bit of a problem with authority. I don't know why, probably because I'm stubborn, but that and the reading and writing problems meant I was never going to be in love with Ashington High.

When I was 12, I stopped staying at home. Both my granddads died when I was young and my grandma had more recently been living with a nice old chap called Bob, and then he died too.

We lived in the next street – we were in Eighth Row and my grandma in Ninth Row. These houses were all built to serve the pit and that's why they were so named. Rows one to six had been knocked down for a new road to go through.

When Bob died, my mam and dad suggested I go and stay with her for a few days to make sure she was OK. It seemed a good idea to me. Grandma was getting some company, I had my own bedroom, I was getting fed in two places, and it was just round the corner.

I ended up staying for five years! In the morning I'd go home, get a lift to school, bunk off, spend all day doing my own thing, and then go back to grandma's to sleep at night.

There were times where my attendance rate was 100 percent, but what I'd do was go in, get my registration mark, and clear off. It was easy. Later, I would stay with mam and dad more.

They moved to a new house 150 yards from the school's front door. I'd listen out for the bell, walk across, go through registration, and then go home again.

Sometimes I bunked off with a few mates and we'd go and play snooker down one of the clubs. Because we were all tall kids, whenever anybody asked we'd say we were sixth formers and had got a free lesson. But a lot of the time I bunked off I was on my own. The school would never have my parents in because neither the school, nor my parents, knew I wasn't there. It was never like mam and dad went into parents' evenings – those letters never got home.

Sport was the only thing I went into school for. It was how I found my way. Sport, sport, sport.

It was the only thing I was interested in. Mainly we played football. When it came to cricket, there were two games a year, and that was only if you won the first, because it was a cup competition. I used to play football with the teacher who did the cricket. "You pick the team," he'd tell me. "I'll drive the bus" – the reason being that by the time I went to Ashington High, I was already playing competitive cricket.

Dad would play football in the winter and then cricket in the summer at Bedlington just down the road. We would go and watch, play on the side, and when I was nine I started scoring. As scorer, you'd often end up getting a game – a player had to work or someone else didn't turn up.

By 11, I was in the Bedlington second team, before moving over to my hometown club as they had a proper junior section. I was always tall and from a young age I would try to bowl as fast as I could. I was raw, just a kid, but by 13 I was playing the odd first-team game for Ashington.

I wasn't daunted by it because three or four of the team were my dad's mates, so it wasn't like being thrust into a team full of strangers. At 13, I didn't really analyse anything like that anyway. For me, it was just a case of having a game of cricket, sitting in the bar, and having a can of pop afterwards. It wasn't a big deal. It wasn't like I was getting any recognition at that age.

At 13 I was only there to fill in at number 10 and bowl a few overs. I was lively but not really quick. I picked up a few wickets but I don't think batsmen were exactly quaking in their boots.

At the same time, I was playing for the junior section at Northumberland, again nothing more than just making the numbers up. There was no chance of playing for the north of England or getting representative honours higher than that. You can't always judge the potential of a player at that age. You have to wait until their body has filled out and there were bigger and better players in front of me.

It wasn't until I got to 15 and 16, when I got a bit bigger, that people took note. That growth spurt also put paid to any chance of a football career, not that it was ever really a choice. I had a bit of talent at football and was at Newcastle United until I was 15, but that was more about the size I was at that age.

I was bigger and stronger than most, decent at defending, but then people caught up physically and they had better speed and technical ability.

If I was going to make anything of myself it would have to be in cricket. Once I got even taller and started to cause people problems, there was talk of me playing senior representative cricket for Northumberland. But at the time there was a bit of the old school tie thing going on. Northumberland Cricket Club was terrible. If you didn't play for a club which was from an affluent area, and didn't speak with a certain voice, you didn't get anywhere near the team.

People at Ashington would ask them, "Why are you not looking at Stephen?", and they were saying, "Oh, well, we're not sure." But I'm pleased I didn't play for them because it didn't look like a very nice environment to be in. It looked more like a private members' club. Even at a younger schoolboy age, getting in the team was quite challenging. If you didn't go to a private school, or play for a club like Tynemouth, you didn't get to bat and bowl in the influential games. It was a strange environment, but thankfully it's changed for the better now.

Back in the classroom, or not as the case may be, it seemed the school had decided it suited them not to have me around. I don't think they were that bothered either way.

I asked the science teacher once for permission to play cricket for Northumberland. He looked at me. "Yes, you can go," he said. "Because you're never in here away." He also told me I'd never make anything out of cricket and that education was the most important thing. I remind him of that because I still see him now!

When it came to my GCSE year, I left school in the October half-term and never went back.

No-one said anything. The school weren't bothered and my parents knew I wasn't going to get any GCSEs anyway. It wasn't that they didn't care. It upset my mam that it had turned out this way and I wasn't going to get any qualifications. She'd had a hard time with it down the years because she badly wanted me to do well, understandable because there weren't many jobs around. But I wasn't lazy, even when I was 12 or 13 I was working on the wagons, delivering coal to people's houses.

I'd get more than £50 a week, cash in hand. I felt there would always be something I could do, and in the end I signed on for a bricklaying course.

All those years I'd been missing school, none of it had ever been about getting up to no good. I never brought trouble to my parents' door. It went no further than the usual sort of kids' stuff, roaming the streets, jumping over hedges, knocking on doors, climbing on roofs, antagonising folk, just what kids do!

Then sport came along. By the age of 13 I was playing cricket five nights a week and Saturday too for various teams and age groups. Football was the same. I wouldn't say sport kept me on the straight and narrow, but I'd have struggled without it because I didn't have any qualifications.

I don't condone what I did as a kid. I recognise the place I have as a role model, and whenever I do anything where there's kids I'll always do my best by that situation. My own kids have never liked going to school – wonder where they get that from? – but we've always made sure they've gone.

I just hated school – and I hated it because I couldn't do it. And no-one took the time to find out why. School made me anxious and that then stuck with me. All these emotions that were going through my head, I never really understood what they were, but they would stay with me throughout my life.

Thankfully, somebody did see my potential.

I was playing an age group game against Durham for Northumberland, and Durham's director of cricket, the former England opener Geoff Cook, came round to the Northumberland coaches – some say he was so excited he even sprinted, but, knowing him as I do, I doubt it! "We'll take him," he said.

Three weeks later, I was in the Durham 2nd XI. Within two months, I was playing first-class cricket. Within another eight I was in Islamabad starting an England under-19 tour to Pakistan.

I can also thank rabbits for my speedy rise, in particular the one whose hole the Durham seamer Martin Saggers stood in and sprained his ankle while playing golf.

With left-armer Simon Brown also out with a dislocated finger, I was chucked straight into action for a Tetley Bitter Trophy one-day semi-final at Scarborough against Yorkshire. Nothing like being thrown in at the deep end! All of a sudden I'd gone from sitting in the tight little dressing room at Ashington to a proper county ground with England internationals like Darren Gough, Martyn Moxon and Richard Blakey across the corridor.

A certain Michael Vaughan was in their team, although I wasn't to know what significance that name would have in future years.

I, meanwhile, was on a team sheet with John Morris, the same John Morris who, along with David Gower, had buzzed the Carrara Oval in Queensland in a vintage Tiger Moth on an England tour to Australia in 1991 to celebrate Robin Smith's return to form – and been fined £1,000 by a somewhat humourless team management for doing so.

While Ashington was a popular club and you could get a good few people down watching, it didn't exactly compare with a festival crowd coming to shout on Yorkshire while having a few beers on a day out. The game wasn't sponsored by Tetley Bitter for nothing!

We fielded first. I wasn't expecting much fuss before we went out, and it was a good job because there wasn't any.

Durham weren't doing great at the time and, to be honest, I was just the latest in a long line of new faces. The county were going through captains and players like nobody's business.

Predictably enough, we got battered, but the thing was I got away with it. I bowled early on and got eight of my 10 overs out the way before lunch when the ball wasn't going round the park so much.

In that time, I bowled Martyn Moxon, the former England opener, and later to be Durham coach, with a fast inswinger, and also had Richard Blakey caught with the first ball of my second spell. Yorkshire racked up 366 in 48 overs, with Vaughan getting a ton, but only 32 came off my 10 overs. On the back of that performance, and Simon Brown still being injured, a few days later I made my debut in the County Championship game against Leicestershire at the Riverside.

Bear in mind that the year previous I was turning out for Ashington seconds in the Bellway Division of the Priory Northumberland County League. To say this game was an eye-opener would be an understatement.

Durham were bottom of the league, they were top. They bowled us out for just over 100, went on to get 516, and then rolled us over again for 139. I bowled nine overs for 77 and the West Indies all-rounder Phil Simmons whacked it everywhere.

Batting didn't go much better. My first ball in first-class cricket, I was hit square on the head by Alan Mullally.

I'd never encountered anything like that speed of bowling and it took me totally by surprise. He probably wasn't even going full pelt. It was a lesson learnt early – move quicker next time.

They beat us by an innings and 251 runs in a day and a half. We started on a Thursday, finished on a Friday, and on the Saturday I was back playing for Ashington against the North Shields club Percy Main.

It all happened so quickly that it didn't really feel like I'd made my debut at all. It was more a baptism of fire. But I wasn't disheartened, because they were a great team and we weren't.

Not only did they have Simmons and Mullally, but Vince Wells, Darren Maddy, Gordon Parsons and David Millns. It just wasn't a contest. There was no sense of anti-climax because at that time I didn't really know what cricket was. I was still 17 – it was all new, I'd barely been around the set-up.

I'd not played any age group games for Durham, hadn't got

a contract – I didn't know what I was doing. It all happened so quickly.

Cricket being a full-time job? I had no idea that was even there. I was quite naïve. At that stage I wasn't even really thinking about it. I'd travelled up the ladder so quickly, had such a massive rise in the space of just four months, I'd had no time to get used to any of it.

In all honesty, at that age I was more interested in football, to the extent I'd missed the first five or six games of the cricket season because football came first. I wasn't interested in cricket in the same way.

I never watched it, didn't listen to it on the radio, nothing. It all happened so fast. I'd gone from playing Saturday cricket, thinking about getting a job, starting my life, to feeling there might actually be an avenue into professional cricket.

It had all happened in the blink of an eye, and it wasn't going to stop there. Barely had I got my head round the Durham business than I was on a plane to Pakistan for an England tour.

When the call came, initially I thought, 'Brilliant, I'm going away with England under-19s!' Beforehand, we were going to the England Academy at Lilleshall – it all sounded so glamorous.

The Academy bit was actually good fun. We were there to do fitness routines, to meet each other, and for the coaches to work on some basic elements of technique.

In fact, for some of us at least, it was one big piss-up.

I was 16 when I properly started to have a drink. My height had come in handy big time for getting served in pubs. I could go anywhere in Ashington, bar the Buffs because everyone knew how old I was in there.

Even before that, when I was 12 or 13, I was slipping the odd can from parties or people's houses. You'd be round at a friend's house while their mam and dad were out and you'd raid the drinks cabinet.

At Lilleshall, though, I found a new drinking partner, a young lad from Lancashire called Andrew Flintoff. We were two working-class lads from the north of England, two people who didn't take life too seriously, and, yes, two people who liked a beer. Something just clicked, or maybe clinked.

In fact, the night before we left for Pakistan we went down to Brighton from our hotel at Gatwick and got absolutely bladdered.

It was a last hurrah because there wasn't going to be any of that in Pakistan. At one point it looked like we'd messed right up as we only just made the last train. Sleep was thin on the ground that night, so much so that we were still drunk when we got on the plane.

Looking back, maybe I was trying to mask a bit of trepidation, but at the time I didn't feel like going to Pakistan was going to be an issue. I had no idea what Pakistan was. To me, it was nothing more than an eight-letter word, a place on the map. I didn't know what it was before I went and I still didn't know what it was when we touched down in Islamabad.

I was soon to find out. My naivety, not just about Pakistan, but about being far away from home, from the people I loved, the place I loved, would soon totally overwhelm me.

I'm not saying Pakistan was a culture shock, but a mile outside the airport there was a dead cow at the side of the road.

For three days we went to training past that cow and it was still lying there. 'What is this place?' That's all I could think. 'What is this place?' Apart from a holiday in Majorca, I'd barely been out of Ashington. Even the county game I'd played had been at home. Yes, there was the away trip to Scarborough, but while the resort has its moments, it hardly qualifies as abroad.

Everywhere we went, there were different smells, different people. There was the sheer busyness of it all, the noise was terrific, the pollution.

Even the air I breathed didn't feel the same. It felt hard to draw in, like you had to physically breathe rather than do it naturally. In all honesty, I might as well have flown to another planet. I mean none of this negatively. It had nothing to do with Pakistan, it was all down to me.

I had absolutely no comprehension of what the culture was going to be. I was a wet behind the ears lad from Ashington and now I'd been dumped into Pakistan for Christmas. To say it was an education would be an understatement.

Whether it hit other people the same, I don't know. Some of the others had already been on tours.

Fred had been to the Caribbean (a little different to Pakistan!) so maybe some were more used to the change. They'd all been around the game longer than me. They'd been on tours with schools, or with county set-ups. I'd had none of that.

If I'd had a full season of playing county or second XI cricket, with all the travelling that would have entailed, it might have been different.

At the time, though, I wasn't thinking of any of that. Put simply, I didn't care. All I could think about was my feelings. Pretty much from the minute we landed I wanted to come home. I felt panicky and unsettled. I couldn't escape the physical oppressiveness of what was happening. Merely to call it homesickness doesn't come near to how desperate I felt.

I managed to play a couple of warm-up games, but with three under-19 Tests and three one-dayers lined up, I couldn't possibly see how I was going to make it although I was playing in a great side. Not only did we have Andrew Flintoff, known to all and sundry as Fred, as captain, but Ben Hollioake, Gareth Batty, Alex Tudor, David Sales, Chris Read – a lot of players who went on to play for England.

But none of that could ever impact the way I was feeling. The cricket was irrelevant. This was all about being away from home in a place where the way of life was a total shock. The experience had turned me upside down and shaken me round to the extent I barely knew what was going on.

After a week, I was lying awake in bed, sleep yet again deserting me, until in the end I got up, went down to Fred's room, and woke him up.

"I want to go home," I told him. It all came pouring out – I proper opened my heart to him. "I've never experienced anything like these feelings going on in my body and my head. I've never felt anything like it. I literally don't know what's going on. I'm permanently anxious, I can't sleep, I can't eat." I can't say I wasn't a little bit worried that Fred would think I was a bit of an oddball talking about all this stuff. I needn't have bothered, I'm pretty sure he was asleep for most of it. In the end, he asked me to give it a week, then if I still couldn't hack it he'd get me on the next plane home.

The fact we'd become mates at Lilleshall allowed me to open up to Fred. I'm not sure I could have done the same with a member of the management staff, or anyone else for that matter. I felt comfortable going and talking to him, to the extent I was waking him up at three and four o'clock in the morning every night. He always jokes now that he spent a week trying to convince me to stay – and then a week trying to convince the management to send me home because he wanted some sleep!

He also says he never realised how bad Pakistan was until I went to him and told him I wanted to go home to Ashington.

Speaking to Fred sparked a good friendship and a good bond, and a good job too, because if I hadn't had anyone to talk to on that trip, I'm not sure how I'd have got through it.

There's no escape in Pakistan, nowhere you can go, and that's totally stifling if you're experiencing problems. To a certain extent you draw strength from each other in situations like that, because I'm sure there were times on that trip when every single person would have found it difficult, but at the end of the day, when you switch off the light, it's your mind you're alone with. You're the one going through it.

I was constantly on the phone to my mum, telling her how I felt and how much I wanted to come home, and I feel sorry now for her. She's told me since how helpless she felt and that, genuinely, if she could, she would have flown out and fetched me. I tell her she did enough by being a lifeline.

It didn't help that I'd also just met Hayley, the girl who'd be my wife, before I left, which meant I was missing home even more.

We'd met at a pub in Ashington through mutual friends. I'd just come back from the last fitness trip to Lilleshall before leaving for Pakistan. It was clear to me that she was something special.

Not only was she great looking, but she was strong and funny. She was exactly right for me, and I hoped I was right for her. We met again the next day and were just getting to know each other properly when Pakistan took me away. Hayley was another big factor pulling me home, something else in the melting pot, another emotion in the head.

It also didn't help that I had developed a back injury.

Not having playing as a distraction, my mind started wandering even more. When the week was up, I told Fred nothing had changed. By this time we were in the Biscuit Factory in Saiwel, one of the most notorious venues in world cricket. Think the sun-drenched acres of the Kensington Oval in Barbados, and then think the exact opposite.

The Biscuit Factory, officially the Montgomery Biscuit Factory Cricket Club, was nothing more than a portable cabin in the middle of a chemical works with a cricket pitch next to it.

The changing room was also your bedroom, dormitory-style, and the pitch was just outside. It was horrendous, rats everywhere, giant insects, lizards. It's the nearest I've ever got to being in *I'm A Celebrity*, and I was definitely shouting "Get me out of here!" There'd be five of us in a double bed for protection, sleeping bags, batting helmets, the whole lot. Have you ever tried to sleep in a batting helmet? Exactly. I lasted two nights in there and that was it, Fred made good on his promise and I was coming home.

I stayed one last night with the High Commissioner in Islamabad, which was slightly more palatial than the Biscuit Factory, and then flew back from there.

Never, before or since, have I been more glad to be back on home soil.

Sport for me was a release, but Pakistan had felt like a prison. The sentence, though, would never be over. They say when you have a mental health problem, you have things that trigger it, and the Pakistan experience big-time triggered the mental health issues that would affect me, not just as a cricketer, but as a person, from that point on.

I was scarred for life.

3

LEARNING

"'Just watch this kid,' Geoff told him. 'He's got something'"

When I got back from Pakistan, the question I had to ask myself was, 'If this is cricket, do I really want to do it?'

There was a big part of me that thought, 'No way, I'm not doing that again.' Why would I want to revisit what could be such a terrible experience? It wasn't like cricket was my job. I hadn't been paid a penny. I'd had expenses but that was it. I was an apprentice bricklayer who happened to play cricket.

It was then that John Morris rang up and asked to come round. He told me not to give cricket up.

He recognised I'd had a bad experience, but he told me I had something, that I should sort an ongoing back problem out, get myself in a position to play cricket again, and take one step at a time.

I'll always be grateful to John for doing that. He was one of a few real good characters I was lucky enough to play with when I started out. I thought the world of him and still do. He drove from Durham to see someone who might never play cricket again. He helped me get over that bad experience. Without John, I might never have played the game again.

As it was, that back injury would eventually keep me out for the whole of the next season. It was so bad that, aside from a few second team games as a batsman, I couldn't even play for Ashington. Basically, it came down to growing pains.

Every time I bowled, I couldn't walk for three days afterwards. The body wasn't supple enough. I was desperately disappointed, but Geoff Cook kept in touch and encouraged me not to give in.

He'd invite me up to Durham for net sessions and was the one who took me to that next level, gave me the understanding of what and who I could be. Geoff's a great bloke. No idea what he's on about half the time – he goes off into the weird and wonderful world of Geoff Cook – but that's what makes him what he is. He'd have this vacant look on his face, it was obvious he was thinking about something and, as a player, all you could do was think, 'Fucking hell, I hope it's not me!'

You'd look at him in the same way that young players footballers would have looked at Sir Alex Ferguson and wondered what on earth was going through his head.

Like Sir Alex, Geoff always seemed to know where you were, what you were doing, what was going on. He was very old school in his processes and methods and yet he understood the modern game, and that's what made him a good coach.

He would always reiterate it was your career; you were the one making the decisions. Then he'd challenge you on those decisions. If a couple of lads went out for a drink the day before a game, he wouldn't shout and bawl and scream, he'd ask them, "Why are you doing that? Do you think that's good preparation for a game?"

He made players come up with their own answers. He understood people, he knew the different characters, some of these players he'd seen come through from 12-years-old.

Norman Gifford, the Durham coach, was another big influence. I never had a grandfather, both of them died at a relatively young age, but Giff would take all us younger ones under his wing.

A former England slow left arm bowler, and a real gentleman, he was well into his 50s by the time I encountered him and he'd played professionally until he was 48, notching up more than 2,000 first-class wickets.

He'd always bowl in the nets, wanting to be in and around what was happening. At the same time, I had a lot more to do with the Durham fitness coach Paul Winsper, a fantastic bloke, infectious in his enthusiasm. He kept pushing me during that summer of 1997 too. "How are you feeling? Come on, stick with it. Carry on." I'd bowl and then I wouldn't be able to do it again for a week.

Paul treated my body differently to other people. He worked with people as individuals, and he put the facets right to put me in a position as a bowler, and that's something I'll always be thankful for.

Perhaps the biggest turning point for me, and Durham, was when David Boon joined at the start of that summer. I was totally in awe of Boony, this little 5ft 7in Australian, 107 Tests, trademark 'tache. I literally couldn't speak to him for three months. I told him that once, and he said, "Yes, but I couldn't understand you for three years!"

I knew all the stories, like the 52 cans of beer he's said to have consumed on the plane back home from the Ashes. I brought it up once when his wife was with him and she went absolutely berserk. Let's just say she wasn't very happy that having not seen his family for three months, he was then incapable of speaking for three days. I found that quite amusing – so I brought it up again a few times again after that.

During that summer, Geoff got me to bowl in a second team net and told Boony to look in from one of the boxes upstairs. "Just watch this kid," Geoff told him. "He's got something."

After seeing three or four minutes of me bowling, Boony came down, put his pads on, and came into the net for a bat. He wasn't due to practice that day, but down he came anyway. He wanted to see at close hand what I was doing. It was a little nerve-wracking to say the least. This was David Boon, for Christ's sake. He had the swagger, the aura, the steel. Fifteen minutes of me he had, and I was just trying to bowl them straight. It must have gone OK because on the way off he told Geoff, "You've got to sign him." It didn't seem likely at the time because I could barely move afterwards.

I still wasn't wholly convinced that cricket was the way forward, however.

Not only was there what had happened in Pakistan, but there were so many ifs and buts. My back wasn't right, and even if it was it seemed a long way back into the team.

Remember, I'd got no real history with Durham and only got picked because other players were injured, plus the team was bottom of the Championship and had nothing to lose by throwing me in. It wasn't like I was a regular with a proven history and a guaranteed place in the team. I hadn't earned a penny with Durham either, the only thing I'd been paid was expenses.

But then were the other options really better? That winter, I worked at a foundry for four months. My uncle Kevin was there and he got me the job. It was the pits. Absolutely filthy. I was sweeping up coal dust and used to have to wash three times to get clean.

Don't get me wrong, it was half decent money if you worked overtime, but the actual lifestyle of working shifts, not seeing daylight for weeks on end, getting a shower at work, a bath when you got in, just so you were clean enough to get in bed?

When those four months were up, I thought, 'There's not a cat in hell's chance I'm going back to that.'

The winter after, I worked with my dad for six months at American Air Filters, basic labouring, acid cleaning of housings with jet washes. The environment was good, the people I worked with were fantastic, and there's every chance I'd still be there now if the cricket hadn't happened. In fact, two lads who started with me are still there now.

There was a point where I honestly thought, 'This is my life now'. In my mind I was going to work 30-odd hours a week, nine to five, support my family, and play a bit of sport.

Alan Shearer's dad, Alan senior, worked in the same factory as my dad. The pair of them were colleagues for 20 years and were good mates.

When I started playing for England, I went back one day after training at Durham to say hello and was sitting with the staff having lunch when someone piped up, "It's amazing, we've got two people here whose sons play for England, and the only time you hear about them is when you read the papers!"

And that says it all. My dad and Alan weren't rooftop shouters. Half the time the only reason I knew my dad was in the ground was because he was giving me a lift there and back.

I'd look over to the crowd and wonder if he was even awake and afterwards, he'd never really mention what he'd seen nor would he ask why I'd done this or that. I've never had that in my life, be it for football or cricket. He was there for support, and his attitude meant I never got too big for my boots.

My dad would give advice when asked, but he'd never put pressure on me to do as he said. He was the same with all of us. He never pushed us when it came to sport.

Ben was a great footballer and had a few clubs looking when he was a kid, but all of a sudden he just packed it in because he wanted to play cricket.

Dad was a football man but he never batted an eyelid. If that's what Ben wanted to do, that was fine, and Ben proved himself right by going on to be a quality all-rounder for Durham and Kent.

Alan senior was the same as my dad – he sat in the crowd, enjoyed his mates' company, and watched his son. His son was an icon, but it made no difference to him. The only way you might have known he was Alan Shearer's dad was the resemblance, the same with Jimmy and me.

I know Alan well and he speaks about his dad exactly the same way I speak about mine, holding him in such high regard for letting him get on with his career. It was all very down to earth.

You get these parents who tell everyone how their sons are the best thing, put pressure on them, arguably live their life through them. My dad wasn't like that. He kept my feet on the ground. I'd be the same with any of my children if they played sport. It's for them to learn the game, just as it's for them to learn their way through life. I'd always be there to offer guidance, but I wouldn't be there to tell them what to do. I'd just be trying to nudge them back on to the track. I didn't need my dad to shower me with praise to know that he was proud of me. I knew that for sure anyway. Sometimes he'd tell me, sometimes it was unspoken. But I knew. My dad was probably my best friend growing up.

At that point, my body was still letting me down, but thankfully, over that winter, Geoff got me in training properly, Paul got me stronger, and eventually they got me in a position to go on a pre-season trip to Sussex and Essex.

I was a surprise inclusion on the team photo, stood rather uncomfortably at one end, in the shadow of Lumley Castle, and then two weeks later I was offered a contract. By this time, I was 19 months into a bricklaying course.

I had five months left and then another two years of training, so it was still a big thing to decide. Had I just wasted nearly two years of my life to throw it down the tube for a chance in cricket? It was a gamble – for a start, cricket was only six months a year. But I reasoned I could always go back to the bricklaying if it didn't work out, so it would have been wrong not to give cricket a go. I'd made my choice. The thought of touring didn't exactly fill me with joy, but the way I began to look at it was that I could be a cricketer without the need ever to return to Pakistan.

I could end up playing for Durham for the next 15 years and

never have to go away again. I was a little optimistic on that score!

With Simon Brown injured, I found myself in the team for the first Championship game of the 1998 season, against Warwickshire. The young lads at that time had to drive the van with all the players' bags and coffins to away grounds.

Me and Paul Collingwood were tasked with taking it down to Edgbaston. When we got to the first service station, Colly said, "I'll drive for the first two hours, then you take over."

"I'll have to get some L-plates," I told him. "I can't drive!"

He got straight on the phone to Giff. "You've put me in the van with someone who can't drive! Now I've got to drive all the way there and all the way back." I suppose I should have mentioned it before.

At the ground, the game felt absolutely massive.

To me it felt like my first-class debut, because the one game I had played lasted a day and a half and that was now two seasons ago. Not only was Edgbaston a Test ground, but the game marked the return of Brian Lara for the first time since he knocked 501 for the Bears in 1994.

Lara at that point was the biggest name in world cricket, an absolute global superstar. Me? I didn't even have any proper bowling boots, I just had this really old knackered pair that progressively fell to pieces over the course of their first innings. I kept slipping and falling over, long hair flapping everywhere.

Kenny Palmer was umpiring and told Giff that I was worse than useless in them and couldn't bowl properly, so he got our club sponsors Nike to send two new pairs to the ground as soon as possible. Not the most impressive of starts!

I didn't get to bowl at Lara in the first innings as John Wood snared him for a duck. I had a few balls at him second time round before Woody again finished him off early. It felt surreal. It was all so new to me. I was a young lad from Ashington. By rights I should have been laying bricks, and here I was bowling at an all-time legend of the game.

On the other hand, I didn't feel particularly out of place.

In fact, I picked up five wickets in the match, including bowling England opener Nick Knight, and from that point on I never looked back.

When his middle stump went cartwheeling back, my life started.

I barely missed a game that season, travelling with senior players like Simon Brown, John Wood, Boony and Jon Lewis. I enjoyed that – I'd been brought up in football, and that gave me respect for the older players in the dressing room. Those four guided me so well. They had good values, they picked you up, told you what cricket was. They looked after me. For a young wide-eyed lad from Ashington it was a pleasure playing in that team with those senior figures.

My good form continued into the next match, at home to Gloucestershire, where I got my first five-for, including four wickets in my opening spell, eventually taking eight in the match. That was the first time as a batsman I came up against serious pace in the form of Courtney Walsh.

If Mullally had been a shot across the bows, this was the moment I truly realised there was no such thing as the fast bowlers' union. Our batting had collapsed and when I walked out we needed 12 to avoid the follow-on.

It was a freezing cold day and I'm fairly sure Courtney, who was somewhere to be found beneath several jumpers, wasn't keen on hanging around. Neither was I. I just went for it. I pulled him for three, and then hooked him down to third man.

He was in his mid to late 30s at that point but he could still unleash some seriously fast deliveries. He was obviously unimpressed by this 19-year-old hooking and pulling and the next one fizzed into my fingers.

I knew about that all right.

He might have been nearing the end of his career, but he still had it in him to fire the cannon. I got the 12 runs, and then was promptly out to the gentle off-break bowler Martyn Ball at the other end. Boony was amazed by the whole thing. "If I had one rule in my career," he told me. "It was 'Thou Shalt Not Hook Courtney.'"

I always joked about my batting that I was there for a good time, not a long one. I wanted to maximise the amount of runs I could get while I was in the middle.

I had a theory with batting – there were two areas the bowler would bowl at, my toes or my head. I'd work out the ones I could hit and get out the way or defend the others. I would try to hit the full ball, golf-style, back towards the bowler. If it was a bit wider, I'd try to pick it up over midwicket. If there wasn't much pace in the wicket, and I thought the short ball was easier to hit, I'd stand back in my crease and try to hit baseball-style as far as I could. Even if the pitch was quick and bouncy there was a chance of getting something on it and edging it for six over the keeper. This was only if I was batting with 9, 10, 11. If I'd got a decent player at the other end, I'd go out with a mattress strapped to my waist, arm guards on, the works, and play French cricket.

I got hit in the bollocks once or twice but the inside thigh is the absolute worst. That really does tickle. It feels like you've been dead-legged from the inside. It leaves a horrible lump as well. Perhaps the most painful blow I had was when Leicestershire's fast-medium Jimmy Ormond hit me on the foot and got me LBW.

I hobbled off but Durham physio Nigel Kent said it was a toe so there was nothing he could do. I put my boots on and went out to bowl but could hardly move. He waved me back in. I found him sitting there with a lighter, heating a stretched out paper clip up. "Where the fuck's that going?"

Nigel pointed at my black big toe. "In there."

"You can fuck right off."

"It's going in there," he repeated, and before I could do anything he'd jabbed it straight in. There was blood everywhere. You know the relief when you've been dying to go for a wee? You've been holding it in for an hour and then finally you go?

It was like that. It was amazing and within minutes I was back out bowling. That's toes for you – a fast bowler's nightmare because they get cut to ribbons.

I'd now played against Brian Lara and Courtney Walsh, and that's how that season felt to me, like I was going round the country playing against superstars.

Next up was Essex with Nasser Hussain, then there was Mike Gatting and Justin Langer at Middlesex. It was Langer who said I had the look of a "white West Indian" because of the way I ran in with high, typically Caribbean action.

I'd been picking up wickets throughout the season and myself and fellow Durham bowler Melvyn Betts were right up there in the county bowling averages, so it was no great surprise when the under-19s came knocking again, for a series against Pakistan, this time, thankfully, at home, starting with three one-dayers.

In all honesty, while it's always an honour to play for England, I wasn't that bothered about turning out for the under-19s. I was learning a lot more with Durham than I ever would in that set-up.

First-class cricket was where I was learning to play proper cricket, and that was what I wanted to do. It was about striving to get better. If somebody is qualified to play under-19s cricket, but he's playing first-class cricket, and the games clash, they should always be allowed to play the first-class game because it's a far better stepping stone and a far better standard.

I wanted to play for Durham, Durham wanted me to play for Durham and all Boony wanted was for me to play 16 Championship matches and for me to learn the first-class game.

As a result, after those first three one-day games, with three Tests to come, Boony told me I was injured so England couldn't have me.

Declaring me injured unfortunately meant I couldn't then play for Durham either but rather than bowling endless overs in pointless games, Boony would rather just have me practice in the nets until the under-19 game was finished and I could then get back in the team.

The under-19s weren't too happy I couldn't play for them and was then turning out for Durham two days later, but Boony was protective of me and I wasn't bothered. If it helps make an excuse, my shins were pretty sore to be fair.

As a man and a captain Boony didn't say a great deal. He didn't have to, he was held in such high regard. There was none of this high five bullshit.

For him, it was just a, "Well done!" and a quick tap on the

backside when you took a wicket. Very rarely did he have a go, although there was one memorable occasion against Scotland where he lost it.

We bowled terribly, fielded even worse, and let them get 200. Boony went mad in the dressing room. "We'd better get these fucking runs," he threatened. "Chasing 200 against these on a wicket like that is fucking disgraceful." We were all shitting ourselves.

Boony went out to bat and was immediately given out LBW. He wasn't happy. In his eyes, no way was he out. He came bouncing back into the pavilion, absolutely livid. We didn't know where to look. We were just intent on avoiding his helmet as it went across the dressing room. There was a box holding the door open into the shower area. He thought it was empty, actually it was full of ECB manuals, rules and regulations. The ECB would send a boxful every year and it would never get opened.

It was never anything other than a great doorstop. Boony went through to the back to have some time to himself and on the way he kicked this box as hard as I've seen anyone kick anything. It didn't move an inch.

He then pushed it with his foot so he could shut the door and all we could hear was him swearing on the other side. "Fucking hell, FUCKING HELL!" We were all creasing up laughing. Eventually, he came back in. He'd actually broken his toe. He was such a hard bastard, though, that he only missed one game. He also never admitted in public to how it happened. He told the press he'd been hit on the toe in the nets by Melvyn.

Boony was a tough man – he played the last three months of his career with a broken thumb – and you took liberties at your peril.

We were playing a four-day game at Northampton when Boony broke that thumb early on in the match and Jon Lewis took over as captain on the field. The rain came during the afternoon on the third day and then carried on all night. We thought there was no chance of any play on the final day so we sat in the hotel bar that night having a drink.

Every now and then someone would say, "Shall we go?" "What are you talking about? It's pissing down." We weren't stopping drinking until it stopped raining.

No chance. We all ended up absolutely hammered.

Next morning everyone was in a right mess. We went down to the ground thinking it was a formality that play would be called off. Word then came back from the umpires that we would actually start on time – something none of us could quite believe.

We could barely get down the stairs and on to the pitch. Fielding practice was all over the place. Thankfully, at ten to eleven it started to rain again. The dressing rooms at Northampton aren't the comfiest of places but I managed to build a nest for myself out of some bags and was off to sleep. I was out snoring for three hours, drool everywhere.

Eventually the game started with about 40 overs left. Even though he wasn't playing, Boony gave Jon Lewis the order to make me bowl non-stop until the end of the match. "He bowls until he drops," he said.

And that's what happened. I bowled 18 overs in a row. We did actually win the game. It finished in the dark when Devon Malcolm was caught with three overs to go.

Back in the pavilion, there were three or four of us who knew we'd fucked up badly. Boony looked at me. "You are very lucky," he told me, rightly so. "I won't be doing that again, Skip," I promised.

Well, I was only young at the time.

There's a lot said about the drinking culture in cricket, and it's right that the biggest phrase in a cricket dressing room is "if it rains..." and any cricketer who says they don't like it pouring down is talking a complete load of bollocks.

John Wood, bless him, you knew what mood he'd be in before you even saw him. If there were dark clouds in the sky, Woody leapt up the stairs into the pavilion at Durham like he was the happiest soul in the world. If it was a clear sky, he was the most miserable man in the world. He wasn't alone.

Back in the day, before grounds had these brand spanking new drainage systems, if it was tipping down when you came off the pitch at half past six, you knew there'd be a very good chance of there not being any play the next day.

Even if it was looking fine going into a match, there'd be full expectation of four good nights out. We used to laugh that you could tell a cricketer driving up and down the motorway because he'd have his four shirts and four pairs of jeans hanging up in the back of the car.

Now they don't even take civvies away with them. They sit on their PlayStations. Was it the right thing? Was it the wrong thing? It was neither. It was the done thing. That came from me being 17 and seeing 35-year-olds behaving in a certain way.

You follow the big men as a young player and so that seems like the norm. Players are like sheep and I was one of them. I came into first-class cricket thinking, 'Four nights away, that's four nights out'. That was the way to go. That's what cricket was like for the majority of the '90s. We all enjoyed ourselves.

Cricket was a fun game then. It wasn't debauchery, a lot of the time I'd just be sat in the corner of a bar watching those old guys and learning what cricket was like on the road.

Trouble was I didn't have the best teacher in Simon Brown. Not for nothing was he known as the Prince of Darkness. He certainly liked being out at night and he could never bowl in London.

I'm not trying to build up how it was. I'm not saying it was all-night benders and gin on your Cornflakes. I'm not saying it was rock 'n' roll. Most nights you had a few pints and a bite to eat, you went to bed, and then you got up and did it again. Yes, it could backfire. There was more than one occasion when I pulled back the curtains and cursed the fact it hadn't rained. In fact, that was most mornings!

But there weren't many times I thought, 'Hang on, I've completely fucked up here.' Usually it was a bit of a dusty head after three or four pints in the bar talking shit with the lads, but after you'd done your warm-ups and had a run round it was gone, you felt as fresh as a daisy.

Those who did push it harder and tried to do the whole rock 'n' roll thing didn't last five minutes. You can't do that over a sustained period and play cricket. You're not going to ride some great cricketing rollercoaster of joy and emotion. You'll get tired, you'll get injured, and that will be it.

Things changed when England brought in central contracts and then county teams also started to get more serious. Also, the rewards are greater now than they were then.

The salaries that were around in the '90s meant a lot of players had jobs in the winter. Now they've got 12-month contracts and fitness is paramount if you want to play. That's good for cricket.

When I started, you were a professional cricketer, but you were only a professional cricketer for six months, either that or you went away and played in the winter. The drinking culture and the socialising went with the low stakes.

It was nearly an amateur sport. Now there's much more scrutiny of professionalism and fitness. Standards are getting better, pitches are getting better, the level of play is getting better, the game is getting faster, and a lot of that is down to professionalism, both on the part of the clubs and the players. Socialising isn't anywhere like what it used to be, and that, to some degree, has to be for the betterment of the game.

Until Boony arrived at Durham, the club could be a shambles at times. Success at Durham before then was not winning trophies, it was winning cricket matches. In five seasons since being given first-class status, we'd never finished higher than 16th in the Championship.

In 1996, when I made my debut, we were terrible. But that was the enormity of the challenge of being a new first-class county. Durham had gone down the route of employing old experienced players at first – Wayne Larkins, Graeme Fowler, Ian Botham, Simon Hughes – but that didn't work. Then they chucked a bunch of kids at it, and that didn't work either. The Durham team then was not in a good position. Teams were coming up knowing they were going to beat them in two days.

The realisation that something needed to change came that year I made my debut in 1996. Boon had taken Tasmania from Australia's Durham; a young new team, outsiders, and turned them into contenders. That experience and know-how was exactly what the club needed. If Durham could get him for three years, they could build the club's foundations on what he tried to do. That's what Geoff Cook and Norman Gifford saw in him.

We were an older team when Boony arrived and he understood the importance of the younger ones like me, Colly, Melvyn and Neil Killeen. At the same time he had some great senior players, especially in the bowlers.

Simon Brown was the best bowler Durham ever had and should have added to his single England cap. John Wood was a great bloke to have around the team and a good fast bowler, and the two of them were key in my development and upbringing in the cricketing world.

Behind the stumps we had Martin Speight. Boony used to call him "The Speed Hump" – he never used to stop them, he just used to slow them down. But he would get loads of great runs for us.

Initially, some people thought it must have been a comedown for Boony to play at Durham after such an illustrious career but his desire could never be questioned. We played one three-day game against South Africa in July 1998, and he was unbelievable. We couldn't shift Daryl Cullinan and he got 200 as they racked up a massive score.

They had Allan Donald, Nantie Hayward and Brian McMillan in their attack, all quick, quick bowlers, and looked like they were going to rip through us. When Donald then hit Boony and broke his grill, we were a tad concerned – if Boony couldn't play this, what chance did the rest of us have?

But second innings he got stuck in and saved the game with a real gutsy 40 not out. At that point he was 37 and he had scored 7,500 Test runs. It wasn't his hometown club, it was Durham. But he stood up and did what he did, in a game that was meaningless for Durham, and that showed everyone exactly what sort of person he was.

He didn't need to bat like he did that day. He could have just nicked off, and that would have been it. But he stood up and performed, and that taught us young players an awful lot. Off the pitch he was just the same.

He'd sign anything and have a chat with people. He loved a beer, but very rarely did you see him out after 11 o'clock. He'd have the same amount as me but just finish them in a faster time! Quarter past ten, off he'd go for his Chinese, Indian, or pizza, tottering down the road with his takeaway.

After that South Africa game, Hansie Cronje sat me down and talked to me about playing for his Orange Free State team. It did sound amazing. I'd have been playing alongside Allan Donald, which is a dream for any fast bowler. Boony, meanwhile, wanted me to go and play for Tasmania. I quite fancied that as well. I felt I would have fitted in down there. From what Boony said it sounded a bit like Ashington – gritty and down-to-earth with no airs and graces about the place.

Me and Hayley sat down and talked the offers over. At one stage we were going to go to Bloemfontein, but then I got picked on an England A tour to Zimbabwe and South Africa and the decision was taken away from us. Hoggy went instead. He had three years with Orange Free State and ended up staying with Donald, a great experience for him.

The England A-team call was hardly unexpected. I was 10 times the bowler I was when I made my debut and after taking 51 wickets in what was my first full year, I was even being mentioned as a long-shot for the full Ashes tour, although I never took that sort of talk seriously.

Nor did I even want it to happen. I didn't have any idea what that world was. It was a million miles away from reality. At the time, I had just bought a flat in Ashington with Hayley. That's what my life was and I was happy. I wasn't thinking of anything else. The next step was Zimbabwe and South Africa.

And absolute chaos.

4

GOING PLACES

"I clocked Michael Vaughan straight on the chin.
Yes, I managed to hit my own captain"

That A-team tour to Zimbabwe and South Africa wasn't so much a tour as an elongated stag do.

Some way removed from the under-19s visit to Pakistan, it probably still ranks as the best trip I've ever been on.

We went in the rainy season so didn't start a game before one o'clock in the afternoon, you could get a beer and a steak for next to nothing, and we saw some fantastic wildlife.

The problems Zimbabwe would suffer, and which would later impact on me and the England cricket team, hadn't yet started. We also had a very good side, captained by Michael Vaughan, who, even then, was clear leadership material.

He could have a laugh with the rest of the lads but there was clearly a steely competitor in there, he was obviously a thinker. We might have partied off the pitch but he always made sure we worked hard on it. Fred was in there, as was Rob Key, who

I knew from the under-19s, a — shall we say — 'effervescent character', with a sharp sense of humour, always with something to say in the dressing room, and already the real close friend he would always be.

Then there was Graeme Swann. Swanny's a cheeky sod and he hasn't changed a bit. He was like that when he was 17, when I first met him, and he's still a cheeky sod now. He's never tried to be anything other than Graeme Swann, which is what I love about him.

He could light a room up by saying something to get everybody going. We also had future England players in Alex Tudor, Chris Silverwood and Chris Read. We were playing against Zimbabwe A when we'd easily have given the Zimbabwe Test team a game.

The cricket was never hugely testing, but off the pitch there was the occasional issue.

After the second Test in Bulawayo, we were in a rugby club bar. There was this one guy dancing round in his boxer shorts. Fred, naturally, pulled them down, an act that wasn't received very well. In fact, it properly kicked off. Arms were swinging and punches were thrown.

Our female physio got smacked on the jaw. It was all going off and got a bit scary, people swinging everywhere, me among them, except instead of hitting a rugby player I clocked Michael Vaughan straight on the chin. Yes, I managed to hit my own captain. He never said anything. Luckily, we were all too busy trying to get out of there to dwell on it. We'd also had a few so he might not have clicked it was me — which I was glad about!

The rugby players were keen we should go outside and have a proper fight. We had other ideas, managed to find another way out, and made a hasty exit. That was the night before we went to

South Africa − a good time to get out of Zimbabwe. We heard later that some ex-Zimbabwean cricketers had set up the whole thing and made sure there was going to be trouble that night.

If I thought South Africa was going to be any quieter, I was wrong. It was here I nearly managed to get arrested while I was sitting in a dressing room with my pads on.

It was funny and it wasn't funny all at the same time. We'd been in a bar in Cape Town a couple of days before, sat on a balcony outside. Freddie, messing about, had thrown a glass at me. I'd thrown one back and it had sailed straight over the balcony and through someone's car window below.

I must admit I didn't hang around to see what happened next. Anyway, two days later we're still in Cape Town and I'm padded up waiting to bat against the South African Board President's XI. I'm going through the usual preparations, so not very much at all, when the dressing room door opens and in walk two police officers, guns, the works, with a young man and his girlfriend.

All of a sudden, I didn't feel so much like I was in a dressing room as an identity parade. The couple's eyes scanned the room, until finally they stopped on me. There was a short pause. My heart was in my mouth.

Then they said it − "That's him!" It became clear they were the owners of the car and were none too pleased to have lost a windscreen to a beer glass. Thankfully, just as I was thinking how I was going to get the prison visiting times back to Hayley, the coach, John Emburey, stepped in and managed to sort it all out with the officers.

I just had to pay for the windscreen instead of suffering the indignity of being frogmarched out of the pavilion with my pads on. I know it wasn't a great thing to do, and I wasn't covering myself in glory, but I hadn't meant it – it was just one of those things. I was only 20. Boys will be boys. You learn from experience. Thankfully, Phil Neale, the manager, never found out. I tried to make amends with four wickets in the second innings.

Aside from that, I enjoyed every minute of that trip. As someone who has borderline insomnia, I'm used to being awake a lot of the time, but on this trip it was for different reasons! It was the second tour I'd been on. One I'd wanted to end the minute I got there. The other I didn't want to leave.

Back at Chester-le-Street for the first game of the 1999 season and the phone rang in the dressing room. "How the fuck do you drive in snow?" It was Boony. It was April and a fair bit had come down in the night. He'd never seen snow before, never mind driven in it, and he didn't have a clue. I wasn't much help. I'd only just passed my test. Before that I was always dependent on my mam, Hayley, my dad and uncle Melvyn for lifts. I spent a lot of time just hanging round the club waiting for someone to pick me up because there wasn't anyone else from this side of the Tyne Bridge. Now I'd passed my test, the club had issued me with a Vauxhall Corsa, the perfect vehicle for the 6ft 5in fast bowler. After three days, the physio overruled it. After that I had an Astra.

This would be Boony's last year at Durham and in some ways it was make or break.

This was the year when the Championship would be controversially split into two divisions, and it would be an amazing achievement if we could be in the top half on the final day. Things, however, weren't going to plan. As the end of June arrived, the wheels were coming off, the worst moment being when we lost to the Netherlands in the third round of the Natwest Bank Trophy in Amsterdam. Boony was at his lowest ebb.

We couldn't win a game for love nor money. Me, Simon Brown, Norman Gifford and Boony were sitting in the corridor of this sports centre where the changing rooms were and suddenly this bloke came up with some glasses and a four-pint pitcher. He just kept filling our glasses up.

We were chatting together and as we did, a few of the other lads joined in. The general consensus was things couldn't get any worse. We'd barely won a game all season. I don't know who that bloke was with the four-pint pitcher, but that was the turning point.

It was tight all the way from then on in. The last game of the season was at Leicestershire and a draw would do it. Luckily, Jack Hampshire was umpiring. He'd played in Tasmania, like Boony, and they were best mates. It was raining on the last day when Boony went in to see him.

A few minutes later, back he came. "That's it. All finished. I've just told Jack we're not going back on the field." And that was it! We'd finished ninth and were in the First Division, Durham's first ever big achievement.

We were in with the top counties and had players on the international radar. And that's how we sent Boony off, because that was the point where his career was finished. I've still got the shirt he signed for me in the dressing room that very day on my wall. He was an immense part of my life, the first lead figure in my career. He thought I was good, he respected me, and liked what he saw. He gave me a chance.

That summer was a double celebration for me. I became a

dad for the first time when Emily was born. Me and Hayley couldn't have been happier.

Our families meant everything to us and we were delighted to start one of our own. Emily was another part of making us complete, and I couldn't have been more proud when I held her in my arms that first time. Everything felt like it had come together. My life had developed in a way I could never have imagined when I was that kid bunking of school, when I was coming home miserable from the foundry.

I had a daughter, I had a cricket career, and I was engaged to Hayley. We'd get married when we could find a gap in the schedule, eventually doing so at Morpeth Register Office. It was the earliest we could manage because the spring and summer were taken up with the cricket season. In attendance were my three brothers, with Ben and James sharing Best Man duties, my sister, Hayley's sister, my mum and dad, Hayley's mum and dad, my grandma, and Hayley's grandma. It was just close family, quiet, which is what we are. We went for a meal, had a reception in Ashington, and that was it.

Everything I had was wrapped up in Ashington and inevitably it led to problems when, at the end of 1999, after further cementing a growing reputation with 64 first-class wickets, I got the call to fly to the England A-tour of New Zealand halfway through when someone got injured.

I'd initially been selected for the tour but had pulled out because I'd hurt my knee at a training camp. I didn't feel like I was being believed, and in all honesty I might have been over-egging it a little, but, whatever the truth, I'd bowled 600-odd overs that summer, and the body was knackered, gone. Not only that but

Emily was only a few months old and the thought of leaving my new family was tearing me apart. The Pakistan feelings were lurking in the back of my mind, and it wouldn't have been hard for them to break through to the front.

Having declared myself 'unfit', I thought that would be the end of it, so when I then got that phone call from David Graveney, the chairman of selectors, my heart sank.

Inside I was thinking, 'Oh fuck. I do not want to go' but I said I would go to buy me some time to think of a way to get out of it. Not that I had long. I had just four days warning that I was going to the other side of the world. In the meantime, my kit was being sent up to the house, and all the time I was desperately thinking of ways I wouldn't have to travel. Not for the first time as it would turn out, the idea of pulling out on somebody at a roundabout and getting a bump – which would delay things for a few days – was on my mind.

As the day neared, I was getting more and more anxious. I still hadn't rung Graveney and eventually the tour was upon me. My bags were packed, the kit was in the car. At that point I was still going on the tour. Then, about three hours before I was due to head to the airport, something snapped. I realised once and for all that I wasn't going. That was when I rang John Wood.

He told me to forget going to the airport and drive to his house instead. I was in bits but Woody was brilliant, like a big brother. He listened as I told him how I was feeling scared and anxious – anxious because I thought not going might jeopardise my chances of playing for England.

How can they pick someone who keeps pulling out? And if they wanted to pick me at home, would they do so not knowing if I would go away in the winter? I knew I was wrecking my chances of playing for England. At the same time, the other half of my head was telling me that playing for England was the last thing I wanted. If I couldn't even bring myself to get on a plane, there was no way I was ready to play for my country.

More than that, though, I was scared of how I was feeling, the thoughts that were going on in my head and body. The knot in the stomach, the lump in the throat.

John sat calmly with me, made me a cup of tea, and told me not to worry. He reassured me I was doing the right thing. "You've got a nice house, a nice family," he told me. "If you don't play cricket for England it's not the end of the world." Suddenly, it all made sense. I was only going to be there for three-and-a-half weeks. Why put myself through all that anxiety, all that fear, for such a short time? I was turning myself inside out over three games.

John wrote down on a piece of paper what I needed to say to David Graveney. "I'm 20, I've just had a kid, I want to play for England, but at the minute I can't bring myself to get going. It's just not where my head's at right now." I've still got that piece of paper now.

It was a massive help to have that there in front of me, but I was still shitting it when I picked up the phone. Graveney answered and I just came out with it. I can't remember what he said. I had no interest in what he said. My mind was made up. I was ringing simply out of courtesy to tell him I wasn't going.

Obviously he wasn't happy. In his eyes, he needed someone out there quickly, so the call didn't last too long. But I knew even if I had gone out there, within two days I'd be back.

He was never going to talk me round. I was not going, full stop. He could have said anything he wanted, it wouldn't have made a blind bit of difference. The minute I put the phone down I felt a million times better. I was fine, because I knew for sure I wasn't going. From there the sleepless nights, the anxiety, finished. I'd stopped the worst of it happening, because I knew from Pakistan that the real nightmare hadn't even begun.

The next winter I was picked to go to the West Indies on an A-tour and again I made myself unavailable, this time with sore shins. I'd had a problem with my shins all year, but if I'm brutally honest I put it on a bit because I didn't want to go. I was saying they were worse than they were. I knew it would have been a better thing for me to go, but there was no way I was getting on that plane.

I didn't have it in me. I've never had it in me to feel comfortable out of my personal surroundings. Emily was only small and to go away for 10 weeks, I just didn't have it in me. Ten weeks is a long time to be away from your family.

For the first few years I was very selfish about decisions I made about going on tour, but a lot of those decisions were tired decisions because they came at the end of a long hard season where I was mentally and physically knackered.

I was a young man. I didn't have the armoury, the mechanisms, to confront the barrier in my head. A barrier on the other side of which, to me, only existed torment and pain. My only thought was, 'I don't want to go. I can't go.'

It was getting to the point where I was thinking, 'What are they even picking me for?' Because they must have known there was a very good chance I wasn't going to go.

For me, there was an element of them picking me in the knowledge I wouldn't go, so then I would pull out and they could say, "Here we go again. Same old Harmison. He doesn't want to go," and I resented that as well. Why do it all so publicly?

In between the two A-tours, I was selected in the squad for England's home Test series against Zimbabwe and the West Indies. I was round my mam and dad's one Saturday morning when the phone rang. Mam answered. "It's David Graveney," she shouted. "He wants a word."

"The squad will be announced in the morning," he told me. "And you're in it."

The call-up came a little bit out of the blue, but I wasn't shocked. I wasn't leaping round the room screaming. I'm not a leaping round the room screaming sort of person. Well, not at nine o'clock on a Saturday morning.

In the approach to any Test series at the start of the summer it's not unusual for someone to make headlines, to be an outside pick, and on this occasion it was my name that came out of the hat. I'd actually had a fairly mediocre season up to that point, but we'd played Lancashire at Durham, with Mike Atherton playing, and I'd done OK, taking four wickets in the first innings. We'd also skittled Surrey for 104 and 85 in the previous game.

I went down to Lord's on the train. There was a group of young people with learning difficulties and they sat all around me. They were a great bunch and their cheery chatter gave me some perspective and helped take away my nerves.

One of the carers was an absolute battleaxe. As we neared York, she was barking instructions about getting off the train and started doing the head count. "One, two, three..." She looked at me. "Are you with us?"

"No, no. I'm on my way to London. I'm playing cricket for England."

She pointed at me and went, "Four."

5

IS THIS ENGLAND?

"Goughy, larger than life, a man who I admired so much, shook my hand and wished me good luck. 'Welcome to the madhouse,' he said"

My first time in an England dressing room made me question whether I wanted to play cricket for my country or not.

I realised very quickly it was very much every man for himself.

Initially, when I got to Lord's, I couldn't help thinking 'Wow!' Walking into the dressing room, they were all there – Michael Atherton, Alec Stewart, Graeme Hick, Mark Ramprakash, Nick Knight, Darren Gough, Andrew Caddick.

People were welcoming and the likes of Stewart and Ramprakash were straight over, saying hello, showing me where I could sit, and explaining where everything was.

Goughy, larger than life, a man who I admired so much, shook my hand and wished me good luck. "Welcome to the madhouse," he said.

But underneath people seemed distant. There was no togetherness, no sense of it being a team. This was a group of individuals who'd been put together. There were invisible barriers between them, one being self-preservation, the other being fear.

It wasn't about being a team, it was about each person trying to hang on to whatever they'd got. There was a little bit of a jealousy element to playing. You looked out for yourself, looked after your own place, and did your own thing.

All week I thought I was playing and the mood music was definitely going that way. England coach Duncan Fletcher spent a lot of time with me talking over how to bowl at Lord's and then on the morning of the game, I got to the ground and all of a sudden the clouds came over.

Once that happened I knew I was out the reckoning – they'd go with Ed Giddins because the conditions were right up his street. Even then there was talk of Fletcher preferring me. He had an eye on the long-term but Graveney always wanted to win the next game and so I didn't have a chance.

The plan was that young players such as myself should hang around for three days of the match to become accustomed to the set-up, but once I wasn't playing I'd sooner have been back with the lads at Durham, especially in the evenings because all the England players would disappear. Two would go off in one direction, three in another.

There were all these little circles, and I wasn't in any of them. It wasn't so bad because at least the hotel bar was busy, there were people to talk to, even if there were very few players to be seen.

It was when we moved on to Trent Bridge, an altogether quieter environment, that I was really struck by how different a set-up this was I'd walked into.

At Durham, for an away game, after play it'd be half six, seven o'clock, in the bar, go for something to eat, game of pool, couple of pints, and back to the hotel, and that's what I thought the norm was. I didn't necessarily think it'd be a couple of pints and going out on a night-time for England, but I did think there would be a social side. I was wrong. First night, down in the bar, nothing. Second night, nothing. I was thinking, going down at half six, I must have been early or late. But I popped back again a couple of times and it was like that all the time. I asked the question the next day, "Did anybody go out for a drink or a meal?"

"No."

I just sat in my room and watched the telly on my own – and that's the last thing I needed. For me, being on my own was the worst thing in the world. It got so bad that one afternoon, after training in the run-up to the game, I was going to drive all the way back home to pick Hayley up.

Otherwise I knew I was going to be there for another three days on my own. I thought, 'This is how bad it is, I've got to go and pick my wife up for company!' She said she'd come down when the game started, but it was the run-up to the game I was worried about.

You've got something to occupy your mind when the game is on. In the end, she came down on the train with her mum and dad. They kept me company because there was literally no-one there. Once the game started – again I didn't play – the dressing room was the dressing room, just like any other, but you could still feel the group wasn't as together as it should have been. It consisted of players who were looking over their shoulders all the time.

Back at Durham, the lads were asking what it was like, thinking I was going to tell them how great it was to be around England. To be honest, though, it was terrible.

I'd gone from a Durham dressing room, not quite 'happy Hampshire' but we enjoyed ourselves, to one that was quiet and intimidating. When I started at Durham we weren't very good. We were an emerging county, but we were a county of mates and we stuck together. England couldn't have been further removed. 'This is not like playing for Durham,' I was thinking. 'This isn't what I'm used to seeing.' To me, you get to know people better, not necessarily by sitting in a bar, but by going for a meal, sitting in the reception of a hotel having a coffee. But that wasn't there.

It just wasn't a consideration during that time. As a first impression of being an England cricketer, it was one I didn't enjoy. But I don't blame the players, I blame the environment, and that had been manufactured by the times those people had played in. How can you build a team spirit when the only spirit you get is actually in combat? For me, you don't build it like that, you build it in other ways.

These were well-established players who should have been world beaters. Instead they had been through a system which, through no fault of their own, meant they were very much looking after their own spaces.

Two bad games, they were gone. I could well understand why

Mark Ramprakash didn't fulfil his international career as well as he had done his first-class career. Same with Graeme Hick. People would say they were enigmas. They weren't enigmas, they were victims of the system.

Put Hick and Ramprakash in the system we had five years later and what a team England would have had. I remember bowling at Graeme Hick in the nets and he was using a half-width training bat. I was bowling at 90mph and he'd basically got a twig. If him and Ramprakash had started when Trescothick did or Vaughan it would have been a completely different story.

Play against them at county level and they'd be different players, because it was a stable environment in which they flourished. There's no way they would have averaged 30-odd. They never had the opportunity to fulfil their potential, and that goes for plenty of others too.

Those Tests in 2000 against Zimbabwe – I was picked for one against the West Indies at Edgbaston too but again didn't play – opened my eyes as to why England had struggled so badly for so long.

Yes, the individual players have got to take some responsibility, but the management and hierarchy and the way the game was run weren't up to the standards they should have been. The buck stopped with the ECB.

When Duncan Fletcher came in, he started to disassemble that failed and deeply flawed system. Nasser also realised England needed a fresh approach but it would take time to flush the mess out of the system, and when I first encountered England the pipe was still down the drain.

The good news was that, back in Ashington, cricket was on the tip of everyone's tongues. Everyone had been pleased for me that I'd been picked, even if I didn't play. It was a big thing for Ashington. For a long time it had been Milburn, Charlton, Charlton. There hadn't been any international recognition since then and all that recognition had been football.

It was beyond the town's wildest dreams to have someone playing cricket for England. Suddenly a lot more people were asking about joining the cricket club and the local media were all over it.

Sadly, that mood of buoyancy didn't extend to Durham. Boony had gone and Nick Speak took over as captain. I got on well with Nick as a person – funny, witty, great guy – but you're either a captain or you're not, and I don't think he was.

The pressure got to him and that spiralled down into the team. We'd gone from being the whipping boys when I started in 1996, to David Boon taking us to the First Division, and now we were slipping downhill again. I was only 21 at the time and with the club not doing well and the atmosphere having changed, my lifestyle went a bit.

I wasn't enjoying my cricket as much as I should and so following on from that I was eating the wrong stuff, not going to the gym. I had one eye off the cricket more than I had both eyes on it. It wasn't as though I was in nightclubs half the night. I've never been a nightclub person. I've probably been into Newcastle on a night out about three times in my life. I'm not a big fan of loud music, all the singing and dancing. I'd rather go and sit in a bar and have a few beers, and over that summer I probably had a few too many. I took my focus off being a professional cricketer.

It was my worst year in professional cricket, the only time I ever seriously considered leaving Durham. Lancashire had been showing interest in me for a while and so were Hampshire.

People were telling me if I moved I'd have a better chance of playing for England. My head was spinning. I knew I wanted to play cricket for England. Was I going to do that at Durham, or was I always going to be on the periphery?

Durham was only eight-years-old and it looked like we were on our way back down. None of that was in my favour. I was being a bit selfish thinking like that, I know. I didn't want to leave Durham. They were the team that had shown trust in me and given me a chance at an early age. But Lancashire had Fred, which was a pulling factor, as well as John Crawley, who I'd also spent a bit of time with and got to know. It was also a club with tradition.

But there was a flipside to the equation. For a start, the wicket at Durham was a help to me. On that surface I was always going to get wickets, and if you get wickets you're always going to get spoken about. The other thing was there wasn't the expectation to deal with, like at an old established club such as Lancashire.

I knew my mental health had to come into it as well. Did I want to leave Durham and go somewhere I could potentially self-destruct? I'd miss Ashington. It was my home, where my family were, where I had Hayley and Emily.

In the end, Hampshire came in with the better offer, but I never even contemplated it because it was too much of the unknown. Lancashire, however, retained some appeal, closer to home, and a better wicket.

At the end of that season, though, as relegation loomed, Jon Lewis had been handed the captaincy at Durham. It was a massive factor. I liked Jon, he was a solid bloke, who everyone trusted, and I knew he'd have the support of the dressing room.

He was someone who would pull us all together, like Boony. In the end, I stayed at Durham for a lot less than I could have got elsewhere. But playing was never about the money for me, it was about being happy and looking after myself.

If Nick Speak had carried on I probably would have gone as I didn't want to go through another year like the last one. Another poor year and then my contract would have been up and who then was going to want to touch me? Jon Lewis offered hope, and the new start was confirmed when Martyn Moxon came in as coach.

Sadly, one Durham lad who did go to Lancashire was John Wood. I'd miss him a lot. He was a gentle giant, like a big brother, somebody I loved to bits. I was devastated he was going, but it was a great move for him. It was where his family lived, plus it was a bigger club. John had helped me so much, especially with the homesickness when I didn't want to go to New Zealand. In cricketing terms, he helped turn a relatively young boy into a man. John was one of three or four older players who left at that stage and bizarrely, at the age of 22, I found myself one of the senior players.

For the trip down to Gloucester, I had four lads of 17 or 18 sharing my car. That worried me, but on the other hand I felt I had a duty, as one of the club's higher paid players, to take the responsibility on. Me and Paul Collingwood both grew up a bit at that stage.

We both wanted Durham to be the best team in England. After a stuttering year in 2000 – after the England call-up I suffered a torn side – I bowled a lot more overs in 2001 and felt I was coming back to my best.

That was also the year I first encountered Kevin Pietersen,

when Nottinghamshire came to play at the Riverside. He came in at number six, on a cold day, and worked hard on a tricky wicket for 38. I was someone who had a reputation for being tall, quick and aggressive.

Normally, I'd push people back, but what struck me was Kevin came forward at me all the time. As I was bowling, I was thinking he was lucky but then later, when I had the boots off and the emotion was removed, it occurred to me he did actually look in control.

He never really looked like he was going to get out. I thought maybe I could get him at gully, because he was hitting on the up, but otherwise he was in control. We played a one-day game against them a few weeks later and he did exactly the same, and when I saw that I realised the way he performed wasn't a fluke. This was actually how this guy played.

We always used to joke at Durham about southern teams. In your mind, you could see them coming up in their cars or on the bus thinking, 'Jesus Christ, we've got to stop twice before we get to Durham. Even when we get to Leeds, it's another two-and-a-half hours away. It's going to be no warmer than eight degrees all week and that idiot Harmison is going to be trying to knock our heads off.'

Sometimes they'd be beaten before they got to Wetherby. Notts weren't as far south as others, and they had some good players, but we always felt we could intimidate them. They had big-shot players but not ones who were willing to take it on the body, so for Kevin to come out and play the way he did was something out of the ordinary.

It's clear now when I think back to that Championship game that he'd pre-planned that innings, he was going to take me on whatever the cost. From then on, he was on everybody's radar and by the end of the summer everybody was talking about him.

As for me, after impressing all summer, I was called up to go to England's brand spanking new Academy in Adelaide.

The idea was to replicate the Australian Academy which had turned out a conveyor belt of great players including Glenn McGrath, Shane Warne, Matthew Hayden and Justin Langer. In all honesty, it could have been over for me before it had really begun.

Not 'homesickness' this time. More that two weeks before the flight, I was in a street covered in blood with my face sliced open.

More scars for life.

6

HOME AND AWAY

*"'Write what you want,' I told him. 'Fuck off.' The
story never surfaced"*

I have never been a target for idiots.
That's never happened to me in Ashington. It's one of the
things that's so good about the place. Also, I was a cricketer
and football's the number one round here. I never put myself
in that position anyway. I would only ever drink in one or two
places that I knew, still do.

Surround yourself with people and an environment you're
comfortable with and you'll be fine, you won't ever get a
problem. The way I see it is if you want to go and find trouble,
you'll find it. On this occasion, however, trouble found me.

I'd been watching my brother James play football with
Bedlington up the road. Afterwards, all the lads had gone for a
night out in the town and I was with them. As we walked into a
bar, it was apparent something was already kicking off.

One of the Bedlington players got nutted in a random act,

there was a lot of commotion, and the lad who did it came out of the bar and hit the first person he saw. It calmed down momentarily, but then the same lad got a Budweiser bottle, smashed it, went for somebody, missed, and instead caught the Bedlington manager on the wrist and cut the artery. There was blood everywhere.

I was right next to this lad and he was just swinging the bottle around. I had to defend myself and managed to get him on the floor, my left foot on the hand with the bottle.

The red mist had well and truly descended, and I was hitting him, but then I got knocked. The hand with the bottle came free and it went straight up my face and up the side of my nose, missing my eye by a fraction of an inch. My nose was hanging off and my lip was right through. I was bleeding all over the place, in a horrible mess.

The lads were saying, "Come on, we'll get you out the way" – because I was playing for Durham at the time and had a little bit of a profile. Their idea was we'd get out the way and then regroup elsewhere. That wasn't going to work. I could put my tongue through the hole in my face and touch the top of my cheek. I had to go the hospital. An ambulance came and took me away.

With it being two weeks before I was due to go out to Australia, I told the police I didn't want to press charges. I didn't want to have to come back all that way. My dad was the same. "Leave it," he told me. "It's not worth it."

He was right. If I'd had to come back for a court case I'd have been harming my own career. Before I'd even got anywhere, I'd have had some kind of reputation, even if none of it was my fault. But it was hard to leave matters like that, this bloke had caused a lot of distress and pain. I had to go to hospital in Newcastle and have plastic surgery. The injections were awful, four or five just to make the area numb. It was a horrendous experience and I was lucky that the surgeon was an Indian guy who loved cricket.

He knew of me and so I think he looked after me a bit. He did a good job on the scar, but there was always going to be one and that's why ever since I've always had a beard. I don't like it being seen, and I don't like seeing it myself.

However, when Martyn Moxon came to Durham as coach, he brought a rule in where we had to be clean shaven every day. It was officious nonsense of the worst kind – we played for a cricket club, it didn't own us – and I hated it because the scar was there for all to see.

It was the same with the Academy.

I flew to Australia with the stitches in and whenever the official photos were taken I would try to keep out the way. While I was there I got a phone call from the police in the middle of the night asking where I was and what I was doing.

The person I'd had a problem with in Bedlington had been beaten up and they were obviously going through the files. I was out in Australia so it couldn't have been me! "OK. Nay bother," they said, and that was pretty much the end of it.

To be honest, I don't think they were that fussed about following it up and I just didn't want any hassle to come back on me.

The incident made the local newspapers but never the nationals and the only time I ever got asked about it was during the Ashes in 2005. I was in a hotel and a cricket journalist rang my room and said he wanted to talk about the scar on my face.

"Write what you want," I told him. "Fuck off." The story never surfaced.

Over in Adelaide and things hadn't got off to the smoothest of starts for any of us, not just the ones with stitches keeping their face together.

Rod Marsh, the legendary Australian wicket-keeper, stout, strong, himself once said to have been carried off a plane after drinking 34 cans of beer, and not a man to be messed with, was laying out what would be expected of us on the trip – fitness regimes, coaching, games, standards of behaviour.

When he'd finished, one of his sidekicks mentioned that Robbie Williams was playing in town that night if we fancied going. Rod had never heard of him. "Who's Robbie Williams?" he asked.

It was then that Swanny piped up. "He's a fucking singer," he said, adding to what was already a very poor misjudgement with a mock Australian accent. "You ignorant Aussie cunt."

There was absolute silence.

Behind Rod I could see a couple of the coaching staff trying hard not to laugh. We were in front of him and thought it best to keep straight faces. Rod stared at Swanny for 15 seconds and then turned away. It was clear from that moment that Swanny had blown it with him.

I'd like to say this outburst was unexpected, but the truth is this was Swanny all over. All his life his mouth has been three seconds quicker than his brain. He'd say something without ever quite realising the effect it had.

The trick with Swanny was to dip in and out. He was like the Duracell bunny, going from the first minute of the morning to the last minute at night. You could leave the room, come back three hours later, and he'd still be doing the same thing – being Graeme Swann. If you could dip in and out, it was fine. Sit there and listen to it all the time and you'd end up wanting to kill him.

For 15 weeks, the Academy squad would be staying in what soon came to be termed the *Big Brother* house. Downstairs there was a reception area, a massive dining hall with a kitchen, a conference room where all the meetings would be held, and a games room with pool tables.

Upstairs there were just bedrooms of various sizes and containing varying numbers of beds. Rod lived in Adelaide anyway while the manager, Nigel Laughton, and the assistant coach, John Abrahams, were living in these plush apartments down the road. They were in there, and we were in here. Don't get me wrong, it wasn't a dump, but it did feel a bit like youth hostelling.

I shouldn't have been surprised. Before we flew to Australia we'd had a week at another academy – the army's, at Sandhurst.

All of a sudden, facing Courtney Walsh hadn't seemed so bad. Among the tests we'd endured was a night with no shelter in a forest and umpteen assault courses. We'd be in the swimming pool for 6.30am, before circuit training, team-building exercises, zip-wires and lectures on resilience from leading sportspeople and those who'd survived in the harshest of conditions, although not in a dressing room with Graeme Swann. At least at the Academy in Adelaide I could see no sign of any swamps to wade through.

I was rooming with Fred, and I don't think it was an accident. John Abrahams and physio, Kirk Russell, had put me in with him because they were well aware of the troubles I'd been having ron previous tours. They knew I'd have an ear in Fred. While two

6ft-plus blokes in a room the size of a small caravan is always going to be fun we didn't tend to spend much time in there.

For a start we were as messy as each other. The other clinching factor was that there was absolutely nothing to do. If we had any free time we'd either be downstairs watching DVDs, in the General Havelock pub over the road, or on the beach. But there wasn't much time to ourselves because the management insisted on us doing all sorts of thoroughly pointless stuff.

The idea was to teach us life skills, how we should be looking after ourselves, how to cook. I couldn't help thinking, 'Hang on, I've got a wife and kid and I'm getting treated like I'm someone at university. I've got a 25-year mortgage, for Christ's sake. This is for a 17-year-old.' Fred and Rob Key would take the mick out of me because I refused point blank to cook. But what did I want to learn cookery for when I was there to learn cricket?

One night, we had to go to the manager's apartment and put on a *Come Dine With Me*-style evening. There were six of us who had to do it. We had to serve Laughton, Abrahams and us six too. I didn't want to do it. I was extremely reluctant to the point where I'm not actually sure I contributed anything to the occasion.

I had no interest in this kind of nonsense.

All I wanted to do was play cricket and improve myself, but even that was a minefield – there were so many people in your face. For example, early on I was introduced to a young Australian bio-mechanic and right from the start I could see what he was doing – he was cloning people.

In his case, he wanted everybody to be a Brett Lee. One of my big bugbears in coaching is trying to teach everybody the same, but this bloke was doing just that. I was 22, I was looking at him and I couldn't stop laughing.

He was analysing the way I was picking my legs up, the way my arm was coming over and he tried to completely change my action. The one thing I've never done is suffer fools.

"Look," I told him. "I can bowl at 90 miles an hour. Sometimes I've got no idea where it's going. So if I've got no idea where it's going at 90 miles an hour, what chance has somebody 22 yards away got? I might get to 91 or 92 miles an hour doing it your way, but that doesn't feel comfortable to me, so I'm not going to do it."

One, he didn't like it, because he was arrogant. I've met some people who love themselves, but what an opinion of himself this bloke had. Two, it got me thinking, 'What am I doing here? What am I doing around these people?'

It's obvious to anyone that everybody is different, but these people had learnt out of textbooks. We were being taught by people who were little more than schoolteachers. All I could do was laugh.

The only person I was really bothered about – apart from John Abrahams, one of the nicest guys you'll meet, a real people person, who I really liked and respected – was Rod himself. Rod had masterminded the Australian Academy programme which had produced this great new wave of Aussie internationals. You want to work with good people, and he was absolutely one of them.

Also there was Troy Cooley, the main bowling coach, who I clicked with right away. The minute I met Troy and spoke to him about bowling, I knew straight off that he got me. I didn't know if Troy Cooley had ever bowled a cricket ball in his life, but I was talking to a man who not only understood me, but understood the others too. I could see him talking to fellow paceman Simon Jones and he was talking to him in a completely different language to how he was talking to me.

He knew everyone was different. I could see he knew what he

was talking about. So while the bio-mechanic was about as much use as a chocolate fireguard, Troy was different. Straight away we had a rapport. He didn't try to change my action, he just tried to make it as good as it possibly could be for me – not for Simon Jones, not for Alex Tudor, not for Steve Kirby – but for me. He was busy fine-tuning their actions separately.

Yet, it felt like everyone wanted their five minutes. We were being pulled from pillar to post. It was all sports science this, lifestyle that. I didn't want it. I wasn't interested.

All I wanted to do was learn how to play cricket in different countries and different environments, and yet we were stuck doing all that nonsense instead. There were even people keeping an eye on what we had in the fridge, bizarrely sparking another clash between Rod and Swanny.

A big thing about the Academy from a nutrition point of view was no butter. Swanny was having none of that, nipped up the local shop and got a massive tub. Rod walked into the kitchen just as he was buttering his toast.

Swanny was trying to say he didn't realise butter was banned – he'd just thought we were out of it. This time at least he held back on the Aussie accent. Rod was still having none of it. It was duly noted that Swanny was taking the piss. It didn't really matter. We were rarely at the house anyway.

There was a restaurant at the top of the street and two pubs on the corner. As soon as the day finished, we'd eat in one of those. Because of that, next year's intake weren't allowed to go out as much! At one stage Hayley came out – we'd decided to use the trip as a late honeymoon. She didn't stay in the *Big Brother* house, she stayed in the hotel round the corner. I went and stayed with her, but they weren't going to let me.

They clearly weren't keen on a married man staying with his wife in his own time! It was quite bizarre, but eventually they backed down.

A lot of the problem stemmed from a major discrepancy between the Australian and England Academy. Rod was getting paid decent whack to try to recreate the Aussie version. But what the Australians always said was that their Academy was there to provide a decent transition between under-19 and first-class cricket. This was entirely different. We were a total mishmash.

We were treated like some of us had never played first-class cricket, but some of us had played 40-50 matches, several were secure in their county teams and had played for England. At the same time, the majority of us had houses and mortgages, some of us had wives and kids, and yet we had a woman, basically in charge of the building, who was also supposed to be a mother figure. We were grown blokes! It was like having a matron knocking about.

Added to that was the fitness manager, Richard Smith, who was a little lacking in people skills, and the fact that we hardly played any cricket in the first part of the trip.

The whole enterprise was mindboggling.

As always, in the end, Fred got lucky. We'd been there a few weeks when he got called-up for the full England tour of India. Rod told Fred he still didn't think he was ready for international cricket, but he wished him good luck anyway. Soon he'd become one of the selectors.

We went out to mark Fred's departure. I'd bowed out earlier but at about four o'clock in the morning, him and Rob Key were back at *Big Brother* HQ, both with a bottle of bubbly and both singing Frank Sinatra lyrics at the top of their voices. "I get a kick out of you – I get no kick from Champagne!" There was no shutting Fred up. He was celebrating. "I'm going! I'm getting out of this place! I'm going to India – which is even worse, but at least I'm not here!"

And then he passed out. He had to be up in no time to get to the airport for an early flight. I was packing his kit while the management was trying to wake him up.

Eventually we got him off the bed and on to the floor. It was like one of those vet programmes where they've heavily sedated a hippo. The minutes were ticking by. Nigel Laughton told me I'd have to take him to the airport because he wasn't waiting any longer. Eventually we got him up, bag over his shoulder, and he was walking out the door. There was one problem – he didn't have a stitch of clothing on.

"What are you doing?" I spluttered. "You've got nothing on."

He looked at me. "I'm going to put on a smile. Because I'm getting out of here."

I chucked my tracksuit at him. He put it on and away he went. That night I got a phone call.

"Where's my bowling boots?"

"They're under the desk."

"What are they doing there?"

"It's not my fault you couldn't get up. You shouldn't have got so pissed."

Fred was lucky to have found an escape.

I had a couple of weeks until Christmas, when we had a fortnight at home before flying back. I liked the Christmas part. It was the flying back that was troubling me. Having worked hard for those first seven weeks, I vowed that I wasn't going to return after Christmas.

For someone who struggled being away from home, to go to Australia for seven weeks, then come back, and then have to go again, was a big thing. The thought that I was going back to do all this stupid stuff made it even bigger. 'Fuck it,' I told myself. 'I'm not going back. I don't want to go back. I shouldn't have to go back.'

I kept it all bottled up over Christmas. I didn't want to admit to anyone how I was feeling. It was like being in denial, just hoping it would all go away. It wasn't a great idea. One thing I've learnt down the years is that a lot of my mental health issues come from keeping things to myself.

It was New Zealand all over again. All the time the flight back to Australia was getting nearer and nearer. With a day to go, I rang John Abrahams and came out with it – "I'm not going." He tried to talk me round but I was having none of it. He relayed my decision to the England management.

Obviously, there was hell to pay. Instead of flying out with the team, John came to my house. I never for one minute thought he'd succeed – my mind was made up – but in the end he convinced me it would be in my best interests to go back.

He pointed out that England were in New Zealand three weeks later. Their first choice fast-medium bowler, Jimmy Ormond, had fitness issues and it wasn't clear if he was going to make it.

If that was the case, they'd take one of the Academy bowlers who was already nearby in Australia, and I'd have a good chance if I was fit. All I wanted to do was play cricket. I reasoned if there was a chance to play cricket for England and get out of the *Big Brother* house, I'd do it. "OK, I'll go back," I said to John.

It wasn't as if I'd have packed in if I hadn't gone back to Australia, because I knew for a fact whatever happened I'd be back at Durham on April 1, where I was comfortable, where I was happy, and where I'd take 60 or 70 wickets in the Championship. But I knew I was a good bowler, always backed my ability, and wanted to play cricket at a higher level. I just wasn't interested in the bullshit that people surrounded it with.

My whole career, it wasn't my way or the highway, but I always backed my own ability to get me where I wanted to be. That meant sometimes I was perceived as being anti-authority. I was very headstrong, but I wasn't anti-authority. Team meals I was always there. I'd always abide by the dress code.

At times when I played for England, when Nasser Hussain was captain, and then later when Michael Vaughan took over, there were selfish characters in the group who wouldn't turn up for team meals. I would never go along with that.

The situation with the Academy wasn't about causing trouble, it was about wanting to play cricket in the best possible environment. I didn't believe that cooking and 'life lessons' in public speaking and financial management had anything to do with it.

I'd found myself back at school, and I hated school.

Me, Fred, and Rob Key spoke a lot on that trip about how some things you have to go through if you want to play for England. But this time I'd just had enough. None of it was helping my mental health issues. Inside I was struggling. I'd go to bed at night thinking, 'What are you doing here? You're hurting yourself. You're harming yourself. You're doing something that's making you feel bad. You're struggling from a mental health point of view, and then you're going through all this? What's it all for?'

The end goal was I wanted to play cricket for England.

I wanted to be the best I could be and the only way I could test that was in the biggest arena, and yet here I was, striving to get better, thinking this Academy trip was going to be this great thing, and then it wasn't. It just wasn't. It was a let-down, a disappointment, and when you've got a chemical imbalance in your head and those emotions are going up and down, up and down, it's making it 10 times worse than for somebody who doesn't.

That's why I was so headstrong. If I hadn't been headstrong I wouldn't have survived. I would have gone on the downward slope, those feelings would have gobbled me up, and I would never have found the upward slope again.

My problem was I was a northern lad who said it how it was. I wasn't arrogant or disruptive, but if I felt something needed saying I'd say it.

Sometimes it would be good, sometimes bad. I was determined that, whatever came in front of me, and even if I made the wrong choice, I'd be the one shaping my life the way I wanted it to be.

Throughout my career, that ability to work things out for myself was something I was proud of. It was the northern thing in me, my working-class roots, that made me how I was. It came from trusting in and thinking for myself. After Christmas, with Fred gone, I was now rooming with Rob Key – again, probably a wise decision on the part of the management. Keysey also knew the ins and outs of what I'd been going through. In fact, at times I was closer to Keysey than anyone else in terms of what was going on in my head. Fred and Keysey liked playing the fool but there was actually another altogether more serious side to them.

When you're looking at friends who've helped you no end, those two are front of the queue. They could easily have laughed it off, easily have run a mile, thought I was a lunatic, but they never did. Instead, if they could see I was in a difficult place, they'd either be listening or subtly trying to help.

When it comes to people you play cricket with, they're all just acquaintances, you work with them. But your mates are different. Over the course of a career, you'll probably end up with maybe two or three people who you'd drop anything for to go and help out.

Two of my best mates in life are Rob Key and Andrew Flintoff, and no matter what happened I'd back them up to the end of the world. And I know for a fact they'd do the same.

It should also be said that, while I thought they got the Academy system wrong, there were people around the hierarchy who understood that not everyone is the same, that some people have difficulties. I was one of them and to counter that they put two people I was close to in the room with me.

I will always be grateful for that although after I went back, a lot of what I did I did reluctantly. There was a run along the beach and when we first did it before Christmas I came second in 25 minutes because although I wasn't a gymnast, I was naturally fit.

When we did it again after Christmas, when I was at my darkest, it took me an hour to walk there and back. I was trying to make a point – that I hate this.

At training, I made a beeline for Rod and told him honestly what my problem was. I opened up to him. I told him how I wanted to learn, but I didn't like all the bullshit that went with it. "Please," I said to him. "Tell me this isn't what you have to do to play cricket for England."

Rod had to toe the party line, but until that point I don't really think he understood what the whole programme was. He had his time with us, and other people had theirs, but I don't think he fully comprehended what those other people were doing to us.

He'd do his sessions and then go back to his house. After talking to half a dozen players, he got an understanding that people weren't happy with what was going on and said he'd take it on board. By then it was too late for this intake but I hope we improved matters for those who followed after. Next year's intake was noticeably younger, so I think they did learn from us.

In the end, I said to Rod, "If Ormond's fit for New Zealand, I want to go home. I've played every game since I've been out here, worked my nuts off, done everything that's required. I don't think it's doing me any good to be here now."

He wasn't a bad psychologist. "Look," he said. "There's another six weeks left of this trip. You play the next three games and your rest can be the last four weeks of the trip. Everybody else has had a rest, and this can be yours." As it turned out, during the last four-day game I dislocated my shoulder and came home anyway.

Don't get me wrong. I paint that Academy trip like 10 weeks of my life that I'll never get back, and there were dark times, but I actually enjoyed what cricket there was.

Then there were some of the people who were around. Troy Cooley was a big factor in persuading me to go back after Christmas. I held him in such high regard. That Academy trip was also where I first came across Andrew Strauss. We were chalk and cheese. Mine and his schooling days were completely different! Not only did he go to his but it was Radley College, a boarding school in Oxfordshire.

None of that mattered to either of us. I hoped I'd get to play cricket with him for a long period. 'If I was going into battle or a war,' I thought, 'I'd love to have him by my side.'

Even if I hadn't gone back to Adelaide after Christmas, I still think I'd have made it. I still believe I'd have made my debut for England when I did. There'd have been more of a microscope on me because I'd backed out of another trip, but I wouldn't have been bothered. If I didn't get picked, fine, I was never meant to get picked. If I did, then that was the goal in the first place. I didn't need people telling me what to do, how to live my life to make that happen, I could do that myself anyway.

In the end, everything that happened in Australia would be put into perspective by the events of March 23, 2002.

Within minutes, about 15 texts popped up on my phone.

Ben Hollioake had been killed in a car crash in Western Australia.

I couldn't honestly comprehend what I was seeing. I couldn't take it in. It didn't seem real. It didn't seem true. I was devastated. It was absolutely heartbreaking. I knew Ben well.

He was on the under-19 Pakistan trip, and probably the most naturally gifted cricketer I ever played with. His nickname was Pele. It reflected the fact he was a good-looking lad and that everything he touched turned to gold.

That winter we thought Ben was going to come and practice with the Academy but he lived in Australia and so was playing cricket there anyway. It's easy to say such and such would have played a hundred times for England but Ben undoubtedly would have been part of that set-up for a long time.

He was as naturally talented with bat, ball, or in the field as anyone I've ever met. He was a freak of nature, an incredible character, with zero fear. He was so close to his brother Adam.

They lived together in England and Adam was like his dad over here. What Adam must have gone through, God only knows. Sometimes you see brothers who aren't close. Those two were inseparable. They were brothers, mates, everything.

For Adam to lose him the way he did was horrific. It was a reminder that this game we play is just that, a game.

Ben Hollioake – taken before his time.

7

DONKEYS

*"Nasser saw their shoulders going up and down.
'Oi, you two fat fuckers, stop taking the piss!' At
the same time he evicted Key from the slips"*

Iknew I hadn't exactly added a gloss to my CV with what
had happened in Australia, but on the other hand nobody
had a bad thing to say about the actual cricket I'd played.

Also, I'd kicked off well again in the Championship, even if I
wasn't pulling up trees like I was in the first couple of seasons –
inevitable really, as back then I was a surprise package.

In 1998, when I released that ball from 22 yards no-one knew
what they were going to get. Aside from a bit of chat amongst
the players in the dressing room, batsmen were coming in front
of me blind.

The 90mph inswingers, the steepling bounce, the throat balls,
they were all new. Now these players had faced me a few times
they'd come up with a plan, even if it was just to get the hell out
of the way.

At the same time, I knew I had improved as a bowler. If I'd made the England team against Zimbabwe in 2000, it would have been as a raw talent, a shot in the dark. Now I'd been doing this for four seasons. I knew what cricket was. I knew how to deliver in different conditions. I knew I was ready for England.

India were the visitors that summer and I'd missed out for the series opener at Lord's when the selectors went with Simon Jones.

However, Simon suffered a side strain in that game and, in terms of sheer pace, they saw me as the natural replacement for the second match at Trent Bridge. Once again, I got the call off Graveney. It was somewhat lighter than some we'd had in the past.

"I just want to tell you you've been selected and it will be announced in the morning," he said. "Congratulations, all your hard work has paid off, and good luck." The papers seemed to already know, not that any of the nationals bothered coming up to Ashington – they thought they needed jabs to come up this far. I was delighted to have got the call, while also feeling a bit for Simon. He was a good mate and nobody wants to see another player injured. But that's sport, you jump in and take your chance when it comes.

When I saw the full squad, I was even more thrilled. Keysey was making his debut as well and while I was deemed too distant, the newspapers clearly had got to him. *The Mirror's* headline was, 'I was too fat, drank too much, and went clubbing – meet England's new batting sensation Robert Key.'

I've still got the cutting. Fred, who'd pretty much cemented his England place by then, was in the team as well. The two people

I'd drop everything for would be alongside me. Undoubtedly that helped ease my nerves a little, but after my previous experience of England there was still some trepidation as to what I'd find.

Thankfully, I needn't have worried. For a start, after another two years on the circuit, I knew people in the group and Matthew Hoggard and John Crawley were good pals as well.

More than that, though, the whole dynamic had changed. The two-year gap had seen the bitterness, the jealousy, the self-preservatory instinct, sucked out of the atmosphere. It was still in the air a little bit, but Nasser had seen what was wrong, had even been what was wrong, and concluded he had to change the culture to one that was more secure.

He and Duncan Fletcher had dismantled that team – Hick and Ramprakash had gone and Mike Atherton had retired – and taken new players such as Fred, Hoggy, Ashley Giles, Simon, Colly, and now me, forward. They were backing new players over a period of time, rather than the old system of, "Have a shit game and you're out."

Nasser, while not always the easiest of company himself, made the dressing room more inclusive, more welcoming, and that told in the performances of the players. The characters were a lot better. You could breathe in that environment; in the other you were stifled.

Similarly, I wasn't marooned in my room every night. This time around, the players were more my age and not so worried about their places. Me and Keysey were always rather partial to a Nando's and most evenings would head into Nottingham, but even if we laid off the chicken for a night there was always someone to do something with.

At Trent Bridge, I formed a large nest with Keysey in the corner of the dressing room. His stuff was all over the floor – if Rob Key hadn't been a cricketer he'd have been a tramp – and my stuff was thrown everywhere too.

In the middle of all that mess we both felt very much at home. Nasser's idea of a warm and welcoming atmosphere didn't quite extend as far as the cap presentation.

Nasser came off after, as usual, losing the toss, and approached me and Keysey as we stood by the pavilion. "Well done Kent," he said, and threw Key's cap at him. "Well done Durham," chucked me mine, and walked off.

The cap ceremony is now a big thing, but back then it didn't have all the razzmatazz surrounding it. There were no TV cameras, no nothing. Nasser tossing us our caps was all part of his, er, fun and witty sense of humour. In fact, that was quite funny for him.

It didn't occur to me at the time, but looking back I think what it also did was betray the nervousness he had around people. He was thought of as being a bit abrasive when, in fact, he just struggled around those he didn't know so well. Nasser's 'joke' didn't bother me one bit. I didn't care who gave me my cap. What mattered to me was I was standing next to one of my best mates.

We had gone through a lot as we'd progressed through the system together. I'd contributed to him getting his opening first-class hundred at Canterbury by bowling terribly, and in return he'd seen me through some of my darkest moments. Now I was going to play Test cricket for England with him.

It didn't look a bad wicket and India were only ever going to bat. There was barely time for a quick return to the dressing room, a sharp pep talk from Nasser – "Don't let them settle. Let's be on our game from the start!" – and then we were out there. I was stood at mid-on, looking round, wholly aware of what a big moment this was for me. I looked at the three lions and the 611 on my chest, signifying I was the 611th person to play for England. Rob Key was 612. I didn't want 613 to be either of our replacements but Fred and Keysey didn't appear to be taking things quite so seriously.

The way they were going on we might as well have been playing for the Dog & Duck on the park. Before we went out, Duncan Fletcher was wondering where Keysey should field. "Put him in the slips," said Fred. "He's a great slip fielder."

Truth was, Rob Key had never fielded in the slips in his life. Fred just wanted to have his mate to talk to. As it turned out, Keysey took a great catch early doors, straight in, he was flying. A few overs later, however, a catch came to Fred – straight down. At the end of the over, I was walking mid-on to mid-on, as they were going slip to slip. As we passed, Key said to me, "Fred's favourite TV series – *Drop The Dead Donkey*!" Fred was chuckling a little bit and I have to admit I was laughing too. Then, of course, Key goes and drops one, so Fred's in the driving seat.

As we passed the next time, Fred piped up, "Rob's favourite wrestling move, drop kick!" I was trying not to laugh, but Nasser saw their shoulders going up and down. "Oi, you two fat fuckers, stop taking the piss!" At the same time he evicted Key from the slips.

No two ways about it, I was nervous when Nasser finally chucked me the ball.

At the time I'd only ever played in front of one man and his dog in County Championship matches, and a couple of bigger crowds of between three and five thousand in Benson & Hedges Cup ties, but nothing like a Test match in front of 18,000 at Trent Bridge.

As it turned out, it wasn't too bad. My first four overs were maidens – they just couldn't hit the thing because I bowled so wide outside off stump! First day nerves taken into account, I thought I'd acquitted myself quite well and was just starting to cause the Indians a few problems when the umpires offered the light and they came off.

The other major difference between Test and county cricket I noticed was how tired I was at the end of the day. Back at Durham, I could bowl 18 overs in a day, have five or six pints and a Chinese, go to bed at 11 o'clock, wake up and do it all again. In a Test match, I could bowl 15 overs, have room service, a lime and soda, and be in bed for nine.

Physically, it's a bit more demanding, but mentally it zaps everything out of you. You can't switch off for one minute. It's much more intense and while you may not consciously recognise the scrutiny you're under, the pressure to perform is a constant companion.

For players now, it's even worse, because they have even more scrutiny to contend with. Everybody has an opinion, not just the crowd, journalists and commentators, but the millions and billions out there on social media. I tried not to read much that was written about me, but that doesn't mean you're shielded from it. People, be it players, coaches, journalists, or maybe just a bloke in the pub, will mention it to you.

I've always said I've never been bothered about anything

anybody wrote about me, but underneath, who knows what effect it has?

Breaking the Test duck was always going to be a massive moment, and when Nasser tossed me the new ball the next day, it felt like my big chance had come. A few moments later they were hitting the replay button in the commentary box. Sadly, not for a wicket.

My hand had struck my knee in the delivery stride and the ball was now some distance behind me on the grass. No-one, probably deliberately, made a big deal about it. It was treated as just one of those things – keep calm and carry on. My nerves soon settled and the big moment eventually happened.

My first Test wicket came when Ajit Agarkar was caught by Mark Butcher. When I tell people that, they always say, "Oh yes, Butcher, great slip fielder." It was actually caught at third man from a wide long hop that he slashed at. Parthiv Patel, the wicket-keeper, was only 17 at the time, a rabbit in the headlights, and was caught off a throat ball by Flintoff in the slips, and then I got Harbhajan Singh too.

The game itself fizzled out after we racked up a mammoth 617 and then Rahul Dravid, Sachin Tendulkar and Sourav Ganguly took root. Any bowler who played for England with Michael Vaughan from that point on would never hear the end of the fact that it was him who eventually bowled Tendulkar through the gate, much to his glee – "If I can do it, why can't you?"

Ganguly, meanwhile, was on 99 when Fred went off for a toilet break. While he was facing the porcelain, I nipped one through the Prince of Calcutta's defences. Ganguly was playing at Lancashire at the time and, seen as a little aloof, he wasn't very popular.

As he was walking off, Fred timed his run back on to the field so he could give him a volley and tell him what he thought of him. There was a lot of Lancashire politics in that volley.

A debut is never easy but as the game went on I felt more and more at home. The nerves had disappeared a bit and I could just enjoy the experience.

As my career progressed, I would always find India or Pakistan Test matches at Trent Bridge or Edgbaston particularly amazing. After a few years, you'd see the same faces sitting in the same places. If we were playing India or Pakistan, they'd have those shirts on, but when we were playing South Africa, Australia or the West Indies, they'd have England tops.

I hoped I'd done enough to be retained for the next Test at Headingley, but the selectors were chopping and changing at the time. Andy Caddick and Alex Tudor came in and I didn't play another game in the series, but I thought my five wickets on debut gave me a reasonable chance of making the Ashes tour that winter.

In the end, I was proved right. I'd played one Test for England and now I was on the biggest tour of them all. I was delighted, naturally, but at the same time I knew it was going to be hard. Hayley was pregnant again and I was clearly going to be away from her and Emily for a long time.

When I picked up my bag and headed for the door, Emily was in tears. If I'd thought leaving home was hard before, the sight of my devastated three-year-old was a million times worse.

My hope was I'd be back home in six weeks for the birth because the trip had an unusual schedule. There were three Tests, then a two-week break for the one-dayers, and then the last two Tests, more one-dayers and then the World Cup.

I was hoping to play the first three Test matches, come home, go back for a bit and then that would be it because I hadn't played one-day cricket for England at that point.

Darren Gough had been touch and go for the trip with a bad knee that had kept him out virtually all summer, but in the end England had taken a gamble on him.

You need your big characters on a trip like this and Goughy was undoubtedly one of them. I've never met anyone who could talk about themselves so much. In cricket, you often see people bigging themselves up and you think they're a twat but Goughy was brilliant.

He was the only person I know who could big himself up and yet not upset anybody. The first time I met him, he told me, "My nickname's Rhino."

"Oh yeah, why?"

"Because I'm as strong as an ox."

As much as I ever had one, Goughy was my cricketing hero when I was growing up. He's another whose shirt adorns my wall. I love the bloke. Even now, if ever I'm feeling down I'll ring him up, because I know for a fact he's going to brighten me.

The other thing about Goughy is that he likes his money too. "Recession?" he asked me, when I rang him the other day. "What recession? Can't print it quick enough in Gough's household. I'm seeing the Queen's face more than I'm seeing my own." Little things like that make him so funny. I'll hear him on talkSPORT on the radio in the car, but I'll not be listening to what he's saying. I'll be wetting myself remembering things I've heard him say before.

In many ways, Goughy reminds me of Alan Shearer.

They're both people I looked up to when I was growing up

who I then got to spend time with when I was older. Sometimes you meet your heroes and they let you down. I was fortunate that both of mine excelled themselves. Alan's quieter, but with a great sense of humour – he takes the mickey but with a stone face – and then there's Goughy who just doesn't care and says things that are totally off the radar.

I've been lucky enough to know them both. I'd like to think if someone was looking at me as a hero or good role model – God knows why! – if they got to meet me, I'd be like that. I'd give that person the chance to walk away thinking, 'I met him and he was everything I wanted him to be and expected him to be.'

As it was, I hardly saw Goughy in Australia. My last real memory of him on that trip was in the third warm-up game, against Western Australia, in Perth.

Nasser Hussain was stressed out early on as it became increasingly clear that we'd boarded the plane with a squad whose only hand luggage should have been a walking stick.

Freddie was coming back from a double hernia operation, Vaughan had ongoing issues with his knee, Simon Jones had suffered constant injury issues throughout his career, and now the team's most potent fast bowler was looking like he could miss the entire series.

Eventually something snapped in Nasser and he and Goughy had a real bust-up, with the England captain throwing his kit at Goughy about his fitness struggles before Goughy dished plenty back. I was thinking, 'This is great. Our senior players are fighting with each other, and in a few days we've got to go and face Warne, McGrath and Gillespie, and their top seven is the best to have ever played the game. What chance have we got?'

Goughy was never going to be fit. It was inevitable from the start. It was sheer desperation on behalf of the selectors – of which Nasser was one – that meant he was in that dressing room at that time.

Nasser knew that when he blew up. He was a passionate man. His biggest fault was he wanted England to win too much. He was obsessed by it and when things didn't go well the frustration he felt, and the way he expressed it, could upset people. Most of us, though, had played enough with him to know that he'd be fine in a minute and the best thing to do was just let it blow over. He got a lot of respect from us because we as a team were getting a lot of stick from outside and it was him who was absorbing it. He was protecting us.

When he exploded, some people would give it back, but I'd keep my head down. Concentrate on what you're doing and you've got half a chance of making the team better. Goughy never regained fitness and was eventually sent off to the Academy in Adelaide, for intensive treatment on his knee injury. Poor sod, he never came back.

Meanwhile, I'd actually already had my own brush with injury. In the first game, the traditional curtain-raiser against an Australian Cricket Board Chairman's XI at Lilac Hill. I was chasing a ball and was just about to slide for it on the boundary when I saw loads of kids sat at the front.

I didn't want to go in feet first and cut anyone up with my spikes so I went front first instead. I pulled the ball back and, as I did so, not being the most co-ordinated bloke on earth, went headfirst into the rope.

Ropes, let me tell you, are harder than they look. I was seeing

Tweety Pie, the works. I ended up going off for five minutes, a bit dazed, but then went back on because, this being early in the tour, I wanted to prove what I could do and have a bowl.

With the blazing heat as well, I just couldn't get going. My radar was all over the place. I bowled wide after wide, 16 in seven overs, and seven in a row at one point. The crowd were giving me a bit of jip – "You're supposed to bowl it on the cut bit, mate" – but I didn't care.

In my head I knew I hadn't bowled badly. They weren't massive wides, they just kept swinging and slipping down the leg side. If they'd been big wides I'd have been worried, but in reality they weren't too far from what I wanted them to be. Nasser wasn't bothered. "Keep bowling fast," that's all he said to me. "Keep bowling fast."

On that trip I was bowling six or more wides a game, but Nasser would always say, "I'm not bothered about that, I just want you bowling fast. You're in the team to take wickets."

Mentally, I wasn't bothered, because I knew there was nothing to worry about, but the Australian press were always going to make a big deal about it. That's what they're like.

At the warm-up game in Perth, we were doing catching practice, trying to acclimatise because the ball comes out of the sky quicker over there, and Duncan Fletcher actually praised how well we'd done at the end of the session.

It was a really good 25 minutes, all in all we dropped about six catches – and on the news that night they were all shown. It made us look terrible. So we knew what could happen, and that's all part of touring Australia. Go there and you feel like you're taking the whole country on.

Have a good day against Australia, it's mentioned about five pages from the back of the newspaper. They have a good day and it's the last five pages and sometimes the front page too. Lilac Hill was just one of many things to go wrong throughout my career, but I've always found a way to get through them, and I pride myself on that.

The first Test at Brisbane is remembered by most for Nasser winning the toss, choosing to bowl, and the Aussies piling up 364-2 by the end of the day.

I remember it for entirely different reasons – as does Simon Jones.

Early in the match, Simon chased a ball to the boundary, he slid in to make the stop only for his right leg to jar horribly in the soft outfield. I knew straight away it was bad. We all jumped up. The physio was straight on.

The screams coming from Simon and the gasp of the crowd when they showed the replay confirmed something truly awful had happened. I rushed down to the pitch and, while none of us wanted to crowd him, it was clear the injury was an absolute shocker.

When the stretcher came out, myself and Jason Gillespie helped carry him off. Simon was visibly distressed, covering his face with his cap. He knew something was seriously wrong. It was terrible, heartbreaking, to see. I'd gone through the whole England cycle with him, under-19, A-tour, Academy. I'd already made my debut against India because he'd got injured.

As I was carrying Simon off, somebody threw an empty plastic Coke bottle at him. I saw the bloke who did it, and I was ready to go in.

I properly lost it and wanted to get in there and sort him out. He knew I'd clocked him, and when I came back out after taking

Simon in for treatment he'd gone. I found the security guys. "That man should not be anywhere near a cricket ground," I told them, and they went off to look at the CCTV. I was so angry about it. How could anybody behave like that in that situation?

When we got Simon back to the dressing room he was distraught, red-faced, sweating.

It wasn't just the pain, it was that he knew this wasn't going to be something remedied by a bandage and a fortnight off. He'd had to combat serious injuries all through his career, and this was another one. For those of us who knew how hard he'd worked, it was heart-breaking.

Me, Fred and Keysey were devastated as we tried to comfort him. "Come on, mate, it'll be all right, you'll get through it," I told him, but we all knew what a long road he faced back.

More than that, though, this was one of our mates lying there – cricket was secondary.

It turned out that Simon had ruptured the anterior cruciate ligament in his knee and for the team it was a disaster. He'd been the most threatening member of our attack. Just to rub it in, later they put the 10 fastest balls of the day up on the big screen – Simon had only sent down 42 deliveries and had bowled all 10. None of that mattered, though.

All that really mattered was Simon. Yet again, his career had hit a brick wall. I felt terribly for him. Simon was a bloke I always liked being around, a funny, funny bloke, at net sessions especially. I often ended up in the net next to him, and you'd just hear him chirping all the time.

You'd have these young whippersnappers, Academy lads and net bowlers, who'd run up and try to knock your head off. At least twice a session, I'd hear him muttering at them, "You put your fucking pads on, I'll fucking bowl at you. I'll knock your fucking head off." I'd be absolutely pissing myself. He was priceless. Simon's problem was his body. He had an athlete's body. He just wasn't built for fast bowling. But he had serious talent.

There was the usual dose of farce to add to the occasion. Flintoff, Mr Double Hernia, had been sent on to the field because Duncan Fletcher thought he'd be at slip, but at 300-1, the ball never looked like going to slip. It went past the Australian bat twice in five days as they beat us comfortably. At one point, the ball went down to fine leg and Fred was hobbling round to get it. Nasser was going spare. "What the fuck are you doing on this field? Get off! Get off!"

Troy Cooley was still working for the Academy, and so when we got to Adelaide for the next Test, I rang Rod Marsh and asked if I could see him.

I wasn't the only England bowler to rate Troy, a lot of the others were too, and eventually we told Fletcher that we wanted to bring the bloke in full-time. Troy helped me tweak a few things, but what probably clinched my selection was giving Nasser a bit of a going over in the nets. I thought it wouldn't hurt to remind him that I had 90mph express pace that couldn't be found anywhere else in England, let alone in the team.

I had him hopping around a bit, gave him a bit of a going over, and then I also broke Ashley Giles' wrist. I felt terrible, but nets aren't there just for a quick mess around.

We were on an Ashes tour and were already one down in the series. You have to have some intensity in the nets or else you're just going to go from bad to worse. You can never replicate what it's like in the middle but you can at least try to put things right in your game, gain a little confidence, or keep yourself in decent nick. Ashley didn't hold it against me, but we'd lost yet another bowler from the tour. As it was I got Damien Martyn and Adam Gilchrist in that match but any chance of grabbing more scalps was denied by them crushing us by an innings.

Just before the next Test at Perth, my mam rang me to say Hayley was going into hospital to have the baby. It's at times like that you really do feel the distance as a cricketer.

It's a gap so wide that it's difficult even to mentally breach, let alone physically, and I couldn't have felt further away from home. I constantly had to remind myself of the bigger picture. There was the selfishness of wanting to get better and play for England, but more than that it was also about what this life could give to the long-term future of my family.

That was one of the biggest reasons I got through it, because I knew what being an England cricketer could mean to my children and family.

I was frantically ringing round relatives, before eventually my mam rang to say Hayley had given birth to a healthy baby girl and everything was OK. Even now, when Abbie wants something off my mam, she'll say, "Grandma, you were there when I was born, weren't you?" She loves really laying on the emotion and she does the same to me, except she reminds me she was the only birth I missed.

This was before smartphones had really taken off and so I didn't see a picture of my new daughter for two days. Even then it was one that had been scanned and emailed.

I printed it off in Australia and stared into her eyes. It would be three months before I could do that properly. My plan to go home for the one-dayers and then return was kyboshed when England's mounting injury list saw me selected for the limited overs side. I could have pulled out but then that would have meant I'd have missed out on the World Cup which followed immediately afterwards in Zimbabwe and South Africa. It sounds terrible, but all these things had to be taken into account from a financial point of view.

I didn't know how long playing for England was going to last. The roll-call of injured on this tour alone told me that. This was my – our – chance. As an England player I had to establish myself, had to be available, and the money I could make if offered a central contract could set us up for life. The flipside of that was Abbie being three-months-old the first time I saw her. It was horrific.

The plan was that Hayley would travel out to Australia to join me for a few days when the second lot of one-dayers were on, but only with Emily. Abbie wasn't old enough to fly at that point and had been left at home with grandparents. Barely having given birth, that was desperately hard for Hayley.

I'd then go back to England with them, have four days at home, and then go to Africa for the World Cup. In the end it turned out to be five because snow meant the flight was delayed. I've never been more delighted to see the white stuff. That was it – I saw my newborn daughter for five days in six months.

To be fair, Nasser and Fletcher were always great about family. Nasser had gone out two weeks early on that trip so his wife could give birth in Australia and the baby would already be there.

As a coach, Fletcher was always a family-orientated man and I was grateful for that because I knew that people before, like Mike Atherton, would never entertain having wives and girlfriends on a trip, and a few others had been the same before.

Bob Willis still goes off on one about it now – how it just never happened in his day. More recently, Michael Vaughan got a lot of stick when he left the Headingley Test against New Zealand in 2004 to attend the birth of his daughter Tallulah Grace at a hospital in Sheffield.

These people who complain about things like that either haven't got kids or don't like kids. They just don't understand. Idiots like that say things for effect, to get their names in lights, to enhance their reputation by slagging off someone else, or have an agenda against the person in question.

The truth is you cannot detach sportsmen from other sides of their lives. We're not robots. It's easy saying, "You can't do that." You try putting yourself in their shoes.

I firmly believe that if you want to get the best out of professional sportsmen, then their personal and family lives also have to be taken into account. The management knew I needed my family.

Although by the time we got to Western Australia, I'm not sure that even seeing Hayley or the children would have helped my bowling or my mindset – on the field and off it.

8

STRANGERS

"Nasser was panicking and stressing, fighting with senior players, and we were playing the greatest side the world has ever seen"

U npredictability is a hell of a thing to have in your armoury, and at Perth for the Third Test, no-one was less predictable than me.

There was a drain right down the middle of my run-up. I was trying to go one side of it, then the other. It affected me badly and I got the yips, losing my run-up, stop-starting, little steps, big steps, and bowling at just 80mph.

It must have looked comical. I could barely get to the crease, running up on the inside of the umpire and then jumping out at the last second. In the end I was just managing my steps to get to the drain and then starting my run-up again.

Halfway through my third over, I was walking back to my mark and Ricky Ponting said to me, "I've absolutely no idea when you're going to let go of that ball." I stopped. "I've got no idea either – and if I've got no idea then you must be shitting yourself." He just laughed.

On the pitch, Nasser was great. He never stopped supporting me. "You've got to keep bowling," he told me. That was because a few bad balls didn't compare to the long-term psychological damage I could have suffered.

Afterwards, he told me, "You had to keep going because if I'd taken you off, mentally it would have killed you. It worked as well. I was pissing myself laughing watching you, but actually you were getting better."

That was hugely reassuring of Nasser. When the match was on and the pictures kept showing Nasser talking to me, trying to get me through the bad patch, it was misinterpreted as him nagging me.

Ian Botham said if he'd done it to him, he'd have been tempted to throw the ball back at him. But I didn't mind Nasser. I was a young lad who needed a bit of guidance. Some of what he said just went in one ear and out the other, but all he was trying to do was mould individuals, of which I was one, into a team. It would take a little while yet. Once again we were beaten by an innings.

Later I heard that Nasser had a go at Stewie in Perth. He called him selfish. I was with him at the end of the second innings, at a point where Brett Lee was bowling at the speed of light.

I'd come to the crease just as he'd put Alex Tudor in hospital after hitting him on the head. Stewie was going well at one end and generally in these circumstances, the senior batsman will try to farm the strike.

However, he'd tickled it to third man twice early in the over and taken the run, leaving me to face these bullets. I was bowled by one of them and Nasser was far from impressed. He had a pop at Stewie, who, a bit like Goughy, was more than happy to put his point across too.

When I heard about their argument, it was another point where I was sitting there, a young lad on his first England tour, half lapping it up, and half thinking, 'What the bloody hell is going on?' Half of our team wasn't fit, Nasser was panicking and stressing, fighting with senior players, and we were playing the greatest side the world has ever seen.

What chance did we have against Australia when we couldn't even stop fighting each other? Personally, I wasn't even bothered about what had happened with Stewie. I've never shirked the strike in my life. My approach was always the same; I've got a bat in my hand, same as everyone else, so just get on with it.

As the one-dayers kicked in, myself, John Crawley and Rob Key were the only ones who didn't have family out over Christmas. Every time we saw the others, we felt like the outcast uncle who pops in for Christmas Day and then disappears again, so instead of hanging around the hotel, we spent Christmas afternoon in a Melbourne casino playing blackjack with most of Japan and China. Very festive! We couldn't even have a Christmas drink because we were playing the Boxing Day Test the next day.

At the Melbourne Cricket Ground, Nasser seemed to think that if we couldn't beat the Aussie team then we could at least show some fire to their fans.

At the MCG there's the infamous Bay 13 where the real rough, tough Aussie fans go. Of course, Nasser, being Nasser, when it came to warming up, declared, "Right, we're going to take this lot on." Over we went, right in front of them, looking them in the eye while we were doing calf stretches, all the usual warm-up stuff. It was working OK until one of the Aussies piped up, "Oi! Hussain! Saddam's more popular in your country than you are at the minute."

That was it. Nasser's mood changed a little. "Right, come on!" Off we went and practiced somewhere else.

By this time we had only three fit pace bowlers, reduced to two when Craig White broke down with a side injury in the first innings. Mark Butcher made up the numbers as we were crushed again, although we might have had a chance when, with the Aussies making hard work of their small second innings target, Steve Waugh nicked a fast rising ball from me, a proper big nick, and no-one heard, because it was so noisy.

The Barmy Army were making so much racket it was ridiculous. The very next ball Waugh was caught by Nasser at mid-off. He went ballistic, bellowing, throwing the ball high into the air, only to find it was a no-ball. If ever a man wanted the ground to swallow him up.

There was no doubting Waugh's brilliance in the next Test at Sydney when, famously, he reached an incredible hundred off the last ball of the second day. It was an incredible performance.

Waugh was under severe pressure at the time, an all-time Aussie great with the media on his back, berating him for his poor form. People were saying he was finished, that this would be his last Test match, but he could feel the crowd was behind him and it made for an unbelievable atmosphere. We could sense something was coming.

He knew he had to get the hundred that night because at that point in his career he was struggling to start off again after breaks. He didn't want to be overnight in the 90s. He got a big proportion of his runs after tea and, as he neared the landmark, it really did feel like being part of a moment in time. The last half an hour of most Test match days, the game is slowing down, people are starting to make their way home and trying to beat the traffic – but nobody left that ground in Sydney. It was heaving all the way through. The noise when he reached the ton was all-encompassing. All we could do was stand and applaud in appreciation of an amazing achievement.

Most of us thought this would be Stewie's last Test because he was nearing the end of his career and he'd missed the previous one at Melbourne with chickenpox, but on the morning of the game there was no sign of him.

All of a sudden, with barely 45 minutes until the start of play, the door swung open and there he was, pristine as ever, grin on his face. He'd come fresh from the doctor's and declared himself fit to play. Stewie hated missing a game.

Our second innings again ended up with me and Stewie at the crease. Again Nasser wasn't happy about Stewie's ability to farm the strike, and again it all blew up.

It would have been sad if Stewie's last game had featured a bust-up and thankfully the announcement of his retirement never came. My dressing room untidiness would irk him for another two seasons to come.

The game did, however, see the end of Andy Caddick, despite him bowling us to victory in the second innings. Caddick was a very different sort of character to Stewie.

He was bitter at the end. I don't believe he enjoyed other people's success. I never thought he was out there to help me.

He wasn't out there to help Hoggy or Simon either. Caddy was out there to help himself. I was expecting more from him when I came into the England set-up. But I'd heard stories before I got there that, when it came to Andy Caddick, playing cricket for England was very much about him, and he was jealous of Darren Gough.

Whether that was because Goughy got all the plaudits and his larger than life personality meant opportunities came his way, I don't know. There was just something about Caddy that rubbed people up the wrong way. You'd listen to him and you'd just think, 'You didn't really need to say that.' It's said that once when Goughy had four wickets in an innings at Lord's, Caddick was saying to teammates that they had to make sure he didn't get the fifth so he wouldn't get on the honours board.

I can't imagine ever thinking that about a teammate. You cannot overestimate the ramifications of something like that in terms of dressing room harmony. The unit we had from 2003-05 would have been trying to help a colleague reach a milestone, not obstructing him.

After Caddy finished his international career, he made some comments to a newspaper about myself and England, making out I'd only done well on bowler-friendly wickets, the usual stuff. I can usually let these things go, but his comments had riled me as I thought they were unnecessarily aggressive.

It was basically the end for me and him as far as I was concerned and I was looking forward to playing him at Taunton a few weeks later. The game was hit by rain and I was playing cards with the Durham lads in the lunch room when I saw him come in. He couldn't avoid seeing me – bang, there I was straight away. He just stood there staring. He didn't know what to say.

"All right Cad?"

He looked outside as if to say, "It's not looking good is it?"

"No," I said. "But I'm looking forward to getting out there

and playing against you." He just turned and walked away. It saddened me in a way. I played quite a few games for England with Caddick, and looked up to him as a junior to a senior. It shouldn't be like that for teammates.

Sydney saw Michael Vaughan score his third century of a golden tour and we went on to do what so many England teams had done in the previous 15 years, win a dead rubber of a series in which we'd been thoroughly outplayed.

Afterwards, we were invited into the Australian dressing room, dripping in history, cold brickwork offset by the warmth of wooden benches and lockers. Nasser was adamant, "I'm not going in there!" But there was no way I was going to miss out.

The bus was leaving in 20 minutes but I didn't care. "Go without me – I'm going in." We literally sat there for about six or seven hours, just getting tanked.

I was talking to Glenn McGrath, Jason Gillespie, soaking up every word they said, be it about bowling or just life in general.

I learnt so much from those few hours, it allowed me to see them as people as well as opponents, to hear how they lived their lives away from the cricket field, how they relaxed and dealt with the pressure.

I sat next to Steve Waugh for half an hour, the same with Brett Lee and Shane Warne – absolute legends of the game. I can understand that from Nasser's point of view, as captain, he might have felt awkward. He was a proud man and he'd just had his nose rubbed in it by the Australians, as we all had. But anything that happened on the pitch was forgotten. I've never taken anything off the pitch with me, never, and this was no exception. I was never going to miss that opportunity to listen to the greats of the game talking – because these were greats. They weren't preaching, they weren't arrogant, at that point we were just a bunch of blokes sat having a laugh and a few beers together.

Beating England hadn't been personal. Their team was at its best then. They were beating everyone, not just us. I loved every minute.

At the end, there were five England players left – me, Rob Key, Mark Butcher, John Crawley and James Foster, and we had no means of getting back to the hotel.

As we 'walked' out of the SCG, there was a golf buggy with a trailer on the back. On closer inspection, it was the drinks cart they used during the match. Without naming names, the left-hander from Surrey got in the driving seat, John Crawley next to him, and me, Keyesy and Fozzy lay next to each other like logs in the trailer. We were all egging the Surrey left-hander on, and next thing we knew we were off.

Eventually, about 500 yards down the road, Butch, from somewhere, actually found a conscience. We realised this probably wasn't a good idea. Getting beaten 4-1 in an Ashes series was bad enough without the ignominy of then ending up in court for being drunk in charge of a golf trolley. We dumped the vehicle and set off on foot.

Walking wasn't a great option either. It was one step forwards and three steps back because we were all three sheets to the wind.

Luckily enough, some England supporters were driving by and they picked us up at the side of the road and dropped us back at the hotel.

I came out of that series with loads of confidence. For England, it was a bad tour, but I was young, naive, wet behind the ears. There was no pressure on me. The pressure was on the big guns. I'd played against a team that had gone unbeaten for years and hadn't disgraced myself. I'd also played in four successive Test matches in an era where, to some extent, people were still playing one and getting left out. I'd held my own, had Steve Waugh jumping around, had him saying not bad things about me, so my thoughts were, 'If that's the best, I can live with anybody else.' I had the knowledge I could get good players out. I was also thinking that, hopefully, I'd be ready when we next met – which would be 2005.

The others went home but me and Keysey still had the one-dayers, one of which was back at Sydney.

As we got off the coach, we were approached by Rocky, the dressing-room attendant at the SCG and one of the great characters of world cricket, a true gent, who always had a word of encouragement for the visitors. "You two pinched my buggy!" he spluttered. We denied it but in the end caved in under questioning. We made amends with a good bottle of wine and he forgave us.

By the time this second lot of one-dayers started, I was all over the show mentally. I still hadn't seen Abbie and it had already been a long tour. I was all over the place and in Adelaide, on one of the hottest days of the year, I chased a ball and badly sprained my ankle. I couldn't play the remaining games and it was still a problem when I finally got on the plane to see my new daughter for the first time.

When I held Abbie that first time, she felt big. She was quite clearly not the newborn baby that I still held in my mind. It was a shock and really emphasised just how long I'd been away, just how little support I'd been able to offer, just what I'd missed.

Cricket is a great life, make no mistake, but no other sport requires the participant to be away for such a length of time, to miss so much. Aside from those four days at home, I'd gone away in early October and wouldn't be back until the end of March. That life isn't easy. A lot of sporting marriages go under.

The highest divorce rate in any sport is cricket, and considering the pressures it's not surprising a lot of people don't last the journey. Anybody who says being married and playing cricket is easy is lying. It is hard, more so on the women than the men. All they get is disruption. It never gets easier.

That's why, when I look at a sportsperson, I always wonder what's going on in their head, whether they are having a good day or a bad day, what burden they're carrying, what worries.

Cricket is simple, it's about bowling a ball and hitting a ball, but in those six hours between the start of play and the end, a hell of a lot of stuff goes on between your ears.

9

SECRETS AND LIES

"As soon as I saw him my head dropped. He was immaculate – shirt, tie, England blazer. The only problem was he'd still got the Castle Lager tattoo on his forehead"

IF England had been smart, they would have got a replacement for me for the 2003 World Cup.

I knew I wasn't going to play. I was tired, my body was tired, and my ankle still wasn't right. The thing was, they'd had to pick the squad by the end of December not realising that, by the time the tournament was scheduled in February, I would be on my knees.

After flying home to see Abbie, I rejoined the rest of the team in Cape Town. Almost straight away I found myself walking into a shitstorm as we found ourselves stuck in the middle of a major terrorist threat. England's first game of the tournament was in Zimbabwe and the political situation under President Mugabe was unstable to say the least.

Threats had been made to the England team and our families if we fulfilled the fixture, threats that the ECB had known about for weeks. They had initially been dismissed as a hoax, but the ECB now had to come clean after a letter from one protest group, the Sons and Daughters of Zimbabwe, had been made public by the ICC.

"Our message to you is simple," read the letter. "COME TO ZIMBABWE AND YOU WILL GO BACK TO BRITAIN IN WOODEN COFFINS!

"Come to Harare," it continued. "And you will die. And how safe are your families back there in the UK? Even if you survive, there are foreign groups who are prepared to hunt you and your families down for as long as it takes, and they will do that in your very own country.

"Our advice is this: DON'T COME TO ZIMBABWE OR YOUR PLAYERS WILL BE LIVING IN FEAR FOR THE REST OF THEIR LIVES."

In the meantime, we'd been told by Fletcher, who had played for Zimbabwe, and Nasser that two Zimbabwe players, Andy Flower and Henry Olonga, were going to wear black armbands as a protest about what was happening in their country.

Their families, we were told, were fleeing at that very moment. That was happening at the game prior to the one we were supposed to be playing, and was only likely to make the situation even worse.

The upshot was we found ourselves marooned in a conference room in a Cape Town hotel while various security officials and

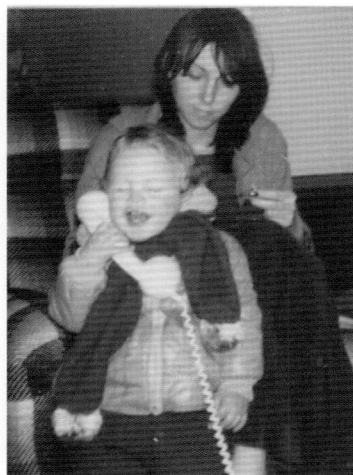

Head and shoulders: (Far left) Me and Dad – he's been a wonderful father and friend and has worked so hard all his life

Mum's the word: Mum has always been there for all of us and she's just an incredible woman

A family affair: (Above left) Me kitted out in Yeovil Town's kit on the pitch with dad, (above middle), trying on dad's Great North Run vest – he always kept himself very fit, (above right), me and James look so innocent, although I'm sure mum wouldn't agree!

It was only a Coke! Me, aged 15, with dad on a family holiday to Majorca

Local pride: When my first-class debut against Leicestershire finished early, I went back to play club cricket for Ashington CC v Percy Main CC the next day. I'm on the back row while my younger brother – and Durham teammate – Ben is front left, in his scorer's tracksuit!

The big day: James, Ben, myself, Hayley, my sister Joanne, mum, dad and Darren at my wedding in Morpeth in 1999

Fresh faced: Me and Durham teammate Melvyn Betts on the day we were named in the England A squad for the Zimbabwe tour in September, 1998

High action: Running in hard against Warwickshire in April, 1998. I never set out to be a cricketer, it just happened

Snow way: Me and Paul Collingwood improvise as the first day of the 1999 season is abandoned due to snow at the Riverside ground. A lot of teams used to hate coming up to the north-east, especially when they realised we were still a few hours north of Headingley!

A whippet of a thing!: Relaxing at the Riverside after receiving my first senior England call-up for the opening Test against Zimbabwe at Lord's in May, 2000

Young guns: Rob Key was a wonderful cricketer and remains a great, great mate

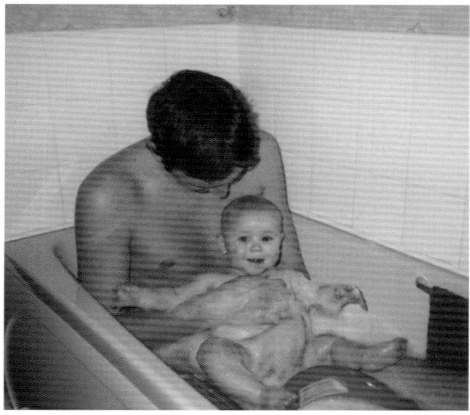

Bubbles and bathtime: I was a young dad and I loved every minute of it

A local lad: Walking out of the Riverside gate to face Lancashire in May, 2000

Preparing: The build-up to my first Test against India went great, despite my nerves

You always remember your first: I celebrate my maiden Test wicket, Ajit Agarkar, caught by Mark Butcher. Michael Vaughan was the first man to congratulate me. He would go on to become a fantastic England skipper who knew how to get the best out of all of us

A Test to remember: Look at that perfect cover drive! I always enjoyed my batting and should probably have got more international runs. (Top right), making Sachin Tendulkar hop around in his crease, (above right) me and Simon Jones take some time out in Queensland

A tour to forget: My first England tour Down Under (above and opposite) was a hot and humid disappointment. This was a feeling I would have to get used to when in Australia

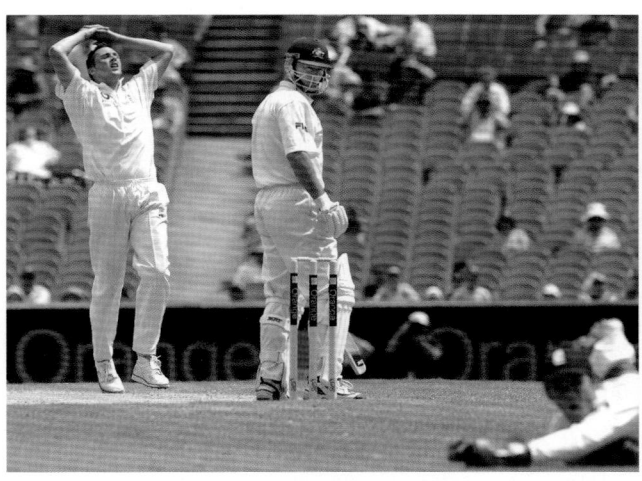

Blood sweat and tears: Anybody who tells you that fast bowling doesn't hurt is lying. I decide to have a little rest in the third Test against South Africa at Trent Bridge in August, 2003

Pleasure: I make sure the England team starts to hydrate properly as we celebrate levelling the South Africa series with a win in the fifth and final Test match at the Oval in September, 2003. All the lads who won the Ashes in 2005 know they owe the likes of Graham Thorpe, Alec Stewart and Mark Butcher a huge debt of gratitude

representatives of the ECB and ICC bombarded us with totally
conflicting information. No-one seemed willing to either tell us
exactly what was going on or make a decision. The whole thing
was an absolute shambles.

Everyone who should have made the decision kept passing
the buck. All the politicians, the officials, proved themselves
utterly hopeless. It was obvious what was going to happen – it
would be left down to us.

In the midst of this nonsense, one man shone out – Nasser.

During that time he was brilliant. Nasser might have had
people who didn't like him in that room, but they'd never be
able to say that he didn't do a fantastic job for the team. He
took all-comers on.

There was no way he was going to allow anyone to pull the
wool over our eyes. If anyone thought they could just come into
that room, tell us a load of rubbish and we'd just swallow it all
wholesale, they hadn't reckoned on Nasser.

For four days, we had different people coming in giving us
different presentations. A lot of them just lied to us – security
'experts', chiefs of police, they lied.

Malcolm Speed, head of the ICC, came to see us at one point
and afterwards he accused Nasser of swearing at him. Nasser
didn't swear at him. He didn't say very nice things to him, but
he didn't swear.

Nasser simply asked Speed what was going on and he came
out with this drivel and bullshit that didn't tell us anything.
Nasser told him, "There's a bloke outside with a white towel on
his arm waitering and he could have told me more than what
you've just told me." I thought that was quite good for Nasser.

Arguably, Nasser took too much on, but he was the frontman

of the England cricket team and he wasn't going to let anybody get to us. He had some young players in that room. I wasn't very old and neither was James Anderson. Then there was Hoggy and Ian Blackwell. It was a lot to take in for some of us. We were cricketers, not politicians.

There was some brief escape from this nightmare in the form of the opening ceremony.

Before it began, some of us went to the Sports Café by the harbour for a bit of refreshment. The result was one of the funniest nights I've ever had playing for England.

We were walking round the Newlands Cricket Stadium absolutely bladdered. Nasser was the exception. He was the flagbearer and can only have been thinking one thing – 'What is this rabble I've got here?'

After the ceremony we got shovelled on to a train back to the hotel. Vaughan was coming off his ridiculous run of form in Australia and Fred was singing, "Michael Vaughan, superstar, scores more runs than Tendulkar!" We knew there were other teams on the train but weren't overly sure who they were. We soon realised India was one of them when we looked up and saw Sachin sat further down the carriage.

The fun was short-lived. Back at the hotel, we had meetings for hours. Our World Cup was about to start and we hadn't touched a bat or ball in days. It all got on top of us.

One bloke told us that in Zimbabwe if there was a demonstration it had to be planned. People needed permission to demonstrate. If they demonstrated without permission, the police could use ultimate force. Another chap then told us there hadn't been an application for a demonstration. In fact, there hadn't been a demonstration in Zimbabwe for a while.

The next person who came in then said there'd be at least one demonstration on the day of the game. "Hang on," we said. "If there's a demonstration and they haven't got permission, then the police can shoot them." We didn't want that. We were playing cricket. Cricket's not that important that someone should die.

We were all frazzled but eventually we were told we'd have to make a decision – but before that we were told to have some lunch. "Go away, come back in two hours." We again walked down to the Sports Café. We didn't know what to do.

We were Arthur and Martha. There was a waitress walking round with a big jug with a beer tap on it. I was looking at it. There were three or four of us, Hoggy and Fred included, who had the same idea. "Bring two of those over," I said.

We went back in the meeting after having a quick pint but by that time I didn't care what happened. I, and the rest of the lads, were just all so worn down by it all. We were bored of all the bullshit. We were cricketers, not politicians. When we got back in, Nasser had a plan. "I don't want to see a hand raised," he said. "I want each of you to tell us why you don't want to go." He paused. "The youngest go first."

That was me and Jimmy Anderson.

It came as a bit of a shock. I knew I didn't want to go to Zimbabwe but I was just going to say what one of the senior guys said. Jimmy went first. He said he didn't want to go, that we couldn't 100 percent say the letter wasn't genuine. I was the same. "How can we go if people might be killed when we get there and also there's a risk that something might happen to our families?"

Nasser went round the room. Ronnie Irani was the only

one who said he wanted to go, but then that's Ronnie Irani. It confirmed what I already knew – never to go on a tour of which he was in charge. Still to this day I don't know why he wanted to go. They should have let them try to shoot him! Alec Stewart abstained. He was 40 and it was his last World Cup. He wanted to go but had seen how the others had voted.

If the vote had gone in favour of going, I would have gone. You're a team, and if the team says they're going, you go, you stick by it. It's like the toss, you might not like your captain's decision, but once it's made you go with it.

If the vote had been 14-1 to go, and I was the one who disagreed, I would have gone.

Nasser asked the ECB to come back in to tell them we weren't going and, surprise, surprise, it was at that point the ECB then said they were pulling us out because the threat was real. They'd waited for us to make a decision and then jumped on the back of it.

By this time there were a few tears knocking about. Hoggy was upset, as were a few others. The emotions were all coming out. The threat to our lives was real. Somebody really could have had a pot shot at us.

I resented the fact we'd been put in that position. Why were we left to make a decision of such importance, one the government should have made for us? They were, after all, giving everyone else the travel advice that they shouldn't be travelling to Zimbabwe. So why should the cricket team be any different?

Nevertheless, there was a relief it was over. We weren't going to get the points from that game, reaching the next stage would be hard for us, but at least now we knew what was going on.

We were always behind in the tournament from that point on.

The Zimbabwe situation had knocked the stuffing out of us. We were still in with a chance when we easily beat Pakistan, a match most notable for the performance of Somerset all-rounder Ian Blackwell – who wasn't even playing.

It was in this game that Shoaib Akhtar is said to have bowled the fastest ball in world cricket, 100mph, although personally I think the speed guns on that trip were revved up by three or four miles an hour.

Nick Knight was facing when Shoaib bowled the 100mph delivery. The big screen went crazy – '100mph – Fastest Ball Ever!' – and the whole crowd erupted.

There were lights flashing, the works. At this point, Blacky went back into the changing rooms and started rooting in his bag. Eventually he emerged with his camera.

You could tell what was going through his mind. The view from the players' viewing gallery at Newlands makes the perfect picture. You've got Table Mountain in the background, and then a big electronic scoreboard in front.

He wanted to get the once in a lifetime shot – the scoreboard with 100mph and the stunning backdrop. Knight was opening and Blacky was stood behind Vaughan and Hussain, both padded up ready to bat three and four.

"Go on Shoaib," bellowed Blacky. "Bowl another one!" Nasser went apeshit. "You what? You fucking useless twat! Get out! Go take your camera and fuck off!"

We were pissing ourselves. I wasn't playing anyway. I didn't care if he was bowling at 100mph or not. Blacky was the same. We were in hysterics. That was Blacky, though. You never quite knew what might happen. Same trip he smashed a shot on the golf course straight through the golf buggy. Luckily the glass was down.

I got to know Shoaib a bit the next season when he joined Durham on a short deal until the end of the season. We never knew what we were going to get with him. We were playing Yorkshire and Steve Kirby, a proper tail-ender, was batting. It was getting dark, Shoaib had already hit him on the head twice, and Kirbs wasn't happy about it.

He squared up to him. Shoaib then went back to the end of his full run, steamed in, and bowled Kirby a beamer at 90mph from around the wicket – and he meant it. Thankfully, the ball went straight through and missed everything. Kirby, meanwhile, had hit the ground and bounced straight back up.

His helmet was all over the place and gloves off ready for a fight. Shoaib was trying to say it was an accident, trying to apologise. Kirby was having none of it but no bones were broken in the end.

On his day, Shoaib could be devastating, but not all the time. He could be hard work and occasionally needed telling to pull his finger out.

At Worcester he was moaning about bowling into the wind. I swapped ends. He then started moaning about bowling at the other end. So I swapped back. It was worth pandering to him because if he got it right he could blow teams away. The ball then got hit to the boundary and as Shoaib fetched it he gave it a massive scrape on some concrete.

It was all roughed up on one side and a piece came away, which he then started working on. I was all for changing the ball as it was going out of shape but he was having none of it. "Right," I despaired. "You've got two overs. You'd better pull your finger out and do something with it." He was hooping it round corners, Worcester were gone in no time. "If you'd done that earlier," I pointed out. "We could have been home yesterday." He was OK,

Shoaib. He just had things going on in his head that nobody else could comprehend. People have called me an enigma but he truly was one. He was also the fastest I ever faced.

I came up against Allan Donald at his lightning quickest, but at no point with Donald did you ever lose sight of the ball. Brett Lee was the same. But Shoaib, because he had a slingy action and a kink in his arm, caused batsmen to lose sight of the ball for a split second. You knew it was coming but you didn't quite know when or where from.

Thing was, you never knew which Shoaib was going to turn up. He could bowl at 75mph one day and roll his arm over at 95mph the next. When he was on, though, he was breathtaking.

In the World Cup match against India, Fred's Tendulkar chant came back to haunt us. We were on the arse end of the toss in Durban and Sachin belted us for 50. When the lights came on, the dew appeared and, batting second, we didn't have a chance.

We might still have made it to the next stage had we finished off Australia at Port Elizabeth. At 135-8 chasing 208, it looked like we had it in the bag, but Michael Bevan wasn't known as the world's best finisher for nothing, and with Andy Bichel he saw them home. For me, any faint chance of contributing further down the line had disappeared.

With the tournament gone, me and Fred decided to have a few drinks. Six months away, with Hayley giving birth and barely looking like getting a game, something had to give.

A few players were required to go on a trip with a travel agent's tour party. Me and Fred were among them. Thing was, one of Fred's friends in the Barmy Army was having a six-a-side up the road in Port Elizabeth, an event sponsored by Castle Lager, and invited me and Fred along.

Even by our standards, it was an early start. We had our first lager at half past nine in the morning, and kept going from there. As part of the promotion, you got a water bottle, T-shirt, straw hat and temporary Castle Lager tattoo. I had mine on my arm. Fred had his on his forehead.

We left the Barmy Army boys at five and had to be on the tour bus, suited and booted, at six. We got back to the hotel, in through the fire exit, up the side stairs and into our rooms – this would become a well-practiced routine. "We've got to be on it, Fred," I said. "We've got to make sure no-one twigs we've been drinking. Once we arrive it'll be all right – we can say we got pissed a bit quick while we were there."

I got cleaned up, showered, suit on, down in the lift, sitting, waiting, rocking a little bit because it had been a long afternoon in the heat. The management kept asking me, "Where's Fred?"

"He's coming, just give him a minute."

Eventually, the light lit up above the lift. The number counted down from 10 to one, and then on zero the door opened.

As soon as I saw him my head dropped. He was immaculate – shirt, tie, England blazer. The only problem was he'd still got the Castle Lager tattoo on his forehead.

There were two buses, I got on the first, he got on the second, and we set off. As we U-turned away from the hotel, there was Fred standing by the hotel, like a lost schoolboy, waving at me. It transpired that the England manager, Phil Neale, had told him he couldn't go in the state he was in.

As far as I was concerned, that was it. "Stop the bus! If he's not going, I'm not going!" Fred found himself up before Duncan and captain Nasser. I was trying to defend him. "He's had a few," I told them. "But he's all right. It's a garden party we're going to, he's a funny lad and they'll love him."

They were having none of it. There was no way he was going to get back on that bus. Deep down, I think Nasser was trying to stop laughing, but they couldn't let us go. No doubt they were thinking what the reception would have been if this barbarian and his mate had walked into this nice serene garden party.

Back down in the hotel bar and Fred was swaying on his stool. I looked at him and thought, 'I've pretty much defended the indefensible there!' But he was my mate. It would have been a sod's trick to have left him to face the music alone. More than that, it was his face. He looked like a kid who'd been left behind by his parents. I had to stop the bus.

A short series against Zimbabwe, made special for me by the second Test being the first at Durham's Riverside Ground, was the prelude for the summer's main event, a five-Test series against South Africa.

Before the opener at Edgbaston, Nasser thought it would be a good idea to 'forget' the name of the visitors' new captain. By the end of the first day, with Graeme Smith on 178 not out, I'm fairly sure it had sunk in. When the game ended, there was an odd atmosphere in the dressing room.

Eventually, Fletcher announced that Nasser had resigned and Michael Vaughan would now be captain. Nasser himself was too choked to speak. As I saw him sat facing the press, tears in his eyes, I couldn't help but feel for him. Nasser wasn't everybody's cup of tea. He could be brusque with people and hard on his own teammates, but I loved playing for him. He was exactly what I needed at the time, someone to tell me what to do and how to do it. It wasn't tough love, it was just tough. I think deep down with Nasser there's a very warm guy in there, but when he got nervous he would lash out with his tongue, and that came into his captaincy as well.

As much as anyone wanted to say Nasser was too demanding, too sergeant major-ish, I needed Nasser to be like that. He picked me, he wanted me, he trusted me and he ground me into someone who could operate at Test level.

Nasser was the way he was because he wanted England to win – too much. He was obsessed, but at that time that wasn't a bad thing.

He would kick, fight and scream to make things better. The team Vaughan would build was itself built on Nasser's ruthlessness, his willingness to ditch the old guard and have a punt on young players. The Andy Caddicks, the selfish attitudes of the previous times, all that seemed to go.

Instead we were left with those who Hussain identified as having what it took to take the team to the next level. Flintoff came in, then Vaughan, Trescothick, Hoggard, Jones, myself, Rob Key, Strauss. Those names were swapped for the more selfish characters – understandably selfish after the way they were treated – and Hussain said we weren't going to treat people like that anymore.

They didn't all get there, but the majority did. The nucleus of the 2005 group began when Nasser began to imprint his style and thinking on the team. Then, when he realised he couldn't take his group any further by pointing the finger and shouting, he stepped aside and gave Vaughan, an altogether more laidback character, a go instead. That day at Edgbaston, he said to Vaughan, "It's time for you to take it over. These players aren't kids anymore. They've played a few games, they understand it, they know what they're doing, and they know what they want. It probably needs a more relaxed approach." I needed Nasser to be like he was – and then I needed Vaughan to be like he was too. I'd got a good few Test matches under my belt, had an idea what I wanted to do and how I was going to go about doing it.

A more relaxed approach was exactly what was needed to help me perform. Vaughan came in and allowed me to do just that.

Another thing I'd miss about Nasser was his bat throwing. Forget his Test average, he was right up there with the best in the world when it came to chucking his bat. Nasser's penchant for a tantrum worked both ways. Yes, it could be a pain, but on the other hand you could have a great laugh winding him up.

If you put the commentary on the TV in the dressing room it was like the world was ending. "Get that fucking thing off! That bunch of wankers, what do they know?"

I used to do it and then walk off, waiting for the eruption in the background. Then, of course, what did Nasser do after scoring a hundred in his last Test? He doffed his cap and took his bald head off to do exactly the same thing with the exact same people he had been been slagging off for God knows how many years!

However, before that, Nasser – along with Vaughan and the rest of us – still had some work to do out in the middle if we were to ever get close to becoming a serious force.

10

BUILDING

"After the previous issues over touring, my relationship with Graveney was virtually non-existent. I could barely look at him"

It shows you the class of Vaughan that he wanted Nasser to stay in the team.

He stayed and batted number three. Butcher stayed too and Thorpe also came back into the side. A team was then built around those older characters with the younger players who Nasser and Fletcher had identified as the future. I was one of those players, although I still had hiccups along the way.

I played the first three Tests of the South Africa series and felt I was bowling well when I was left out in favour of the veteran Surrey fast-medium bowler Martin Bicknell.

It seemed an odd decision since we felt we were a team looking to the future and Bicknell was 34, having last played for England 10 years previously.

The afternoon before the match, I'd had an injection in my back, just underneath my ribcage, because I was struggling a little bit with soreness in the lower back and one of my calves.

They said the injection would take away the pain, that way I'd be fine to play. I went along with what wasn't an altogether pleasant experience. I was always petrified of needles and this was a big one. At dinner that night with Vaughan and Giles, it was all good. Vaughan said we'd name the team in the morning but as good as told me I was playing.

On the field the next morning, quarter to 10, he approached me. "I've got some bad news for you," he said. "I've had a word with David Graveney and we're going to leave you out."

I couldn't believe what I was hearing. "You fucking what?" I hit back. "After having the injection? You're fucking kidding me, Mick."

I wouldn't normally blow up like that, but I was absolutely livid. I'd done everything I could to be fit, played the last nine Test matches, and felt I was by now a reliable pick, giving England the raw pace that could change a game in a session. But as soon as Graveney's name was mentioned it all made sense.

After the previous issues over touring, my relationship with Graveney was virtually non-existent. I could barely look at him. But then again he didn't have a great relationship with many people. To me it felt like an unsubtle reminder that I could forget any thoughts of being here to stay, even if I'd thought that anyway.

Nothing ever changed really. With Graveney in charge, if ever there was anyone to be axed from the side, or blame to be issued for a poor display, then it always fell on me. Geoff Miller, when he succeeded Graveney, would just tell you straight. "You haven't been bowling well enough." You might not agree, but he told you why, and that's why he was well thought of as head of selectors, but with Grav there was always a bit of stiffness, a bit of arrogance, and it was hard to get past that to see what he was really thinking.

It was hard to know what he believed in. He didn't like telling people what they didn't want to hear and he hid behind others. I always felt he didn't trust me. There were a few people who didn't see eye to eye with Grav and he wasn't very well respected by the England players at the time.

They weren't big fans of his and neither was I. I'm sure he'd probably say the same about me. It didn't bother me. I wasn't playing for David Graveney, I was playing for the England cricket team.

Graveney had actually played for Durham and was part of that old brigade who'd got brought in at the very start; the guys who'd had their careers elsewhere coming in to have one more crack at it. But forget the Durham link, when it comes to me and David Graveney, we have nothing in common at all.

I was back for the Oval, a track normally suited to the quicks, and had my best Test yet. My figures of 4-33 in their second innings proved to be the turning point as we fought back from a very unlikely position to draw the series.

Almost as enjoyable was the 99 I put on with Fred in our first innings, of which I made exactly three.

During that partnership, Graeme Smith was having a go at Fred because he wouldn't take the single early in the over as he was protecting me. "You don't back your partner then, no?" he kept shouting at Fred. At the end of the over, we met in the middle. "Would you not back me then?" I asked him, tongue in cheek. "Bollocks to that," he replied. "You're number 11 for a reason!"

At one point, Makhaya Ntini bowled Fred a yorker which he kept out at his feet. The rest of the South African team were on the boundary as Fred was pummelling the bowling, and Ntini had to walk all the way up the wicket to pick it up. Smith ran in from long-on. "You like to let the black man do the work, Flintoff?" he shouted.

Smith was trying to play the racism card, ridiculous against a man like Fred, who just stood there laughing at the absurdity of it. Next ball, Fred smashed Ntini for six over Smith's head. As it crashed into the dressing room windows at the Oval, he shouted, "Go on, Smithy. Pick that one up!"

Sometimes I wished Fred would be a bit quieter when he was batting. At Sydney in 2007 I went out with him at the crease, and Brett Lee was causing havoc. "I'm not going to lie to you," Fred greeted me. "He's bowling fucking quick."

"Thanks," I told him, my stomach churning. "I really needed to know that." Next ball, he caught Fred a blinder on the inside of the thigh. As he looked up, all he could see was my shoulders going up and down. He wasn't happy.

After surviving the torrid tour of Australia, and Nasser's tongue, this was actually Alec Stewart's last Test match, and at the end of the game me and Fred were honoured to carry him shoulder high around the ground. Stewie deserved the send-off. He truly was a great, everybody's mate, one of life's good guys, a big booming voice and a real gentleman who, in the era he played in, had to combine talent with a self-preservation instinct to survive as long as he did.

Playing until you're 40 is one thing, keeping wicket at 40, that's entirely another. He sacrificed a lot to play for such a long time but he had the organised mind to do it. He was meticulous with his kit. As soon as I arrived in the dressing room, he instigated a 'No Harmison Zone' next to him.

No way was he going to have me changing anywhere near him. My idea of preparation was to zip open my bag and chuck the whole lot on the floor. My theory then, and now actually – it drives Hayley mad – is if it's on the floor, I know where it is, whereas Stewie would have five shirts neatly folded, pants neatly folded, shoes there, socks there.

Every time I walked in the dressing room I could see him thinking, 'Fuck off, you're not changing next to me.'

Stewie loved his football too and he was always telling me how bad Newcastle were in comparison to his beloved Chelsea.

Even now I speak to him a lot. As Surrey's director of cricket, he rings me up occasionally to talk about Durham players and see what I think.

A couple of players, spinner Scott Borthwick and opener Mark Stoneman have gone to Surrey and Alec asked my advice on them both. I didn't get them for Surrey, but I gave my opinion. They made their own decisions. Even now when I see him at the Oval meeting and greeting people, he's still got this lovely aura about him.

It was a great feeling, that of a team coming together and enjoying one another's company. We all then went out round London, me and Fred dipping in and out of the swanky bars to head for the backstreet boozers we preferred.

Later we found ourselves on the opposite side of the river to where the American magician David Blaine was spending the summer suspended in a glass box over the Thames. We were tempted to go and have a look but the crowds put us off. That didn't stop a national newspaper ringing the next day with allegations we'd been throwing eggs at him. No way. We both had good arms but there's no way we could have reached!

After the six-month epic of the previous winter, the schedule was better this time round. England would travel to Bangladesh, Sri Lanka and the West Indies, between October and April, with a decent break worked in.

After being picked for the Bangladesh and Sri Lanka leg, having by now played 11 Tests, I was hoping that now might be the time I was offered a full-time central contract after spending the previous six months on a temporary version.

It wasn't to be, and so while the majority of the squad in Bangladesh were now fully in the employ of the ECB, it was clear an issue still existed with me. To me it felt like – for some – central contracts were a reward. For me they were a carrot.

Apparently I needed to push on over the winter and show my worth. I, however, felt I was showing my worth, but other people seemed to catch the eye while I didn't. If I had a quiet game I had a bad attitude. But my attitude never changed – I always wanted to do my best for England. I was in limbo, while everyone else knew where they stood. It made me feel like I wasn't trusted.

I spoke to Graveney on the phone about it, not that I was listening because the damage had been done. I didn't play for central contracts. I played as well as I could for England whatever the circumstances.

I just felt I wasn't getting the recognition I should have been.

When I then took nine wickets in the first game at Dhaka, in which I was also man of the match, I ended the year as England's leading Test wicket-taker with 31 scalps. People were finally starting to talk about me as being a real deal frontline England bowler.

Whether those people included the ECB was unclear. I then missed the second Test at Chittagong because of stiffness and soreness, a nightmare scenario because if there's anywhere you need to play to take your mind off the place it's Chittagong. It was horrendous. When you're watching the TV with the lights off and you can see shadows crawling around the floor, you know you're in trouble.

I shouted Colly from the room next door – he'd been to Australia lots of times and liked insects and all that kind of stuff. "Paul Collingwood – get your arse in here!"

"What's the matter?"

"There's three things in here," I said. "And one of them shouldn't be. Find it and get rid of it."

I wouldn't say it was as bad as Pakistan with the under-19s, because it wasn't as unexpected, but there was a familiar feeling of, 'Where am I? What am I doing here?'

I wasn't involved in the one-dayers and went home, the idea being I'd return for the Sri Lanka leg of the trip, but I could feel myself sinking into a dark place mentally.

The knot in the stomach, the lump in the throat, the panicky feeling, the breathlessness, were back. I felt like I'd been put in a bubble, detached from the rest of life, and I couldn't get out of it.

The thought of going to Sri Lanka made me feel ill, not because there's anything wrong with Sri Lanka, I would eventually tour there in 2007 and count it as one of my favourite places in the world.

Nor did it come, as some might have assumed, from the fact I'd been refused a central contract. I'm not petulant. I'm not a child. It came from not being able to handle being away from home, and feeling like I was. I wasn't stupid. I knew that if I was to be an England cricketer for any significant period of time I would have to tour. I wanted to tour. I didn't want to finish my career with 50 caps when it could have been 85. I just had a mental health problem.

In the end, I exaggerated how bad the soreness actually was. I laid it on thick and didn't go. Believe me, it wasn't an easy decision to make. I did, after all, have a chequered past on not wanting to be away. However, I'd dispelled some of that the previous winter when I went away for so long – and had a child born in the middle of the tour – and, after a brief trip home, still went back on tour.

Now I was back in the same position. The selectors asked me to go to the new ECB National Academy at Loughborough for two weeks to be monitored. I felt I was being tested. If I wouldn't go to Sri Lanka, would I go there instead? I didn't appreciate it and told them as much.

Instead I went down on an occasional basis, and that helped me much more because I was working once again with Troy Cooley. He had the technology to properly analyse my bowling and over the course of several sessions he straightened my body at the point of delivery, which in turn led to the ball coming out straighter. The dividends would be seen in a few weeks.

Pulling out of tours, playing cat and mouse with the selectors, these were the issues I was always fighting with. All through my career, I made decisions that the public didn't know about.

Some players knew that I didn't like going on trips, the same for the selectors, and that was always against me.

It meant even more that when I did play I had to perform properly because I had blotted my copybook on not wanting to be away. Immediately, there were questions from the media.

"Does Harmison really want to play cricket for England?" All that bullshit. I never usually bothered what the press said – I always made the joke that I couldn't read – but Derek Pringle wrote an article which I thought was appalling, suggesting I wasn't committed to the England cause, an attitude, he said, which had been noted in the England dressing room and with the coaching staff.

He told me doubts about my commitment had been expressed by the players, the questioning of my desire came from within the dressing room. According to Pringle, there were people in the England dressing room who thought I was skiving, although no-one said anything to my face.

Tres has since admitted he was one of those who doubted my desire. He openly says he thought I was swinging the lead in Bangladesh, that his attitude at the time was very much that if I didn't want to play for England, then I should piss off.

Tres would suffer his own problems later and reflects that in hindsight it would have been better to try to find out exactly what my issue was.

It's never nice to think that players might be talking about you behind your back – just ask Kevin Pietersen in later years – but at the time I was relatively new to the group, and a lot of people didn't know my insecurities and the person I was.

If I'm honest, I was a young man who needed a bit of a break, a bit of head space because things were starting to get to me. Playing for England is the best place to be for any cricketer, but it can also be the worst place to be if you have a problem. The misinformation, the scrutiny, the ill-informed views of others all add up to a very difficult situation.

If I'd had a recurring injury, nobody would have said a word about me missing tours. Because it was something between the ears, people – journalists, players, selectors – found it unfathomable. "Oh, Harmy, he'd rather be sat at home." Really? Is that what you think? Or do you think it might be something that runs a little bit deeper?

If the bloke you sit next to at work suddenly can't do his job and has two weeks off for stress, do you send him a 'Get Well' card or a load of abuse and vitriol?

We need to move away from this idea that sportspeople are somehow public property, treasured when they're polished and performing, worthless when the sheen disappears. We need to be less confrontational and more understanding.

I could understand it was frustrating for those around me, but the truth was I was having a bad time but didn't want to make a big deal of it because then other things have to come out. I was happier to be branded lazy or a shirker than for the full extent of my mental problems to be revealed. Not because I was ashamed, but because I felt sure that if people in the England set-up knew how bad it was I'd never play for my country again. So I did what I normally did, brushed the comments aside, allowed people to say what they liked about me, put up with being branded merely 'homesick', and tried to get on with it.

In the end, having that Sri Lanka trip off did me the world of good because it meant I got fitter than I'd ever been before.

Paul Winsper came back into my life and changed it forever. Paul had already been a massive influence on my career. For four months before my breakthrough 1998 season, I was with him four days a week just getting my body strong, and once that season started I never missed a game. Paul was like Troy Cooley.

He treated my body differently to other people. He worked with people as individuals, and got the physical facets right to put me in a position as a bowler, and that's something I'll always be thankful for. But barely had he started as Durham's fitness trainer than he was off elsewhere.

That was because John Morris was best friends with Rob Lee, who played for Newcastle United, and whose training ground was at the back of the Riverside at the time.

John mentioned to Rob that Paul was unreal and in the space of two conversations he was employed by Newcastle. I kept in touch with Paul because, as a massive Newcastle fan, I was over there all the time.

I'd nip through the fence to watch them in training, and Paul would do the same to watch the cricket, as would Rob Lee, a big cricket fan, who lived in one of the big houses alongside the ground.

Paul had read the Derek Pringle article, as had Newcastle's then manager, the legendary Sir Bobby Robson. Paul had then asked Sir Bobby if he could bring me in to the club. At the time, Paul told me in a different way.

He said, "Sir Bobby has read the article and wants you to come training." He knew it would have more weight if it came from Sir Bobby, although he was kidding no-one – I knew it was really coming from Paul. I couldn't believe it. Newcastle were in Europe at the time. They had all my heroes – Alan Shearer, Gary Speed, Shay Given, all these big players. I was like a kid being offered the keys to a sweet shop.

I went in and met Sir Bobby. He was kind, generous and knowledgeable, just as I'd imagined him to be. "How are you doing?" he asked. "I've seen you play cricket a lot. I didn't like what they wrote about you. Is what they wrote right?"

"No, no, I want to play," I replied.

"Well, use the facilities here." He was a very infectious character and was talking a lot about cricket as we went down to the gym.

"Look at them," he told me. He was pointing at Shearer, Speed and Given, as well as Steve Harper and James Milner. "You spend six weeks here and you'll understand why they're the best at what they do. Train hard with them and you'll be in a good position."

Then he looked round. There was Kieron Dyer, Craig Bellamy, Jermaine Jenas and Titus Bramble. "Train like these four," he said. "And you're going nowhere. I can get rid of you. I can't get rid of them!"

Over the course of that winter, I had my eyes opened to what it took to be an individual in a team in the top end world of professional sport.

Alan didn't really do any upper body weights, but he had problems with his knees and ankles, so worked tirelessly hard to make sure they were strong. Paul Winsper would set out a training programme for him and then Alan would come in and nail it.

The players would be told what to have for breakfast, lunch was the same. One of the first days I was there I thought Shay was going to eat me. I was sitting at the dinner table, having innocently just walked into the canteen, got my food, sat down and started eating. It was only then I realised I was the only one doing so. Shay was sitting opposite me looking longingly at my dinner.

"Why aren't you eating?" I asked him.

"We're not allowed to eat until past one o'clock."

"Oh shit!"

The one thing I didn't want to do was break any rules while I was there. I had total respect for the environment I was in. I never wanted to use Newcastle's training kit or be seen outside because I didn't want my presence to be a distraction.

Being in the gym so much led to one of the most surreal moments of my life. Me and the Newcastle coach John Carver were on exercise bikes while Sir Bobby was walking on a treadmill.

The reserves were playing and Bobby was watching through a window. He became so engrossed in the game he must have forgotten what he was doing, because all of a sudden he stopped walking and ended up flat on his face. Me and John looked at each other. We were both clearly thinking the same thing – 'Did that really just happen?'

We were desperately trying not to laugh as John got Bobby up. He calmly got back on the treadmill and started walking again. It was only when he left that we could let ourselves go.

I saw four or five managers off. Sir Bobby was my all-time favourite but I liked Graeme Souness as a man. I'd never met him before but I knew of his reputation. He was a man's man.

He scared you when he looked you in the eye. He stared you straight through. When Paul first introduced me to Graeme, I didn't know what to expect.

He was, after all, a blood and thunder Scotsman so there was a reasonable chance the delicacies of cricket had passed him by. But, again, he couldn't have been more accommodating. "Look," he said. "I don't know cricket, I haven't got a clue. What I do know is that I asked three or four senior players about you and after what I heard you can train here anytime you want."

That had come from me making a good impression. I hadn't been stupid, I hadn't told stories, I'd come in and worked hard and left it at that. Alan, Shay and Harps were key, because if Graeme had asked them what I was like and they were unsure, he'd just have turned round and told me to fuck off.

I'm always thankful to the people at Newcastle who made me so welcome. It was an amazing gesture by Paul and Sir Bobby, and when I had my benefit year in 2013, the Sir Bobby Robson Foundation, which helps cancer patients from across the north-east, was my chosen charity.

Sadly, Bobby had passed away by then, but his three sons Paul, Andrew and Mark were there at the launch. I was immensely touched when Bobby's widow Elsie said that although I was never actually a Newcastle United player, she thought Bobby would think of me in that light given how much time I'd spent at the club.

It wasn't just at Newcastle United I'd see Sir Bobby. Down the years I'd see him at Durham – you knew he was in when you spotted his Rolls Royce in the car park.

He was in no way flash, though. All he wanted to do was sit and talk about cricket. I couldn't have been more happy to oblige. He'd done so much for me, allowing me into a top Premier League club at a crossroads in my career.

Thanks to him I'd reached a position where I realised that if I wanted to play cricket at the highest level I needed to be better, stronger and fitter than I was, physically and mentally.

It lifted me so much. I wouldn't say I felt like an athlete, but I was comfortable with my body shape. I didn't have any insecurities in my mind as to whether I was fit enough. I was superfit, mentally refreshed and I probably never got to that point again.

However, it did set me off on the crest of a three-year wave from which I never looked back.

11

UNIQUE HARMY

*"I had energy coursing through me from head to toe.
It was an incredible feeling, as if, at that moment
in time, I could make anything happen. I felt
supercharged. I knew there was something special
in the offing"*

Sabina Park, Kingston, Jamaica, Sunday March 14, 2004

I'm stood at the top of my mark. The atmosphere is amazing. The rickety old stands are rocking, people are singing and dancing. As ever, you can smell the weed in the crowd. Stand on the boundary here too long and after a while you need to change position. You're getting high as a kite.

I look down the wicket. It takes a while to sink in. I have never seen a sight like it.

Every England fielder is either level with or behind the stumps. We have six slips, two gullys, wicket-keeper and Nasser Hussain under the lid at *short leg. I smile. I can't help but notice that Michael Vaughan, a man who is to fielding what the Biro is to fine art, has positioned himself behind Simon Jones and Matthew Hoggard so he won't have to catch anything. Not that it matters. I'm bowling at 95mph with outswing. The ball is only going to go into Chris Read's gloves, Trescothick at first slip or Flintoff at second, because of the speed and the bounce.*

A last quick glance at the scoreboard before I start my run confirms why the field is set as it is. The West Indies are 43-9, and I have dispatched six. It's not the West Indies fans that are singing and dancing in the stands, it's the English, bottles of Carib beer in hand. Finally, they're watching an England team on West Indian soil with the upper hand.

Last man Fidel Edwards is waiting for me. He looks jittery, jumpy, as well he might. I am flying. I have known from my very first ball that this will be my day. 'I am going to bowl these out. This is my time. This is my turn.' When you get a day like that you make the most of it – and I have.

I begin my run up. It is hot, humid, on any other day it would be almost overbearing. I feel none of it. I could be in my back garden in Ashington sipping a beer for how fresh I feel. I'm at the wicket now. I've done this hundreds, thousands of times, but never have I felt a part of it like now. I am a machine. Everything is running perfectly. I'm invincible. I could literally bowl all day. I hate the psychological bullshit of 'the zone' but this is my version of it. I am accurate, aggressive, intense, hostile. I know the moment won't last, but it will live with me forever.

The back arches, the front leg lands, the lever comes over, the ball is catapulted at 90mph towards Edwards. He has no time to think before the ball ricochets off the edge of the bat and straight into Tres's safe-as-buckets hands.

From the minute we'd landed in Jamaica we'd been bombarded by West Indians with a love of song. The tune they particularly favoured was, "Lara's going to get you!" There were other variations on the theme, but the basic message was the same – 'We've been crushing you on our own patch for years. Don't bother thinking that this time is going to be any different.'

Put simply, we were just another England team coming over to get their backsides slapped. There was even talk of "licking us down", which personally, as a fairly straightforward lad from Ashington, I didn't like the sound of at all.

I'd never been to the Caribbean before and having missed Sri Lanka, I hadn't heard all the chatter among the lads which generally gives you an idea of what a place will be like. My first impression when I got off the plane was that it was a lot better than Dhaka.

Right from that first minute on Jamaican soil I could see why people so enjoy touring the Caribbean. I threw myself right into the mix, jumping on the reggae buses to travel around Kingston just taking it all in. I say 'bus', but they're actually little vans.

You pay the driver a couple of dollars and they drop you off where you want, with other people jumping on and off all the time. We had one driver, a Rasta, whose bus we used all the time. With music blasting out, this thing was just bouncing. Your insides moved to the thud. Or your outsides if you were a bit heavy. He didn't need to sound his horn, you could hear him coming from miles away.

People would have a bit of craic with you wherever you went. A few times I was walking down the street and there'd be three or four coffin-dodgers sat playing dominoes. This wasn't normal dominoes, though, like you might play as a kid.

This was Ninja dominoes, everyone arguing and shouting at each other at the top of their voice. They'd talk about cricket all the time and were very knowledgeable about the game, constant chatter coming from the little transistors they would also use to listen to the commentary.

Everything was done at backward pace, so funny. You couldn't get upset with them or argue with them because they'd just suck their teeth and laugh at you.

I loved Kingston. It felt real, not too touristy. The tourist part of Jamaica is on the other side of the island at Montego Bay. But 'real' meant it could be quite a tough place too.

We were staying in the more volatile part of town and were told early on to be careful where we went when we left the hotel. "Don't go left, go right. Go left and there's guns and all sorts." If ever there was a time to remember my left from my right.

The West Indies tour was a good time to be an England cricketer because we were an emerging team and were getting better. We were a side that didn't have the weight of expectation on them that teams which came after had plus there was no awkwardness with me coming back into the group after missing Sri Lanka.

No-one mentioned it and there was certainly no problem with Tres. I loved Tres then and I love him now. When people ask who's the best English cricketer I played with I say Tres every time. If they ask me who's the best England player I played with, that's different. Then I say Kevin Pietersen.

Nevertheless, not for the first time in my career, and certainly not the last, I was coming into a trip having received more than a few negative comments in the press. But the only person I felt I needed to prove something to was myself.

I always knew I could perform at international level but my mental and physical health was the difficult side for me. By the time I went to the West Indies, though, thanks to Newcastle

United, I'd begun to understand my body a bit more and what was needed to be an elite sportsman.

Whereas before people had generally said nice things, and I wasn't doing too badly, to the extent that I thought the game was relatively easy, now, after Bangladesh, I'd had a period away from the game, taken the criticism and come back with a steelier and more "Up yours!" attitude to the outside world. I blocked everything off, whereas before I was getting caught up in it and letting it affect me.

All this had come out of training with Newcastle and it was somehow appropriate that I heard I'd been selected for the West Indies tour on the same day I was sat at St James' Park watching the Magpies beat Leeds 1-0.

I had the confidence that if I got myself on the field, bowling properly, I was as good as anyone in the country. In fact, before we left for the West Indies some commentators had been making comparisons between myself and the great Antiguan Curtly Ambrose.

I found such talk absolutely crazy. Even to be mentioned in the same breath as Curtly was ridiculous. But I had actually seen a split screen of me and the great West Indian running in and delivering the ball and the actions were almost identical.

Sadly, from that point onwards there was a slight difference in skill!

It was a good build-up. The lads spent a lot of time with each other, although Graham Thorpe had done his best to maintain a little distance at the start.

Thorpey was one of those people who wasn't very good at

timekeeping. We had to be at the airport hotel at Heathrow for 1pm ahead of the flight to Jamaica at seven to do all the media interviews, sign bats, the usual kind of stuff. It was six o'clock when Thorpey finally rocked up. We were flabbergasted.

Even by Thorpey's standards this was seriously late. His excuse was incredible. "I had an Asian taxi driver," he told us. "And he took me home to meet his family."

"Fuck off Thorpey."

"No, no, he was a big cricket fan, that's what happened."

"Come off it, mate. We're not bothered that you're late, just tell us the truth."

"Seriously, that's what happened."

We were having none of it. He just wanted to turn up at six, get on the plane and miss all the media business. From that point on, whenever he was late for anything, someone would pipe up, "He's had that taxi driver again."

We were a good group, one where everyone got on, and one which I'd have thought was easily led from Fletcher and Vaughan's point of view. Everyone knew their role and bought into the ethos of the trip, which was to work hard and try to make history. The old heads wanted to work with the newer lads and help bring them through.

We worked ourselves very hard in our preparation, to the extent we'd be in bed by nine o'clock. Yes, really! When people think of England in the West Indies, they have this image of drinking in beach bars, games of football on the beach, but there was none of that, certainly not at this stage. As a unit we trained very hard, and everybody bought into it again, including the older ones.

There was a key moment in the transition from Nasser to Vaughan in that warm-up period.

In fact, it was so key I've often wondered if it was staged.

In the last game before the first Test, I was bowling when Devon Smith clipped the ball just past square leg. Nasser was at short leg but didn't chase it.

Instead, Hoggy ran from fine leg, chased it all the way down in brutal heat, and threw it in.

Vaughan just went through Hussain. "You should have gone for that," he shouted. "The bowlers shouldn't be having to chase it." Nasser's helmet came off. He was kicking the dirt, not happy, giving it back a bit.

It seemed that Vaughan was trying to set his marker down and I thought that was a good turning point in the relationship between the previous and the new regime.

Nasser played a massive role in that – he gave Vaughan a bit back, but didn't go over the top and disrespect his captain. After a bit of chuntering, he got back to his job and just got on with it. I wasn't the only one who thought that was gutsy and ballsy on behalf of Vaughan. Nasser was a big character. You could argue that Vaughan, who wasn't exactly pulling up any trees for Yorkshire when he got his break for England, had benefited more than most from the Nasser regime. But he recognised a line needed to be drawn if he was to take the team forward in his name.

A public dressing down is not nice, but instead of that shift in authority being an awkward prolonged process, the job was done in 10 seconds.

From that moment, as a team, we never looked back.

Even being at short leg would have been seen as an insult by some ex-captains but, in all honesty, Nasser was no use anywhere else. His eyes were going and he had poppadum fingers so was no good at slip. In any case, Trescothick and Flintoff were the two best catchers so they were in the cordon. Butch was a great slip fielder too, and so was Thorpe.

All the junior players were bowlers and having big hulking units crouched at short leg is no good for either them or the team. There was only Vaughan or Nasser left to do it, and Vaughan wasn't going to do it because he was captain. If he hadn't been captain, that would have been his position, because he couldn't catch anything anywhere else, and to be fair he admitted it.

For a man who clearly had great hand/eye coordination when he was batting it was amazing. He'd drop them when you were just lobbing them to him in practice. Even the ones he took you'd see them in slow motion and they'd have not gone in properly or hit the wrong part of his hand.

"How did that stay in?" Nasser going into Boot Hill was the obvious choice, but it was still a big deal an ex-captain going in there.

The fact he was willing to go into a position traditionally reserved for the rookie in the team said a lot about Nasser.

Fitness was one of Vaughan's big things. He'd initiated a massive fitness drive in Bangladesh and subsequently, even though I wasn't there, in Sri Lanka.

When it got to the West Indies, and brace yourselves for this, me and Fred even had a self-inflicted booze ban. By the time the first Test came round we hadn't had a drink for three weeks.

Instead we trained hard, and to reduce temptation rarely did we go anywhere.

To fill the gap, we had a little card school going in our room for entertainment. Hoggy, Simon, Fred, me, there was a few of us playing.

We used the plastic studs from the bottom of our boots for

chips, teabags were worth a bit more. "I'll see your plastic stud and raise you a teabag" – that kind of thing.

A lot of the players went along with the booze ban, and they did so because we really wanted to give ourselves the best chance of doing something special. As a bunch of players, it made us feel even more like a solid unit. It reflected how hard we were pushing ourselves. It started in the first week and just kept going.

Golf also played a key role on that trip. We'd train early in the morning and then there was always a few going out on the course in the afternoon.

It all added up to a tight group, and that then shows itself on the pitch. Sounds odd, but I think golf is one of the best ways to prepare for cricket, because you're on your feet for five hours peppered with periods of intense concentration.

Fielding takes a lot out of you. It's tough on the old legs, and the only way you can prepare for that is to physically do it.

I tended to play with Geraint Jones a lot of the time, but there were some keen golfers in that team. Fred, Thorpey and Simon wouldn't play, but everyone else would, even if it was just having a swing and walking off the course after six holes.

I got into golf through cricket. I never played as a kid – it was a money sport, an elite sport. I didn't have the finances to play nor the network. It was always football and cricket for me. But on tour especially it can be a bit of head space, a way of relaxing while enjoying yourself with others.

On tour, the downtime is a lot. You can very easily end up, both mentally and physically, spending a good length of time in a place you do not want to be, so having ways to get out of that is vital. Mark Butcher had his guitar, he was a great singer, can write his own songs, and that was his escape.

Others have PlayStations. Whatever, you need something. Fletcher was a big one for training out of the midday heat. We'd train late afternoon or first thing in the morning. That might be 9am, so you'd be done by 12.30, had your dinner, and then be sitting around wondering what to do. Having a diversion, be it from negative thoughts, the bar, or whatever, is vital.

Some of the Sky boys played golf but we'd avoid them. We tried to keep out of their way. We were there to do our job, they were there to do theirs. It was as if we didn't want to dilute what we'd got together by mixing with them. Paths rarely crossed anyway.

In the Caribbean, Beefy would live on a boat for eight weeks. It wasn't like we had a problem with them, or most of us with journalists in general for that matter. At the World Cup the year before, when me and Hoggy never looked like getting a game, we spent a lot of the time in various bars at night with the journos.

After that I always got on well with the majority of the lads from the written press.

By the time the first Test match came around, the bowling unit was looking strong. Freddie was a force to be reckoned with after shaking off his own injury problems, and Simon and Hoggy were in a good place too.

The series would prove that if you've got a good bowling unit, you've got a great chance of winning games. But in no way was it apparent that I was going to go into that Sabina Park Test match and do what I did. In the warm-up games I got a couple of wickets, but I wasn't blowing teams away or knocking people's heads off.

In fact, in the first innings at Sabina Park I took 2-61 as the West

Indies reached a very respectable 311. If anything I thought the pitch was too bouncy for me, but then as the game went on it got a little bit more uneven which brought me into the game a bit more. In the first innings I was an easy leave, and if I bowled it full I was an easy hit.

Batting first with 300-plus on the board, the West Indies were in the driving seat and with Fidel Edwards and Tino Best bowling seriously fast, Nasser and Butch took some hefty blows to keep us in the game as we inched to 339. It was their bravery and steel which set us up to win. I just did the end bit.

When their second innings came round, I decided to change my length. I reasoned I'd bowled too short in the first innings and let the West Indies batsmen off too easily.

Gayle hit a four at the start – one of the three boundaries that would make up the 12 runs I conceded, but I soon had him back in the hutch thanks to a fantastic catch by Thorpe at second slip which took him so far off his feet he nearly ended up in the Barmy Army.

Hoggy then nipped in to get Devon Smith caught and bowled, before I got Sarwan LBW for a duck, an iffy decision – it wouldn't have hit another set.

After five overs, the original plan was that I'd come off. But I was in no way tired. Far from it, I had energy coursing through me from head to toe. It was an incredible feeling, as if, at that moment in time, I could make anything happen. I felt supercharged. I knew there was something special in the offing.

Coming off wasn't an option. In the end I had one more and that was when I got Chanderpaul, another bit of luck that went my way as he played forward defensively only for the ball to continue through his legs and take the bails off.

If I'd come off the over before, my path in life could have been so, so different.

Once I'd got that wicket, and the way I was feeling, I was bowling all day – or the next hour as it turned out! With me, once I got on a roll I was virtually unstoppable. The speed I had and the intimidation factor meant I was hard for any batsman to start against.

I genuinely felt there was no-one who could play me. I felt every ball I was going to get a wicket. Everything had clicked, and there's only half a dozen times in your career that happens. The ball was swinging, it was quick and it was accurate, on the money every time.

I absolutely knew that nothing could stop me.

I tucked Ridley Jacobs up with one which he could only fend to Nasser at short leg, and then Tino Best was caught behind off a riser.

It was at that point, with seven wickets down, that Vaughan changed the field and put everyone behind the stumps. I've watched it back on YouTube and Michael Holding is astounded. "Well," he says. "I've never seen an England field like this."

I've got news for you, Mikey, neither had anyone else.

It felt like something special was happening but at the same time I was focused on the job at hand, almost too caught up in what was happening to see the significance of it.

In all honesty, I've always been of the opinion that a fast bowler only needs five fielders anyway. The rest are for chucking the ball back. In modern international cricket, you don't get many caught mid-on or mid-off.

You need three slips, a gully and a wicket-keeper. That's where you get your wickets. The rest of the fielders in that slip cordon were never going to catch the ball. The batsmen were only nicking it fine and Tres and Fred at slip were both such big lads, and had such a big spread, they were practically three slips between them.

To have those nine guys there and then Nasser at short leg looked a great picture, but for me it was about sending a message, not just to the West Indies but to the world, that this bowling attack was special.

We could take anybody on.

It was a statement.

Look at these bowlers, Harmison, Hoggard, Jones, Giles, Flintoff, not as individuals but as a five.

That picture is just as significant as my 7-12. It was telling everyone we had bowlers who could take five wickets, take three in half a spell, and between them can take 20 in a game. "Look world, look at this!"

To round the innings off, perfectly proving my five-fielder theory, Adam Sanford and Fidel Edwards were snared at first slip by Tres.

Not only had I recorded the best ever Test match bowling figures at Sabina Park but I was the first 6ft 5in cricketer to disappear under a pack of celebrating teammates.

The game wasn't finished – we needed to knock off 20 – but afterwards I managed to grab a stump and I've still got the ball as well. It was the first time I'd taken seven wickets in an innings since I was 14.

Fred says that in the dressing room afterwards it was as if I didn't realise what I'd done. There was an element of that, but I was also thinking of a good friend, Graham Wilson, who lived next door to my mum and dad.

Graham had died suddenly, aged 46, just before I came out.

I'd played cricket with him at Ashington – first-team opening bowler, give it a bit of a whack at the end – and he was a great bloke, organising all sorts round the club as well as encouraging and supporting me through the years.

The whole of Ashington Cricket Club was devastated by Graham's passing, and, as I sat in that dressing room, kit all over the floor, lads chattering excitedly, I couldn't help but think about him. He'd seen me grow up and had always pushed me to get better. He'd come to watch me at Durham. I would have loved Graham to have seen that last hour.

There was also an element of not quite realising the enormity of what had happened. I wasn't as hung up on cricket as some other people are, so this whole thing of turning the tables on the West Indies, turning them over in their own backyard, after all those years of humiliation, didn't really mean anything to me.

The pundits and the Sky boys were making a massive thing of it because they'd all gone through those bad times, but it wasn't something I recognised. I had never seen it.

I wasn't the only one having trouble taking it all in. Amongst the players as a whole there was a surreal atmosphere, as if no-one could quite believe what had happened.

Bear in mind the whole game had gone from drifting first innings parity to being all over in two-and-a-half hours. I don't think people could comprehend it. The plan had been to get ourselves in a decent position by the end of what was the fourth day, come back tomorrow and try to finish the job off chasing 200-220.

Instead, here I now was with a beer in my hand (the booze ban had come to a sudden end) having bowled them out. It was an amazing achievement as a team. It was never just about me.

I hadn't just blown the West Indies away on my own. Thorpey took a catch, Nasser took a catch, Tres took two, Flintoff, Read.

Hoggy had bowled brilliantly to keep the target batsmen down my end and taken two key wickets in the process. Simon had kept the pressure on and nipped out Ryan Hinds too. If they'd have been going at six an over, it would have been a very different outcome.

As a unit we bowled for each other. If your mate was on one, doing something special, you made sure you did your job for him.

If Hoggy was doing well, troubling players on the front foot, you'd see me bowling a lot of bouncers from the other end. That way I was hiding the ball so the batsman couldn't get any runs and also constantly pushing them back. That then helped Hoggy when they had to make a mental switch back to the front foot the next over. In Jamaica, yes the wickets came my way, and the plaudits that followed. But I couldn't have done it without Hoggy and Simon, any more than I could have done it without the lads who took the catches, made the diving stops, and kept the pressure on the batsmen. That's what good teams do.

The West Indies guys didn't come into our dressing room. They were stunned more than anything else, as were we.

Back at the hotel, I rang home. It was great to hear Hayley's voice. It turned out the whole family had watched the whole thing together on TV. They all told me how proud they were and how Emily had been shouting "Daddy!" when she saw me on TV.

It reminded me how much I missed them, and how again I had struggled at the start of the tour – days of darkness before the light lifted when the cricket began. Thankfully, I wouldn't have to wait long to see them. They were all coming out for the Barbados Test in a fortnight, along with the small matter of a party of 20 from Ashington Cricket Club.

The celebrations had started in earnest at the Buffs too. All the lads had been watching it down there on the Sunday and there'd been a few drinks, to the extent that a few had phoned in sick the next day.

When the cameras then turned up at Buffs on the Monday, three or four bolted out the back door so their boss wouldn't see them on TV. The attention didn't stop there – my grandma Brenda was in the national papers. She used the opportunity to apologise to anyone whose window I'd broken while I was playing in the street as a kid!

Not only that, but Newcastle United flew a shirt signed by all the players out to me. It's one of my proudest possessions. I particularly like the message at the bottom – 'Unique Harmy – Bobby Robson'. It was a time when people were talking about cricket and not football. Everything had been turned on its head.

The Jamaica Test had happened in March, a month before the domestic season, and it was great to hear that grassroots clubs, like Ashington, were experiencing an upsurge in interest. Jamaica came at the right time not just for me, but the England team, and English cricket.

12

HERE TO STAY

"It was the start of people looking at England and thinking, 'Hang on, this team is dangerous'"

Freshened up, we headed for the bar by the pool.

There were some England fans sat by the water and as we emerged from the hotel they stood up and cheered.

It all just added to what was already a very special day. We sat down there for hours and hours, until the sun came up the next day.

Butch had his guitar out, there were a few cigars, and we drank more that night than we had in the three weeks previously put together. We certainly gave it a good go, and rightly so. Even if you don't drink you should celebrate winning. You have to. You have to enjoy that feeling of accomplishment or else what's the point?

I enjoyed winning, and when I won I enjoyed celebrating. But even then it felt like we were only at the beginning of something. Butch, Nasser and Thorpe, who'd all been battered on previous tours to the West Indies, were drumming it into us not only what an achievement this victory had been, but how important it was that we now carried it through for the rest of the series. They spelt it out in no uncertain terms. "Look, we've been smashed by the West Indies for the past 30 years. What we've just done is special. What we can carry on and do will be even more special. Let's stick with it."

I had never truly felt like I was here to stay as an international cricketer, but after Jamaica I finally thought, 'Right, I can pack my kit for a while now. I'm in.'

From a mindset point of view that was a big moment for me. People often ask if it was one in the eye for the doubters who'd been lining up to knock me down over the winter, but none of it was about sticking two fingers up to the critics.

None of that bothered me. I wouldn't give Derek Pringle the time of day. Anyone who says the article he wrote did me the world of good because it fired me up doesn't know what they're talking about. It didn't. It was never a driving force for me. The driving force for me was working together as a team while getting better individually. Putting two fingers up to people is a negative way of motivating yourself. If you're constantly doing that, then your focus is wrong. It's totally the wrong way of looking at it.

Being a not very bright Geordie was quite good for me as a cricketer because I let a lot of things go over my shoulders. When people said nice things about me, it meant the same as people saying nasty things about me. My philosophy was if it didn't affect my teammates and it didn't affect my family, I couldn't care less. All I cared about was doing my job and being the best I possibly could be. It didn't always happen, but I tried. I understand it could be frustrating, but nobody would be more frustrated than me. And whenever anybody wrote something about me, or tried to insinuate something, or labelled me as something, I didn't care.

As captain, Lara tried to put a brave face on things. "There is one good thing about this situation," he said. "It can't happen again." Hmm. The West Indies is never a happy camp and it doesn't take much to put the cat amongst the seagulls. That's Caribbean cricket – there's a bit of selfishness in their culture and when that gets mixed in with inter-island rivalries, and people chasing the dollar, then it's a recipe that doesn't always add up to a good performance on the cricket field.

The true impact of what we'd done at Jamaica only really hit home to me on the first day of the second Test at Trinidad.

Gayle had come out all guns blazing, battering me everywhere, with the clear intention of taking me down a peg or two and putting me back in my box. It worked as well – after stuttering to 47 in Kingston, they reached 100-0 here one-day style.

From the home side's point of view, everything seemed back to normal. Trinidad isn't as overwhelming an atmosphere as Jamaica but they still had the supporters' bar going and the dancing girls in the stands. And the weed. It was then I switched to the other end and immediately had Gayle caught behind, with Devon Smith LBW not far behind, and Sarwan caught by Fred at slip. It had taken a little time to get going, and didn't feel as intense as the last one, but it was happening again, I was on a roll.

Lara was next in. He lasted three balls before I fired one in at him that reared straight in front of his nose.

He couldn't get properly behind it and edged it to Ashley Giles at gully. It was a moment of clear realisation for us all – we're going to beat these, and we're going to beat them well.

Lara looked shot and totally dazed by what we'd thrown at him. In Jamaica, he'd been hit on the hand by both me and Simon, and had come out down the order in the second innings. Now he'd basically been bounced out on his home ground. The great Brian

Lara bounced out on his home ground! We knew what the rest of the West Indies team would be thinking as they saw him there in the middle, blindly fending one off, stuck like a rabbit in the headlights – if that's happening to him, what chance have the rest of us got? We jumped on that. Once we saw that fear, we were all over them. .

With Lara out at lunchtime, that was it, they capitulated, total collapse. I ended up with 6-61 as the light went out on their innings just like it had in Jamaica, but in reality it was more like 6-20, because they'd got those early runs on the board before the collapse.

I felt like I was in the form of my life. Everything went my way. If there was a catch off another bowler, it was dropped. If there was one off me, it was snaffled up. It's swings and roundabouts. It happens like that. The following winter everything Hoggy touched turned to gold and I couldn't buy a wicket. Did it bother me? No. I got my rewards one winter and he did the next.

Once again the old guard came to our rescue when we batted, Butch, Nasser and Thorpe all making fifties. There was an hour period when Fidel Edwards and Tino Best flew in and bowled at Nasser and Butch. We sat on the balcony as the day faded and could hear the slaps and thuds as they were whacked all over the body. I couldn't help thinking that if they got one of them out they could be through us in no time.

It didn't happen and this time it was Simon who cleaned them up with five wickets in the second innings. After carrying him off the pitch at Brisbane, his knee in tatters, and possibly his career, I was more pleased and emotional for Simon than I ever had been for myself. It was real lump in the throat stuff because I'd also seen the rehabilitation work he'd put in at Loughborough, the sacrifices he'd made to get himself back playing again. He could now put that particular demon to bed.

The West Indies is the best place to win because everything about it, the atmosphere, the surrounds, the noise, the islands, is unreal.

I'd love to have won in Australia, but the West Indies is special, a party place, but not nightclubs and noise, little bars on the beach, a relaxed environment rather than the full-on stuff you get in other resorts. It was in one such bar that, after being named man of the match again, the rum and cokes were flying and I was celebrating our victory big time.

I felt it was time for a sing-song and, after very little thought, my ditty of choice was, "Where's your Lara gone?" bellowed, like Noddy Holder with a megaphone, at the top of my voice.

I was very pleased with myself when I finished about the seventh rendition. If ever there was sweet revenge for a threat of being "licked down" that was it. I grabbed my drink, turned round and found a rather unexpected audience member.

There was Brian Lara sat at a table in the corner.

Later we were invited aboard the luxury yacht of Hampshire chairman Rod Bramsgrove. If ever there was a millionaire's plaything, this was it. The boat had several jet skis and we were spinning doughnuts in the sea. People were flying out of rubber dinghies going at silly miles an hour. There were calves popped, shoulders sore, but that just showed the togetherness of everyone on that trip. Barbados is always a big favourite with England fans and this was no different, except that this time a decent proportion of them were from a small pit town in the north-east.

There was the kids, Hayley, mam and dad, a few from the Buffs, and then the cricket club crowd as well. Bridgetown was alive with Geordie accents for five days and it was incredible to see so many friendly and familiar faces in the crowd. All except one. My mam would rarely go to games. She couldn't watch, she found it too nerve-wracking.

Over the years, she'd come on a lot of the overseas trips, but very rarely would she come to the ground. She'd often end up babysitting, by choice, instead. "Leave the kids with me. You go off!" The maternal instinct was never switched off with mam. If there were kids needed looking after, she'd be there.

By now, the West Indies team were done. They looked a dispirited group and we wanted to take advantage. We didn't want just to secure the series in Bridgetown, but go the whole hog and win it 4-0 but, despite their disarray, it wasn't a storyline the West Indies were overly keen to be a part of.

After edging their way to 224, they'd have bowled us out for nothing were it not for Thorpey battling out one of the best ever hundreds by an England batsman.

I should know, I was in the middle when he got it. He put 32 on with Simon and 39 with me – I got precisely three – as we managed to claw ourselves out of dire straits.

The more we crept closer to their total, the more we could again see the energy draining out of the West Indians. It was another kick where it hurts for them. Not only had we hung on but we'd got a lead. That knocked the stuffing out of the West Indies and this time it was Hoggy who inflicted the pain with a hat-trick as they collapsed to 94 all out.

Fred had also wrapped up his first five-wicket haul. Every game, one of the bowling unit had now done something special. The satisfaction was unbelievable. There was no let up. What we were doing to the West Indies, they'd been doing to teams for years. It was relentless. After me and Hoggy there was Fred and Simon

– and that was a massive part of us reaching the summit in 2005.

That was it, we'd won the series 3-0.

The Sky cameras came into the dressing room to watch us celebrate. I remember because I hit David Gower flush on the side of the face with a chocolate bun. He'd knocked my first delivery away with ease, but this one had sneaked through his defences. It was a carnival atmosphere. We sat there for hours. When you've won the best place to be is the dressing room. Don't want to get changed, don't want to leave. You just want to sit there and tell one another how good they were.

Thorpey had been named man of the match and had to go off to another room to do his press conference duties. As he sat waiting, he noticed a journalist in the room who he liked about as much as a fast delivery on the inner thigh.

This particular scribe had slagged him off about his personal life before the trip and now that Thorpe had the upper hand, he was having none of it. "I'm not going to answer any questions," he told the assembled throng. "Until he's out." The reporter could either stay and ruin it for his colleagues or leave the room.

In the end, the reporter left, and instead stood outside. If he thought he was going to get an easier ride out there he was very sadly mistaken. We were all ripping into him. "What are you doing out there mate? The press conference is through the door." He didn't enjoy it one bit. But that was Thorpe's moment – he had just scored a big hundred and he was entitled to send the man out.

After his hundred, Thorpe was knackered and quite emotional, without shedding a tear. He'd not long been back in the team and it showed how much it still meant to him. He wasn't a man of many words. For him, actions spoke louder.

When it came to what was going on underneath, he only really opened up to Butch and Nasser, the guys who'd been with him through thick and thin, but the rest of us could see how much it meant.

After the toss at Antigua, Ian Botham introduced me to the legendary West Indian quick Andy Roberts. "Great fast bowling," Roberts told me. "But you'll not win 4-0." Here we go, another Caribbean great telling us what's going to happen to us.

"Why not?" I asked him. "They're all shot to bits."

He looked at me. "It won't bounce. I know, because I prepared the pitch!" I had no idea he'd taken this rather unusual route of fast bowler to groundsman.

Roberts might have been proved wrong had umpire Darrell Hair heard the noise the rest of us did when Brian Lara subsequently nicked off from my bowling on nought. I was spewing when it wasn't given.

When he got to 80, though, we knew we'd had it. You could see from that point on, there was 300 coming here. We were only a hundred out. The St John's Recreation Ground was home from home for Brian Lara, the flattest wicket you'd ever seen.

He'd bedded down here more often than he had at his house in Trinidad, most notably 10 years previously when he eased his way to a then world record 375 against England. Australian opener Matthew Hayden had surpassed that feat with 380 against Zimbabwe at Perth in 2003 and it soon became clear that Lara saw this Test match as a very good chance to get the record back.

Not only that, but he'd failed all through the series and was due.

I'd been warned about Lara's love of a big one before I set off. Durham were on the receiving end when he got his world record

501 at Edgbaston. That was before my time, but Simon Brown told me he was unbelievable.

Gareth Batty was the spin department in Antigua. What a game to make your debut. He needed 15 fielders. Whatever Vaughany did it made not a blind bit of difference and they had to call Securicor to take the bowling figures home with us.

Vaughany would bring a fielder in, Lara would hit it over the top. Move a fielder sideways, he'd hit it through the gap. If he didn't fancy that, he's just run down the pitch and hit it out of the ground.

Set a 7:2 offside field to try to choke him, and he'd step across and hit it on the leg side. He was never going to get out. The only time he looked vaguely vulnerable was against the new ball – the three times we had one! – but not to the point we ever thought we'd got him.

I bowled 37 overs in that innings but, in the end, I was barred from the attack by Hair for running down the pitch. I forgot I'd been warned previously.

When I got warned the second time, I looked at the scoreboard and just pissed myself.

I was just on the verge of going for a hundred when I had to come off. I could see Fred shaking his head, telling me, "You bastard, you did that on purpose." A few moments later Fred went for his. I clapped him when he brought it up. If you look you can see me stood there, shoulders going up and down, laughing. He scowled at me and was a bit off with me for the rest of the day – "I'm not bowling your overs again." Even now, when someone goes for a hundred he reminds me about it.

The innings spanned three days, with Lara easing past Hayden's mark on the third morning. He kissed the pitch and, as in 1994, when Sir Garfield Sobers strolled out, play was delayed as all sorts of people started walking out to congratulate him. There was the mayor, the prime minister of Antigua, everyone. This was in the middle of the game! I was thinking, 'Hang on, we're trying to play a Test match here.'

Thankfully, on 400 he put us out of our misery and declared. It's an odd situation. You clap the first century, clap the second, clap the third, and in the end you're just thinking, 'Get your 400 and get off!' He was unreal and all you could do was watch with a mix of admiration and frustration.

It was a phenomenal achievement. It's hard enough for a team to reach 400, let alone one man on his own.

After three days in the field, I took the opportunity to get some rest. I always liked lying down in the dressing room, and the best thing about Antigua was it actually had a bed – a little one in the corner, which reflected the sheer unorthodox nature of the Recreation Ground. I've played at Lord's a few times but never have I seen an old guy singing in the stands, swinging from a chandelier, with his stilettos on.

In the background, you've got the drums banging away, and then you've got the prisoners watching from the side – sometimes they'd let them in to watch a day's play. Three or four of us even went in the prison gym because there was nowhere else to use.

There was an entrance off the side of the ground so me, Simon and Hoggy went in that way. A couple of prisoners were in the gym with us, but we weren't worried. To be able to use the gym they must have kept their noses clean. They loved their cricket too, so they were fine. When Lara got going I was wishing we could have stayed in the jail and sent the prisoners out to bowl.

Unsurprisingly, after being out in the field for two-and-a-half days in blistering heat, we ended up following on, even though

Fred got a brilliant 102, but batted solidly in the second innings and in the end easily saved the game.

Antigua was a little bit of anti-climax for us considering how the three previous Tests had gone. We'd have liked to have played on a pitch like the others that offered a little bit more of a contest between bat and ball. But it was understandable the West Indies went the other way because the last thing they wanted was to get beaten 4-0 in their own backyard.

It was also the Test which saw the only bit of upset in our camp.

Vaughan and Fletcher had decided that Chris Read wasn't the right man to keep wicket for England. Fletcher had already reached the same conclusion about another great keeper, James Foster.

Both were suffering for what Adam Gilchrist was doing for the Australian team at the time and also what Alec Stewart had done for England. Whoever came in was going to have to bat and keep, and Fletcher didn't believe they had what it took with the bat.

In the glove-work department they were incredible, but it wasn't enough. Their faces didn't fit and that was that. Read was dropped for Antigua and I found that difficult to take.

Fletcher had taken Trescothick from relative obscurity, Vaughan the same, but for every one of those players, he turned his back on several others and made quick judgements. If he liked what he saw, he backed it. If he didn't think you were very good, or didn't like you, that was the end of it.

He wouldn't entertain the idea of you being in the team. He could be influenced by senior players, but if he didn't like something in somebody, that was it. You were gone. I could see what Fletcher and Vaughan were trying to do, which was get in somebody who was a better batsman, but as a bowler I was quite keen on the better keeper. Having said that, Read's replacement, Geraint Jones, became a vital member of the group as we went forward to the Ashes in 2005.

We'd have liked to have won the series 4-0 but, essentially, Lara had done what he'd wanted and taken the opportunity out of our hands. It was his way of dragging some kind of positivity out of the series, although even then it was a personal kind of glory rather than something to be shared by the team.

It had been a difficult series for the West Indies captain. He was a superstar in an otherwise decent, but not brilliant, side.

When everything goes well, that's great. When things start going wrong, all of a sudden it's a problem. Sometimes the separation between him and the rest of the team was tangible.

At the end of the trip, after the one-dayers, some of us went to play golf at the Westmoreland Club in Barbados and were flying home that night. Fred was in the pool bar when we left and I thought playing golf was a good way of stopping myself sitting there all day next to him.

I didn't fancy all day in the sun drinking, then getting on a plane, getting off at Heathrow, and on another plane to Newcastle. I'd have been a jibbering mess by the time I got home to Hayley and the kids. The West Indies were playing Bangladesh in a couple of days so they were heading off on the bus from the same hotel to practice. Brian Lara came down to the restaurant, and saw us. "Where are you going?"

"We're having a game of golf at Westmoreland," I told him.

He pondered this for about 20 seconds then went over to the West Indies bus. "I'm not coming to training," he said, preferring to play 18 holes than go for a net.

The lack of togetherness he displayed there I felt had come from what we'd done to the West Indies team that trip. When I saw him do that, I didn't want him playing golf in the same place as us.

I didn't like what he'd done. I was always for the team, and to see him do that to his teammates when they were at such a low ebb, and he was captain, left a bitter taste in the mouth.

It did feel as if he lived one life and the rest of the team lived another. When he scored his 375 against England at Antigua in 1994, he was given a load of land above a big roundabout in the middle of Port of Spain. The house he built was massive and beautiful. I'd like to give you a guided tour, room by room, but to be honest the only time I went there the whole thing was a blur.

The one-day international was rained off in Trinidad and so I met a pal of mine and watched the Newcastle match on TV in a bar instead. Because of the time difference, this was about 10 in the morning. We had a couple of beers, those couple of beers turned into a liquid lunch, which turned into a hazy afternoon, and then in the evening there was a party at Brian Lara's house. All I can remember is we turned up smashed. He had a big marquee in the garden and we were swinging around on the poles holding it up. How we didn't bring it down I don't know. As I say, a guided tour is out of the question. I certainly couldn't tell you what art he had in the bathroom.

Over the years, it has been said that my 7-12 in Jamaica was the start of the three-year purple patch that England had but I've always disagreed with that idea. It's just too simple a conclusion to jump to. There were a ton of reasons we won in the West Indies and, for me, that Test – and that entire tour – was the first sign of what the England team as a whole could do.

Over the course of the series we showed resilience with the bat and our new-look bowling attack became apparent. It was a very powerful and potent bowling unit, as we would go on to prove in the next few years. It was the start of people looking at England and thinking, 'Hang on, this team is dangerous.' Because if you've got a good bowling attack, you've got a good chance of taking 20 wickets.

As a team, we were fit and strong, nobody stood out, we all worked well together – and we got on. We had an absolute ball on that trip, and it helped our cricket. The group togetherness was something else. It was a relaxed atmosphere, on the perfect tour, the Caribbean. The way we got on was vital, not just for then, but for the future. We had so much belief in the unit. Whenever anyone then came into the team, it was a good environment for them to step into. What happened in 2005 was built on that West Indies trip. That was the foundation, benchmark, stepping stone, whatever you want to call it, for English cricket to move forward.

When we left for the West Indies, we had no idea things would pan out as they did. I had no idea I would have such a bearing on the outcome that I'd be named man of the series. But when it's your day you have to make the most of it.

You're happy when it's someone else's day, but when it's yours you absolutely have to enjoy it. As it turned out, it wasn't my day, it was my month; a month that would set me up for the rest of my career. Whether people say that career was good, bad or unfulfilled, it was that month in the West Indies which confirmed me as having arrived. For me as a person, though, it didn't change anything. I was still the same. I went back to Ashington, closed the door, spent time with my family, and went down the Buffs. It was other people's perceptions that changed. I was just happy to have stepped up and made a difference.

The West Indies in 2004 was my greatest tour. It gave me confidence that I belonged in the team. "I'm here," I could finally say. "I belong here, and I'm here to stay."

13

AND YET, AND YET...

*"Vaughan was a good captain, but any captain
is only as good as his bowling attack, and we had
a great bowling attack, as good as any in world
cricket"*

S omething strange was happening in English cricket.
The national team was actually becoming something
the country was proud of.

It was a year when, yet again, the England footballers had
failed at the Euros. Sports fans needed something to rally around
and, increasingly, that thing was us. We didn't disappoint either.
In 2004, we just couldn't get beaten, no matter what situation
we found ourselves in.

We saw off New Zealand in three Tests and then the West
Indies in four, and that was the best year ever in English cricket

in my view. England were in a place they'd not been in for 20-plus years.

Fred had more than a little to do with the side's raised profile. The public had waited a long time for someone they could truly call Botham-esque, and he was now really coming to the fore.

Both in personality and talent, the whole country had caught on to Fred big time, but their growing attachment to the England team wasn't based on him alone.

Michael Vaughan was also huge after what he'd done the two previous winters, smashing ton after ton against the Aussies, albeit in a losing cause, and then captaining England to victory in the West Indies for the first time since 1968.

Unlike Nasser, who seemed bolshey and intolerant a lot of the time, the replacement skipper was a PR man's dream. He was approachable, always had the good lines, and was out and about doing things in the public eye, not taking himself too seriously.

Vaughan was one of the best captains I ever played under, and one of the best liars! He'd say anything if he thought it would get the best out of you!

He was the ultimate man manager. If he could see a player was struggling, he knew exactly what to say to get them to relax. If I was going at six or seven an over, I knew I was bowling shocking, but he'd come over, say something, maybe about cricket, maybe something else, about Newcastle United or his own Sheffield Wednesday, and suddenly the tension would be gone.

He knew exactly what to say at any particular moment. As a captain, I never really knew what he was feeling or thinking, but when he came up with a plan, we all believed in it.

It was the art of Michael Vaughan. He was the master at getting the best out of a team.

The other thing to factor into our improvement was that while I had always known cricket as a working-class sport, something played between the mining communities of the north-east, I knew for many in England it was seen as slightly elitist.

In some areas, the local cricket club was deemed to be snooty and, like golf and tennis, a bit superior. The England team at that time, though, was a living, breathing example of why that attitude could be misguided. It was a team that, far from being old school tie, look down your nose, was full of realistic and normal people that kids and their parents could relate to.

Fred, Hoggy, Simon and myself were a bowling unit from working-class environments, same sort of upbringings, similar sort of characters, and people latched on to that. We were the toilers, putting in the hard yards, sometimes for no reward, and it's not difficult to see how people could see a bit of themselves in that scenario.

At the same time, we didn't take ourselves too seriously and were never distant from the support. We were part of them and they were part of us.

That's not to say it was all about class. Not everyone was from the world of sweat and industry. It just meant we had a good mix, a representative mix, and one that was never less than harmonious.

Andrew Strauss, with his public school background, came into the side that year and was as close to his teammates as anybody. Us northern working-class lads could comfortably take the piss out of him – "Shut up, you soft southern git" – but he could just as easily do the same back. "Sorry, I don't speak Geordie," he'd tell me on more than one occasion. Ed Smith was the same. The Middlesex batsman, who came in against

South Africa the previous year, was from completely different roots, Cambridge University educated, and with a list of qualifications as long as your arm, even my arm, graduating with a double first in history.

The way he spoke was like living in an episode of *Downton Abbey*. Initially I thought, 'He's going to come in here and look at Flintoff and Harmison, two northern idiots, and think, 'What's going on here? Who are these two?' But the Test matches Ed played, he was never away from us.

As a group we took people at face value, background was never an issue.

We always tried to make new people feel comfortable. After both having been plunged into an England dressing room that had all the warmth of an ice bath, me and Fred felt strongly about that. During this time we didn't need team meals, we all ate in the same place anyway. We were all best mates.

In 2004, we were at a point in our careers where we felt safe in our places, knew if we were in form we would play, but also that we couldn't rest on our laurels. It was a time when you never wanted to get injured because everybody realised how great this was and could be.

A lot of the players were at the peak of their powers and there was no sense of anyone playing for themselves. When Strauss came into the team at Lord's against New Zealand and immediately made a hundred, followed by 83 in the second innings, Nasser, despite making a ton in that game, promptly sacrificed himself to create a long-term spot in the team for the newcomer. Nasser could see he was the past and Strauss was the future. It was an honourable gesture that took some doing, although, to be fair, Nasser did owe Strauss one after running him out on the verge of a historic pair of hundreds on Test debut.

Nasser didn't tell anyone he was going at the time, although he hinted at his plans while having a celebratory beer. "It would be great to go out on the back of a moment like this," he noted. We thought he was just thinking out loud, like you do, but clearly he meant it.

Strauss repaid Nasser by continuing the good work he and then Vaughan had started. Under Cook it then went a step further, all the fruition of central contracts, the fruition of stable management, and the fruition of stable thought processes, born out of that period under Nasser.

Thanks to Nasser, what New Zealand and then West Indies came up against in England in 2004 was a team of good characters, great experience, energy and drive, combined with mavericks who could win the game at the drop of a hat.

They didn't stand a chance. Gone were the days of chopping and changing, largely it was the same characters who put their hands up in the Caribbean and would go right through to the end of 2005. Together, we had one common goal – "Let's win the game, and win it as quick as we can."

They were in the way of an unstoppable boulder.

For me, the wickets just kept coming. Against New Zealand, I took eight at Lord's, seven at Headingley and six at Trent Bridge. Against West Indies I took nine at the Oval. It was one of those summers where no-one ran away with big bowling figures, it was threes and fours, illustrating what I've always said – when you see a bowler who's taken a lot of five-wicket hauls, it's worth looking at who they were playing alongside.

A lot of the time there's one person in the attack who stands out as the main man. He gets five wickets, the others get twos and threes. We didn't have that in 2004 and 2005.

A lot of the time the bowlers didn't have the time to get five wickets. One would have a spell, nip a couple out, another would do the same, and all of a sudden teams would be six or seven down. We never gave each other a chance to get five wickets because of the pressure we created together.

Vaughany was a good captain, but any captain is only as good as his bowling attack, and we had a great bowling attack, as good as any in world cricket. We could take anybody on. We were virtually unstoppable, and if you've got a bowling attack as good as that, the pressure to get 400 runs on the board is not as high.

If we got 300, we'd got a great chance of winning, 250-300 we were still in the game, because that unit would still knock them over. Not that getting a total was a concern. We were more than adept at putting runs on the board and taking the game to the opposition.

From that point of view, Tres was massive for us at the top of the order, but everyone was capable of adding a score. They had to be. Fletcher hated the concept of the traditional tail. He didn't want an occasional wag, he wanted contributions all year round. I even chipped in myself!

We were winning from every point. In the summer of 2004, we chased 280-plus against New Zealand twice. Those were games that England would have lost five years before. Now we didn't know how to be beaten. We didn't know how to lose.

Against the West Indies at Old Trafford, Fred and Keysey had to chase 230 to win on a fifth-day wicket which was up and down.

In the past, the tension would have been awful, but for about an hour, every time the camera focused on them they were laughing. I was just so proud that two of my mates were out there, together, finishing the match for England.

You could tell they were having a great time and I knew that their conversations out in the middle were about absolutely everything other than cricket.

Whenever I batted with Fred, we'd talk about any old rubbish – about a bus going past the ground or some daft sod in the crowd – and I still believe the reason we got over the line in that game was because they each had a mate at the other end.

That was what we had in that team. A lighter atmosphere in the dressing room isn't the enemy of a cricket team, it doesn't lead to laziness and complacency, it doesn't lead to cliques, it strengthens the unit.

The dressing room at that time was amazing.

When you're winning, and everyone is doing well, characters feel freer to reveal their true personalities. There are no eggshells to tiptoe around, sensitivities aren't so unwittingly upset. People are themselves, not the edited version of themselves they might otherwise display.

They don't take things so personally, they don't feel the need to be selfish and protect their place. If there is someone they don't get on with they tend to be more tolerant. Why upset the apple cart? Rarely was I ever in a dressing room, England or otherwise, where people openly didn't get on, but at that time and into 2005 it was better than any I can remember.

Away from the dressing room, it wasn't bad either. I had a massive friends network travelling to games. They'd be on the first train from Newcastle on Thursday morning to wherever the Test was and get the last train home on Friday night.

Despite their best intentions, it wasn't unusual for my lot to 'miss' the train home because they were having such a good time. There was one night when two of the lads rang their girlfriends to tell them they weren't on the train. One said the train had left, the other said it had electrical problems and was cancelled. It might have worked had their girlfriends not been sat next to each other in a bar.

My exploits against the West Indies in the Caribbean had rocketed me up the world rankings, and my nine wickets in the final match of the home series against them saw me named the number one bowler in the world.

It was hard to take in. Behind me in the list were Muttiah Muralitharan, Shaun Pollock, Shoaib Akhtar, Glenn McGrath, Shane Warne, Anil Kumble and Jason Gilllespie.

Just being mentioned in the same breath as them was amazing, let alone someone saying I was somehow better than them. A lot of these blokes had been around for years, I felt I'd only just arrived. Yes, I was now an established bowler, capable of turning over any line-up in the world, but there was also part of me that didn't feel too far removed from that long-haired kid running around Ashington. But it wasn't me saying I was better than them, it was the rankings.

Don't ask me how they work these things out, but the rules applied to them as much as they applied to me. In 2004, I'd taken 67 wickets in 13 Tests, at an average of 23.92, and that was enough to put me on top of the world. You don't complain when those things happen, and I always said I was as good as anyone on my day. But while rankings make good talking points, players don't pay that much attention to them.

The accolade didn't mean a great deal to me. Yes, it's great to be called the world number one, but it doesn't make any great difference on the pitch. It might intimidate one or two people, but, if anything, it could spur batsmen on to try to knock you off your perch.

And yet, and yet – when I was named world number one, I was in no position to celebrate. I was in no position to do anything.

As this great summer of 2004 had gone on, I could feel the brightness being replaced with a cloak of darkness, as if someone was draping thicker and thicker curtains over a window in my head. It was the middle of summer and all I could see was grey. It came as a shock. I couldn't work out what it was, or, more likely, I hardly dared admit it. To do so would make it even more real.

The horrible truth was those same feelings that had consumed me on trips abroad were overpowering me again, and this time it had nothing to do with being away from home.

This was happening right now in the middle of an English summer, and a very successful English summer at that. I was scared. When these things happened overseas, that gave them a reason. There was at least an explanation lurking underneath – I had a serious mental health problem about being away from the place and people I loved. I couldn't apply the same rationale this time.

The demons hadn't bothered to travel, they'd come to get me at home.

That's the thing with depression. It doesn't care. It doesn't give a shit who you are, what you are, where you are. It's very open-minded from that point of view, there's no sense of discrimination.

If it feels so inclined, it will get you, and that's that. It doesn't care if you're a millionaire, a successful doctor, a nurse, postman, airline pilot, Miss World, Mr Universe, whatever.

It doesn't care if you're the number one bowler in the world.

If it decides you're going to get it, then that's it. There's no point telling it you've got a great wife, brilliant kids, and a big car in the garage, it just won't listen. There's no exact science. It's there, you get it, it breaks you, and, if you're lucky, you get yourself through it and manage to get yourself into a position to carry on and come out the other side.

From the middle of that summer, the cloud built up constantly, reaching a peak at the last Test of the West Indies series. Prior to that Oval Test match, I was feeling really down and low. I had no energy and trying to get myself motivated was very difficult.

I would have to lie down in the dressing room because that would help ease the churning in my stomach. I was masking my true problem by saying I had a bad back and I needed to stretch it. Sometimes I'd lie on my front and push my back up. I'd be complaining it was stiff, but all I was doing was trying to ease the awful sensations I was feeling.

It worked in that it helped me get through those periods when mentally, physically and literally, I was on the floor. But it was no solution and in the end this would be the summer I 'came out'. I'd bottled my mental state up for so long it was time, not to tell everybody, but open up to certain people and say, "Look, I've got a problem. I actually need help."

I spoke to the England team doctor Peter Gregory, who was aware of the problems I'd been suffering throughout my international career, and I also went to see a consultant psychologist at the Priory clinic in Manchester. At the start of the treatment, I was asked a series of questions, one of which was, "Have you ever considered harming yourself?"

Wow. That frightened the hell out of me.

They were asking if I'd ever considered suicide. In layman's terms, "Have you thought about doing yourself in?" The honest answer was, "Maybe," never a categorical, "Yes." I can't say there haven't been some dark times where I thought it'd be easier if I wasn't here.

Easier on me and easier on those around me. But it never went further than thoughts. I never actually contemplated it. Yes, things went through my mind, but when I was lying in bed and couldn't sleep in the middle of a prolonged episode, everything went through my mind.

When I was absolutely exhausted, the lights were off and my head was on the pillow, there were millions of things going on inside my head and I just couldn't switch any of them off. Even the stupidest of things wouldn't go away. If I'd been sitting in a restaurant or bar, the last song that had been playing as I walked out would be going through my mind over and over again, 5,000 times on fast forward, and I couldn't stop it.

I'd be thinking about things, churning them round and round, not sleeping. It's then you start wondering whether it's worth putting up with it.

The pressure of the game probably didn't help. Arguably, it made it a little bit worse because I was constantly thinking about ways of getting better, wanting to improve, striving to be the best I could be. But often there was nothing there. The body clammed up, the mind clammed up – I was just thinking, 'I need some sleep here.'

But it never came, and once that happens everybody knows how irritable you become, how down you become, how emotions rise to the surface. In the dark times, it was exhaustion more than anything that was my problem.

That plagued me throughout my career. Even now, I struggle to sleep. I hardly sleep at all. I don't go to bed until one or two in the morning, then I'll be awake again at half four, and then again at seven when the kids are up. I tend to sleep more in the day than I do at night.

The Priory doctor described the symptoms of clinical depression – low mood, feeling sad, no energy, lack of interest in activities you used to enjoy, sleeping less, low self-worth.

It was as if he was describing me. In my head I was thinking, 'Yeah, that is actually me – this is the same, this is what I've got.'

We sat and talked. He knew nothing about cricket, had never heard of me, and I was glad. If he'd mentioned cricket I would have got up and walked out. I wanted to be seen like everyone else.

I didn't want my playing cricket for England to be any part of it. Instead, we talked about me as a person, my life, my family, what I did with myself, my daily existence, how I felt about my place in the world, and how I felt about me.

It was clear I was clinically depressed, and medication, the subject of which had already been raised by the England set-up and my GP, would be the way forward. I've been on it ever since. I've got a repeat prescription.

I felt no stigma about going on anti-depressants. All I was bothered about was making me feel better. I could be hooked on them for the rest of my life, I do not care. If I have to pay eight pounds every couple of months to get a prescription, fine. That money couldn't be better spent, because it is going on something to help me feel better.

And if it's going to make me feel better, I'm having it. All I ever wanted was to feel normal, and that's all I want now. I take my medication when I get up and hopefully it will get me through the day. Whether it works I'm not sure. It's probably not for me to say. Prior to the anti-depressants, on tour I was on sleeping tablets to knock me out and get me over what I thought was just homesickness. The thing I found hard on overseas trips was sleeping. I thought if I could get into a decent sleeping pattern, I'd be sorted.

I knew now I'd just been addressing a symptom, rather than the cause of it – sleeping pills was a battle I still had to come.

The minute you mention the Priory, people get the wrong impression, like it's all celebrities coming off the booze, going in for two-week detox sessions. It was never like that for me.

I went six times for between an hour and 90 minutes. I didn't stay overnight. The reason I went was because the doctor concerned had been recommended to me as the best consultant going.

He could have been in Timbuktu for all I cared. The first couple of times I went, it clicked, I felt happy, and from that point on, if ever I felt bad, I would go back and talk things over. I would go for a bit of a top-up in terms of counselling and to discuss where I was at.

Talking had always helped. Fred, Keysey, Neil Fairbrother, Kirk Russell, John Morris, all these people were a massive help because they would sit and listen to me tell them what was going on. They couldn't do anything practical, they weren't a doctor, but because they were listening it was helping me to get better. They were probably thinking, 'Fuck me, here we go again! Take the shoelaces off him!' But to me their support was huge. When there was no-one there I would let it all pour out on to a notepad, because that felt like telling someone too.

Ultimately, though, it's me that has to go through it. It's me that has to put up with it. And it's me that has to come out the other end of it. A severe depressive episode remains a twice a year occurrence for me, even to this day. It comes, you get through it the best you possibly can, and you come out the other side. There are millions of us doing that all the time. You may very well be one of them.

Strange to think that the game at the Oval was my best of the summer. Maybe the cricket offered some respite. I recorded my highest Test score, became the number one bowler in the world and got my 100th Test wicket – it had taken me two years and 11 days. For England, only Ian Botham had done it quicker – by under a week.

That year, 2004, was the best I would have as an England cricketer. Perhaps the best year ever for English cricket as a whole, one in which we'd won every Test save for an impossible pitch at Antigua. We were untouchable. We were unbeatable. At the same time, this was the year that would prove my absolute nadir when it came to my mental health.

Maybe I needed to be depressed a bit more often!

The only thing that let us down in 2004 was the ICC Trophy at the end of the season. How we lost that final, I still don't know. With the West Indies 147-8 chasing 218, the silverware was ours, but they somehow crept home. If anything, though, that galvanised us even more and gave us another push, another boost, to go that one step further.

It was during this tournament that another clash with the management occurred.

England were due to tour Zimbabwe for five one-day internationals, but after what we'd been faced with the previous winter, there was no way I was going. I told Vaughany and Fletcher as much after the ICC Trophy group game against Sri Lanka in the dressing room at the Rosebowl.

They wanted me to keep it quiet but I didn't see why I should.

All this cloak and dagger stuff had got us nowhere last time, aside from four days of torture in a Cape Town hotel. I knew the ECB, in its unwillingness to rock the apple cart, was perfectly capable of landing the England cricket team in exactly the same situation again – which eventually they did.

The players who did go were once again stuck in the middle as the ECB suits put morals to one side to try to satisfy the ICC and not get fined.

I got letters from politicians and members of the public commending me on my decision, but it was nothing to do with politics.

I was looking at it from the point of view that I'd made a choice the year before not to go somewhere because it wasn't right, it wasn't safe. We got knocked out of the World Cup because we didn't go to Zimbabwe. If we didn't go then, because of the threats and the domestic situation, why should we go now? Is that situation better? No. Is the country more stable? No. Have any of the reasons I didn't go a year ago improved? No. I'd have felt hypocritical going back.

After what Nasser did and how he protected us during those four days in that hotel, with everybody basically coming and lying to us, it would have been wrong for me to forget what he'd done for us. It didn't matter if my place was secure or not, or even if it would have ended my career, I didn't see anything in the time that had elapsed that told me we had either made a wrong decision or the situation had improved.

If anything, it had got worse and more volatile. It wasn't a case of why the team shouldn't go, it was a case of why I shouldn't go. Eventually, they said they weren't going to take me anyway as they were going to rest some senior players. But yet again the ECB had allowed themselves to get in a terrible tangle by not stating their position from the start. Fletcher, Vaughany and the players were once again left stranded in the middle.

What really mattered to myself and the rest of the England team wasn't a few one-dayers in Zimbabwe, but the main business of the winter in South Africa.

We knew that if we could get a positive result there then the world really was going to open its eyes to what we'd achieved in the last 12 months.

People never believe us when we say we weren't thinking of the Ashes in 2004, but we genuinely weren't. If we'd thought about Australia we'd have got beaten by New Zealand. Vaughan and Fletcher would have been thinking about Australia, because that was their job, they were forward planners, but no-one was talking about it in team meetings. Australia had nothing to do with the games we were playing then.

We weren't going to change the way we bowled at the West Indies because Australia were coming next year.

We weren't bothered about Australia.

If we carried on winning, it would be Australia that was bothered about us.

Yet, first of all, with the blackness getting worse by the day, I had to somehow leave the house, leave the country and try and take on South Africa.

14

BETWEEN THE EARS

*"To be told I had clinical depression wasn't great,
but at least it gave me a platform to work from"*

It was like putting an Elastoplast where I should have had
stitches.

Swallowing a few sleeping pills on that plane and hoping
I was going to wake up a different person was optimistic in the
extreme. If it was that easy to get rid of a head full of negativity,
everyone would be doing it. One in four people wouldn't have a
mental health problem, they'd be asleep.

As mentioned in the first chapter, when we flew to South Africa
in late 2004, I was already on anti-depressants. But, while some
people might think you take these things and they offer almost
instantaneous relief, like Paracetamol with a headache, the truth
is far, far different. People don't walk into the doctor's depressed

and come out whooping and clicking their heels, these things take time.

Depression is a chemical imbalance in the brain. You can't just lift the bonnet and top the chemicals up, like brake fluid in the car. Anti-depressants work over a period of time, and everyone is different. Some find a medical treatment best, others find it's pills combined with therapy. Finding the right solution for every person is important. You have to hope your doctor is more Troy Cooley than Australian biomechanics guru.

So while I'd been on medication for a few months before we went to South Africa in December, these were early days, and maybe it still hadn't clicked with me quite right. We were still finding our way.

Depression is a complex thing. Even when the right drugs and procedures are put in place, they can only ever be a help. Bad episodes can still return. Ups and downs remain a constant part of existence. Not many people with depression can honestly say they know they'll be OK in six months time.

When I was put on anti-depressants in 2004, it by no means meant that the South Africa trip was going to be a stroll in the park. In all honesty, I have never felt worse.

This was as low as I could go.

Sitting in that car on my drive, everyone would have assumed I was a man who had it all. Not only was he married to a great woman, who had given him two beautiful girls, but he was the number one person at his job. Everywhere he went, aside from perhaps David Graveney's house, he was lauded for his brilliance, showered with praise, held up as an example of how far talent and a bit of hard work could take a person.

What was actually sat in that car was a broken shell, a person who had turned himself inside out in despair that the thing he was so good at was also the thing that made him ill, that took him away from everything he loved.

At times like that you can't see further than two centimetres beyond your own face. You are consumed utterly by feelings that are physical as much as mental. You have lost control to something else, something that has got its hooks in and isn't in any rush to let go.

When it does, it will leave an array of scars as a reminder that one day, in all probability, it will be knocking on your skull and will be right back in there.

When I say I was thinking of crashing the car on the way to the airport, I am serious. Imagine the thing you most dread in your life, and then think what you would do to stop it. That's how it was with me. A nice little shunt on a roundabout, a bruised leg, whiplash, and that would have been me for a few days. But how do you control these things? And creating that scenario wouldn't have been just about me. There was the other driver to think about.

Pulling out of the tour would be easier, but then that would have spelled the end of my international career. After all those other incidents, how could they possibly plough on with me after that? The selectors wouldn't have needed an excuse to give up on me. Also, however I felt about going, there were other implications. I was a lad who left school with nothing. Playing cricket for England had given me the chance to build something amazing for my family.

My children had security, I could give them a solid foundation for their future. Do I really just turn my back on all that? Hayley never put any pressure on me on the money and security front. In fact, she was exactly the opposite. She'd said it before and she said it again in the run-up to this tour. "If you feel this way," she told me. "If it's as bad as this, don't go, don't play. We'll still be here. We'll still manage. We'll move on and life will be OK. If it's killing you, there's no point. Life doesn't have to be like this."

It was an amazing thing for her to say. But that's Hayley, a truly amazing woman. Talk to her even now and she'll say she wishes I'd never played cricket. Yes, we've got a nice house and the money has given us stability, but if I'd had a normal job, our lives and the children's lives would have been more structured.

They would have had a far more normal relationship with their parents, rather than so much being put on Hayley while their dad nipped in and out of family life, not being there for days, weeks, months on end. It's down to Hayley that they've grown up as well as they have.

The children are lucky because they've got a mother who loves them as much as any mother there's ever been. They've got a dad who loves them just as much but has often done so from afar. That's how it was again this time. Hayley, Abbie and Emily existed on the end of a phone line or on the photos and videos that had accompanied me on my laptop.

There are times when photos make things better, times when they make things worse. This was both. It sounds like a cliché, I know, but looking at those pictures of home I was smiling through the tears. I would ring home constantly.

People often ask if that might have made things worse. I don't know, possibly it did, but I was the dad of two little girls. Am I expected to ignore that? They and Hayley were my world. Yes, if I heard Abbie crying, I couldn't do anything, and it wouldn't help my emotion at that time, but if one of my kids had hurt themselves I needed to know. The events of the previous summer, when I was told I was clinically depressed, did at least help me make sense of how bad I was feeling.

To be told I had clinical depression wasn't great, but at least it gave me a platform to work from. England team doctor, Peter Gregory, and physio, Kirk Russell, really came to the fore and I can't praise them enough. What I put on Kirk especially over the years is mind-boggling.

He knew I had long-term issues because he was another I'd confided in so many times in the previous three or four years, another I'd raised from a slumber more times than I, and probably he, would care to mention, on trips ranging from Academy to A-tour and England.

He knew I'd been having to take sleeping tablets just to get to sleep, so was aware there was something not quite right. He'd seen me struggle down the years, although when I broke down in front of him in South Africa, I couldn't help but feel he must have thought I was an idiot, a grown man crying.

Kirk, of course, was far too good a man to judge me like that. Around most people, I was quite good at disguising my feelings. Where I'd struggle was at night. When my hotel room door closed at 11 o'clock, midnight, whatever, that's where the problems were. When I was around people in the day, I'd just go and talk to them, non-stop, babbling, wittering, this mad Geordie going on and on to take his mind off his true feelings.

I just kept going because it was a method I'd found to stop my mind racing to somewhere either it shouldn't be or I didn't want it to be. I was self-taught in how to manage it. It was a way of life to save my life, to get me through a day, and that's what the start of a tour was for me, just getting from one day to the next.

There is very little happening at that time, usually no games, a lot of it is about acclimatisation, and you spend a lot of time in your own head. Once the game starts it gets easier. At that point I had something to occupy myself. Emotionally, it was a case of walking before I could run on each trip.

Get off the plane, get in a position to start walking, and then start running. Every tour I went on, my preparation and acclimatisation came not just from the cricket side, it came from the mental side as well. How was I going to get myself into a position where I could play cricket? Because once I could play cricket I was OK.

It was when I wasn't playing and I was in my own mind, that's when I wasn't in a very good place. It was then about chalking off chunks of the day.

Just to add to the issues, Johannesburg is the little matter of 1,700m above sea level, and one thing about anxiety is it makes you short of breath.

That, combined with trying to train, being tired and struggling mentally as well, was the perfect storm. In the end it all just went, 'Bang!' in my head. There was a week where I really did think it could be the end for my England days. I knew that if I went home that was it.

At the same time, I knew if I could just get through it I could play. I'd proved that before, although there was no denying this time it was worse. Me and Kirk tried all sorts to sort the breathlessness out. We went to see this one lady, part-psychologist, part-hypnotherapist, who said she could help.

We were invited into her 'clinic', a weird place with smoke billowing, herbs all over the place, all in the dark except for candles. It'd never catch on in Ashington. I was lying on the couch while this woman was hovering her hands over me. "Breathe," she was saying, in a thick South African accent. "Deep breaths – draw in the air," trying to get me to inhale properly.

I was expecting Jeremy Beadle to pop out at any moment.

To be fair, she understood what I was going through, and taught me some breathing techniques for when I was feeling anxious, but overall the advice she gave me boiled down to one thing, "Go home."

She recommended I go back to my nice comfortable house, recover, and then come back again. But cricketers don't have that sort of luxury. When I came away I wasn't any better, but the fact I'd gone to her in the first place just showed how desperate I was to get rid of these feelings.

I was constantly with my head down, a lump in my throat, a burning sensation in the middle of my stomach. I didn't want to eat. I was basically a zombie. I'd worked out from experience that each episode lasted two-and-a-half weeks.

I just had to get through that period. Just! I'd be in a bad place for eight or nine days and then, all of a sudden, I could feel myself start to come out the other side. From there I'd feel better day by day until it was gone.

Those dark periods would always come at the start of the trip. New environment, away from the family, the weather, the food, the culture, everything was different and I'd been suddenly plunged into it. Add in the anxiety of going away, and it was something that for me was always going to be difficult.

But South Africa was by far the worst. What saved me in the end was that, deep, deep down, I knew I wanted to play cricket. I couldn't give this game up. Those who said I was lazy, or didn't care, or was a shirker, might want to take note – that was the determination, the secret determination, I had to play for England.

Perhaps it was the hangover of this awful start that made it such an unmemorable series for me. I went into it as number one in the world and ended it clinging on to the top 10. South Africa played me very well, Jacques Kallis especially.

Early on in the trip, unless the ball was on the stumps he wouldn't even try to hit it. He waited until my third or fourth spell, when he'd tired me out, and then hit it – all over the park.

I felt I had to live up to this number one tag. It didn't feel like a weight round my neck, but when I'd blown teams away for the previous 12 months, I'd begun to expect to do it, so when it wasn't then happening my mindset was very much, 'What am I doing wrong? How am I going to put this right?'

It's then you start trying things you shouldn't. When they backfire, the ball starts hitting the boundary. Averaging 72 in that series was below the standard I set for myself. In cricket there's a mental battle, for batters and bowlers, between panic and patience – and I was coming out on the wrong side of the equation.

I didn't have the patience that Jacques Kallis had against me. He stifled me, others did the same, and instead of just carrying on bowling my line when they were leaving it, testing their patience, I was bowling balls I shouldn't have been, short balls, full balls, and was getting hit for four.

It's a vicious circle. Instead of sticking with the same mental processes that have got you where you are, you're telling yourself you shouldn't be doing this, shouldn't be doing that.

As a sportsman, the good times don't just run on and on forever. It's getting through the bad times, that's what defines a great. In the end, even with a bit of waywardness on my part, we won that five-Test series 2-1.

South Africa didn't help themselves, their quota system leading them to leave out the hugely experienced Mark Boucher until the fourth Test at Johannesburg, the same game my mam and dad flew over to watch.

At the time, because I'd gone out there as number one bowler in the world, I was getting some stick off the Bullring crowd, to the extent that, when I was fielding on the boundary, the people behind me in the seats were singing, "Harmison's a wanker!" I looked round and then all of a sudden, in the bottom corner of the stand, I clocked my mum and dad. "What were you doing sitting in there with them lot doing all that singing?" I asked her later. "I used to watch your dad play football," she replied. "I've heard a hell of a lot worse."

On a more positive note, in terms of the Ashes series to come, that winter in South Africa taught me a lot. South Africa were a good side – tough players, tough people, tough characters. Up and at 'em old school players. It was the first time South Africa had been beaten at home since they'd come back into the international fold post-apartheid. Playing against such a hard side before Australia was spot on.

We could now go home and say, "OK, Australia, in you come. We're going to give you as good as you give us." It should also be remembered that during that period my body was trying to get used to anti-depressants.

They were in my system and perhaps there were subtle, possibly even unnoticed, differences that brought. So much of that trip was about learning more about myself, how to manage my body and my emotions, because I couldn't have been any worse than I was at the start.

Sadly, the series saw the last England appearance by Mark Butcher, one of the finest people, let alone cricketers, I ever toured with. Nothing was ever a problem to Butch. He breezed through life. "If we need six an over, we need six an over, that's fine,"he'd say, totally relaxed.

On a night out he was great company, always laughing, always good fun. Not in a Graeme Swann way, going over the top, just a nice relaxed atmosphere, good chat, and then out would come the guitar.

Many's the time I would sit in the corner of Butch's room and just listen to him play, so, so relaxing. For me, he should have been England captain. He had a great cricket brain although we did have one interesting moment.

After he finished playing, he made a comment about me in the media, and it didn't come across very well. He was saying England should leave me out, possibly questioning my desire and commitment. In two weeks time I was playing against Butch. 'Right,' I thought. 'This is going to be interesting.' It wasn't a case of revenge but I did remind Butch of what he'd said when he came out to bat – on a freezing cold day at the Riverside on a corrugated wicket.

I dug one in, and it veered back in at him. He couldn't get out of the way and it smacked him on the head by the ear. The damage didn't stop at bruised pride – I perforated his eardrum.

I felt awful. Whatever he'd said in the newspaper, he was still a good mate. We still laugh and joke about it now – although there wasn't much laughing at the time. He spent the rest of the game wearing a woolly hat and unable to hear out of his right ear.

Butch was eyeing a job in the media at that time and so was maybe trying to enhance his chances by getting some headlines. But if you're going to do that, make sure you're not then playing against the person you've been talking about – especially if they bowl at 90mph.

It was also the end for Rob Key, a player I feel massively sorry for and whose chances, I believe, were unfairly harmed because he was close to me and Fred. He was one of the best players in England and should have played more Test matches than me or Fred.

But, for Key, or rather for the team management, me and Fred were the problem. He was guilty by association. Me and Fred were larger than life characters. Two they could tolerate, three was out of the question. He was deemed as being a larger than life character and that wasn't PC for the ECB.

He paid a big price for his 'crime' of having a personality. It wasn't that me and Fred were not conforming, but we liked having a laugh. We didn't take very much seriously. Key was seen as being part of that same group. As time went on, there was a big push to keep members of that group small, not only from the coach, but from other players who didn't want that group to be stronger.

There was an element of people coming into the dressing room and keeping their place by saying the right things to the right people, and that was to the detriment of Key. People didn't say Key was bad news, but they drew a picture with Fletcher of who he was friends with in the team. Rob didn't operate like that. He wasn't the sort to say stuff behind other people's backs. He was honest, straight-up and wore his heart on his sleeve.

He knew what he wanted, understood the game, didn't suffer fools easily and was always after a challenge. Every net was like a World Cup! To Key, everything was a contest. He was a winner and was never going to adversely affect the group.

That's my only disappointment with that time with England in 2004-05. It saddened me a lot because on that trip to South Africa, when I was at my worst, if it wasn't for Keysey I might have gone under. He was so good to me. He knew I was struggling and he did his level best to help. That's why I feel so negatively about the way people went about getting into Fletcher's head, to tell him not to pick him because he was one of us.

The management couldn't get rid of me or Fred as we offered something unique to the team, and so instead they decided to isolate someone close to us. In doing so, they lost a future England captain. I just couldn't understand it. Me, Fred and Keysey weren't disruptive – we were nowhere near being disruptive. It was just that we weren't people who took life massively seriously, but that didn't mean we weren't going to give 100 percent on the pitch. In fact, if anything, it helped, because we were relaxed.

"Disruptive" would become a familiar theme down the years for me and Fred. As soon as something started going wrong, the cry went up – "They're disruptive!" I didn't hear anybody saying that in the Caribbean in 2004 or in the Ashes in 2005, but as soon as the team performance dropped a notch and the blame game started, the focus would always fall on us.

When we were winning, it was, "Aren't they great for team

spirit? Isn't it great for teammates to have people to bounce off?" and when we were losing it was, "They're starting a clique. Those two are making a splinter group." Bullshit. We weren't like that. No way. Quite forceful with opinions, but everybody has to be sometimes.

If players don't make their feelings known, that's a sign of weakness in an international environment. You can't have that weakness if you want to beat the best in the world. In a cricket dressing room, as in life, everybody spends time with the people they get on with. That's just natural. Vaughany and Colly used to spend a lot of time together, Colly again with Strauss, Vaughany and Trescothick were close – none of them were any different.

Me and Fred had grown up together in cricket. We knew each other inside out and outside in, from a family as well as a personal point of view. He was someone I spent a lot of my time with. But that's not to say it was us and then everyone else in the dressing room. I never saw it like that and I can't see why anyone else would see it that way. We were all part of the same team, a single unit, and I never saw it as anything different.

If anyone should have been complaining about Fred, it should have been me. So much of what Fred did ended up at my door. He always had something to say about me being from Ashington. "If we're going to see a film tonight," he'd tell the lads. "We'll have to get one with subtitles for Harmy." Then if someone else tried to join in he'd jump on them – "Oh aye! A posh lad from Sussex!"

All of a sudden, he's got two people on the go, the dressing room is laughing, any tension, be it on the field or off, has been totally diffused. Do you think he somehow contrived to do that by accident, time and time again? He was clever. He knew how to break the ice in any situation. There's this impression that you had to be a big gregarious character to be mates with me and Fred.

It's just not true.

Take Geraint Jones, me and Fred were close with him all the way through his England career. Geraint is far from a big loud character. He's actually quiet (most of the time), clever and a sensitive bloke.

When Shaun Udal was picked late on in his career for the tour of India in 2007, even now he says if it wasn't for me and Fred he's not sure how he would have handled it.

He didn't have much in common with the others because of the age he was at. Nobody really wanted to get involved with him, but me and Fred tried to embrace him and hopefully made the trip more enjoyable for him. It sounds like there were nine blokes and me and Fred, but that's not how it was. I got on well with everybody. Whether everybody got on with me, I don't know. I've not heard many bad reports.

Those who had gone were soon forgotten by the media when a new face came into the England side for the one-day internationals.

I'd seen him before once or twice, mainly when he was trying to take me on at the Riverside. Kevin Pietersen, with an orange streak in his hair that looked like he had a dead animal on his head, promptly smashed the South African attack all round the park and occasionally outside it, for three incredible centuries.

Kevin had made his debut the previous winter in the ODI series in Zimbabwe that I'd pulled out of, having already made a bit of a reputation for himself on the county circuit with a spectacular falling out with his teammates at Nottinghamshire, to the extent that Jason Gallian and Graeme Swann had chucked his bag off the dressing room balcony. I was surprised when I heard that because Jason, in particular, wasn't that kind of character.

I don't know what Kevin was like on the inside, but on the outside he was running over with confidence. In Bloemfontein, when he got his first hundred, the crowd turned their back on him as he celebrated. That's a big statement, hurtful as well as pointed. In the dressing room we could see him taking his helmet off. "Don't do it! Don't do it!" we were shouting, but then he did. He went and kissed the badge. "Fucking hell! What are you doing?"

Then, after the last one-dayer at Centurion, he went and got a Three Lions tattoo with his player number underneath it. He'd threatened to do it all series, saying he was going to copy Goughy's – the two of them were inseparable that series. He couldn't wait to show the rest of us. In he waltzed, "Look at this boys!" We couldn't believe it.

Not so much that he'd had it done. Even in the short time we'd known him that was Kevin all over. We were more concerned that it was lop-sided. The fact that Kevin had kissed the badge, got a tattoo, didn't change one bit that he was South African. No getting away from it, he was a born and bred South African. But that was nothing new in the England team.

There'd been Allan Lamb, Robin Smith, and more than a few others, so the fact he was keeping an Englishman out the team didn't bother me one bit. He'd served his qualification and earned his chance to play for England. The fact was that he was deemed good enough.

If a bowler had come into the side who was South African, I wouldn't have been saying, "I should be playing because I'm

English", I would be saying, "I should be playing because I'm better than him" – if I was better than him. That might not have been everybody's outlook.

There were a lot of people in England who resented KP – slightly less after the summer of 2005 – but ask yourself why they had a go at him. My view is they started screaming and shouting about Kevin to enhance their own reputations.

They tried to increase their own standing in the game, be they players or commentators, by kicking Kevin Pietersen, and I didn't like that. They were wilfully misunderstanding the situation. "He thinks because he knows the national anthem and has got a tattoo that he's English!" No he doesn't.

He knows he's South African. Am I bothered a South African has got an England tattoo? No, fair play to him, I don't care. He was qualified to play for England and that was the end of it. Having Kevin Pietersen playing in England made English cricket better. Kevin got all the publicity in that series but he got it because he deserved it.

The one in East London, where he completed the then fastest hundred by an England player in a one-day international off 69 deliveries, was just ridiculous and was one of the best innings I've ever seen. There was no doubting it – he was box office.

There'd be many times from that point on when I'd be having a kip, hear a wicket go and Kevin was in next. Not much got me up off that nest, but if Kevin was in I'd be there watching. I'd never done that when someone like Nasser was batting. In fact, I slept a lot when Nasser was batting!

When it came to the summer of 2005, though, whoever was in the middle, I wouldn't be doing much sleeping at all.

And neither would anyone else.

15

CUTS AND BRUISES

*"After all the build-up we were like 11 dogs
being let off their leash. We were playing for our
country, we wanted to get out there and go"*

Y ou've got to be joking!"
Fred was glaring at me down the wicket. I'd fired
in a bouncer at him, which blatantly hit him on the
shoulder, and was now appealing raucously for the catch.

The umpire was Steve Garratt, who'd never done a first-class
game before, brought in as a replacement for the scheduled
umpire, injured on the day of the game.

This wasn't England v Australia, it was Lancashire v Durham,
a hard fought early season battle between two good teams that
could have gone either way.

The game was in the balance in the second innings and Fred

was going well when I came on to bowl. When the ball lobbed up off his shoulder, we all erupted. We needed a wicket, but the umpire gave it not out – good decision – but I was using every trick in the book. "You've got to be joking," I berated him. "It was off his glove. Look, he's wringing his hand."

"I know you're new and you're doing your best," I continued. "But I'm sorry you've missed one there. You can't be doing that, this is a big game and he's an international player."

The very next ball, a more orthodox delivery, Fred lunged forward, massive stride, and it hit him just above the knee roll. It wouldn't have hit another set outside off stump and would have gone over by another set as well.

We erupted again. And the umpire gave him out! Halfway through him raising the finger, we were absolutely pissing ourselves. I was in stitches laughing. Fred looked at the umpire, looked at me, shook his head, off he went, and we won the game quite comfortably.

This is where I was at the start of 2005. I was a having a good time, I was having fun. I got a hat trick against Worcester, only the second in Durham's history (I got the first one the year before), and it just seemed that everything was going the right way.

Everything in my life was going swimmingly. And that was the springboard for the summer to come against Australia.

The South African trip had made us realise we were a very good side, but there was always room to add to it between then and the Ashes. Bangladesh came over for two Test matches in May, but the games proved little more than a confidence booster.

We were ruthless and blew them away. They even made them

play one of the games in the freezing cold at Durham. For the players and the British public alike though, this was merely a starter, in fact probably not even that. It was a quick bag of nuts on the way to the restaurant. The Twenty20 game against the Aussies at the Rose Bowl was the real starter, and it gave us a taste of things to come.

Forget cricket, this was more like a football match. The Australian scoreboard read 31-7 at one point – it's normally the other way round. The atmosphere was stupendous, the noise, the positivity, the support, it was all-consuming. It felt like right from ball one of that Ashes summer there was an expectation, not just a hope as in previous years, that England were going to give the Aussies a fight.

Even getting to the game was madness. The Rose Bowl is always a nightmare to get in and out of but this was especially ridiculous. People had swarmed down there early – they wanted to see a battle. What they got was even better, an Australian team battered into submission.

We skittled them for 79 but it was actually Darren Gough – who would play no part in the Ashes – who laid the marker down that day.

After getting Gilchrist and Hayden in successive balls, Goughy was on a hat-trick. But rather than try and bowl new batsman Andrew Symonds one of his famous yorkers, he bowled a bouncer that hit him hard. Goughy just stood there, larger than life – even larger than life than he normally is – staring at Symonds, giving him a massive volley.

That for me was the tick in the box that let Australia know they were here for three months, they were in for plenty more of the same and that there was no escape from an England side desperate to show what we could achieve. The Aussies didn't seem their usual selves that day, a suspicion reinforced when they lost to Bangladesh in the one-day series five days later, with Symonds dropped from the team on the morning of the game after a night on the lash.

A day later, we faced them at Bristol, and KP smashed yet another astonishing innings of 91 off 65 balls to take us to another famous victory. I chipped in with five wickets – and to think people used to say I couldn't play one-day cricket!

One of those wickets was the unbelievable catch by Colly that removed Hayden. It was one of the best catches I've ever seen, he just grabbed it out of thin air and Hayden's face was a picture as what he thought was a certain four was actually the end of his innings.

Colly's effort sent the crowd wild and it just added to the idea that this England team was capable of doing anything.

I had a few mates in the crowd to watch me that day. Eight from the Buffs came down from Newcastle on easyJet. At 9am I got a call. "Right, we're all here!"

It was already baking even then, and would be the hottest weather I've ever played in here in England.

"OK, what's the problem?"

"None of us have got hats."

So I'm then going round all the players trying to round up hats. Later, Kevin caught Damien Martyn off my bowling right in front of where the lads were sitting. I was running down to KP to congratulate him and I could see an empty seat where my lot were. I asked them about it later. "Oh, it was your brother James. He was being sick underneath the stand." Bear in mind Australia batted first. The heat, the beer, the excitement of

Kev's innings, all added up to another unbelievable occasion. Days like this hadn't been witnessed on an English ground for years. It really did feel like something special was happening, but we knew we wouldn't win the Ashes on atmosphere.

Something similar happened in the one-day game at Edgbaston when Simon Jones threw the ball back at the stumps but instead hit Matthew Hayden on the chest. Simon immediately apologised but Hayden was having none of it. "Fuck off," he screamed. "You threw it straight at me."

Collingwood was straight in his face and Strauss came in too to back up his mates. The noise was so loud by now that I couldn't hear anything and all I could think as I looked at Hayden, and then looked at Colly and Strauss, was, 'Well, now he's got a starter and a main.' But it showed the Aussies we weren't backing down.

We wanted to show Australia that we weren't like the previous 20 years of England teams who flattered to deceive in the first Test, then got battered, and then might show up again in the last Test when it was all over bar the shouting.

That's what had happened so many times, but, if we had our way, not anymore.

No-one thought for one minute during that series in South Africa that KP would walk out at the first Test at Lord's. I don't think even Kevin in his wildest dreams thought that.

Until the one-dayers, Thorpe looked in the box seat. He'd filled his boots against Bangladesh and played his 100th Test, but then that was it. Pietersen had clearly got the management and selectors thinking. Not only had he shown he could perform under pressure, but his batting added another dimension. That was when the realisation came that this bloke has to play in the Ashes.

It was impossible not to pick him because of what he was doing to the Australian bowlers. Gillespie, anything back of a length, short, six. He was running at McGrath, and when he eventually came up against Warne he took him on too.

Kevin had another important asset. One of Vaughany's big things was not to have players who were knowingly or unknowingly carrying mental scars of previous Australia clashes.

I'd been beaten by Australia myself, but I was different from some of the other players. I was a young emerging bowler when I played the Aussies in 2002-03, the mental scar of constantly getting bombarded by defeat wasn't there. I came out the other side knowing that, while I'd not been great, I'd held my own.

We were in a position where we'd been one of the best teams in the world for the past 12-18 months, but there was always that nagging feeling at the back of our minds that it was all very well beating the West Indies, who were on the decline, New Zealand at home and, of course, South Africa away, but that would be nothing compared to what this was going to be like.

Australia were, after all, still arguably the best team that had ever played the game.

That's not to say that leading up to the series we didn't have the belief that we were going to win. Not for one minute did we think we were there to make the numbers up, or think that losing 3-2, or 2-1 with a couple of draws would be a good achievement.

This team had come through some tricky situations, we'd chased good targets to win matches. We had an inner belief that no matter the situation we were going to win any game we were involved in. But there has to be an element of realism. It's always in your mind who you are playing.

Not that the members at Lord's seemed to have any worries.

When we went out through the Long Room that first morning, I'd never heard a noise like it. Posh people cheering. It was bizarre.

It's not like the roar at Edgbaston or Trent Bridge – posh people cheering is a noise in itself. It's not something a lad from Ashington hears very often, that's for sure. But it did help to really get us going.

Normally you walk through the Long Room on the first day of a series and you've got a couple of people eating sandwiches at a table, half a dozen hiding behind newspapers more or less asleep, and the ones who are awake thinking, 'Fuck me, they've picked him again!'

When it got busier, sometimes you had to fight your way through people in a way that was quite odd. You were the cricketers, you were the ones playing, and the ones who had to get out on to the field, and yet these people in the Long Room would look at you like you were intruding in their private members' club.

On the first day of the Ashes, though, the Long Room was roped off to allow a walkway. Here were all these old boys cheering and shouting. It was another realisation that this was massive, huge. This series had truly captured the nation. It had even woken a few MCC members up – that's how big it was.

Not a lot had been said in the dressing room that morning. Vaughany had done his talking the night before, but even then it was calm and relaxed and he was great at easing the tension. "Embrace the experience," he told us. "And go out there and enjoy it." After losing the toss (naturally), he gave us a little reminder. "You know your jobs, you understand the plans, now it's a case of executing them."

The key was not to build the whole thing up into something

too big but that was easier said than done. Nerves were jangling, there was nervous excitement and after all the build-up we were like 11 dogs being let off their leash. We were playing for our country, we wanted to get out there and go.

What happened at Lord's that first day wasn't so much intentional, it just happened.

It was seen as us – well, me – being deliberately aggressive, and for certain I wasn't holding back, but when it came to the blows I landed on the Australian top order, it was more about them getting in bad positions than me doing anything particularly different.

When I hit Justin Langer on the arm, it was my natural length. It just bounced on him and nipped back up the hill. He didn't shape up to play it very well and it hit him. I never tried to hurt anyone, but it does have an effect. It creates uncertainty in the eye of the batsman, and when he's only got 0.4 of a second to decide what he's going to do that can be the difference between success and failure.

As well as that, a physical blow against the old enemy gets the crowd up. It was barely possible, but the atmosphere now was even more electric.

One of the reasons I consider Ricky Ponting the best batsman I played against is that he always took the short ball on.

At Lord's, though, I did him for pace and struck him right on the side of the face. When it hit him, I turned and went back to my mark.

The England team didn't check him out either and a lot was made of it at the time. Justin Langer was shouting over to Andrew

224

Strauss, who he'd played with at Middlesex the year before, "Is this a war? Is this what it's come to?"

But to be fair to me and everyone else in the team, we didn't know the ball had drawn blood. We only knew when Ricky took his helmet off and lifted his head. By that time I was nearly at the top of my mark – and that's 58 metres from the stumps.

It was only then that I looked at the big screen and saw there was blood all over his face. It was only then that there was a realisation – "Oh shit." It wasn't too late to check if he was OK, but that split second where you go over to the batsman had gone. When some of the lads did subsequently go over, Ricky told them to do one. I've expressed regret for not checking Ricky was OK a lot of times. But, in that instant, the moment had gone.

This idea that I'd deliberately try to cause damage was one that never sat easy with me. It's one of the reasons I never liked being referred to as GBH. I didn't mind the whole thing – Grievous Bodily Harmison – but the abbreviation I hated.

The term 'GBH' was something I didn't want to be connected with. It was the *Mirror* cricket man Mike Walters, a great friend of mine, who came up with it, and I told him I didn't like it, but there's nothing you can do about it if other people want to say that sort of thing. I'd rather talk about the ball that got Ricky out. A very fast, aggressive bouncer followed by the perfect length ball is a fast bowler's dream. It was the perfect delivery. That's how you got Ricky out, by drawing him forward and bringing the slips into play. That's one of my favourite wickets of all time because of who Ricky is, what he stands for, the player he is, and how it was set up.

Hayden got hit that morning as well, but he was no different to Ponting or Langer. He got one that got big on him because he was in a bad position. They were just balls that any fast bowler bowls, back of a length, bouncers, trying to draw the shot.

It was the way the Aussies played the bouncers that made everybody think we had a plan to rough them up. If Ponting hits that ball for four and doesn't get hit on the head – same with Langer and same with Hayden – we would have bowled with the same intent but nothing would have been deemed untoward or said afterwards.

I didn't say anything to Ricky afterwards. I've seen him a few times since, but I've only ever mentioned it once.

He was playing for Somerset and he came into the Durham dressing room to see his great mate Michael Di Venuto, who was playing for us. "I should have checked you out, mate," I told him. "I'm sorry." Ricky kept his head down and just brushed it away. "Long time ago, forget it." It wasn't uncomfortable but I could see that was the end of it. Nothing more needed to be said.

He understood it was a game, the heat of the battle, and that was that. I've always liked Ricky. He epitomised Aussie grit, a tough, tough man. He got some stick off the England crowds that summer, but he took it with good grace and just carried on doing his job. Now I'd like to see him on British TV more because he has such knowledge, he's easy to understand and he makes relevant and good points.

I took 5-43 in that Australian first innings as we bowled them out for 190. We were overjoyed in the dressing room between innings, but it hid an undercurrent of tension and nervousness.

By the end of the day, that tension was no longer hidden. We were 92-7 and never got back in the match. The difference between the two teams at Lord's was Glenn McGrath.

This was his stamping ground – at Lord's he'd always been

phenomenal. Fred said afterwards that he bottled this game, that he was caught like a rabbit in the headlights, but I'm not sure that's what happened. The ball he got from McGrath in the first innings he couldn't do anything with, the same with Vaughan and Trescothick. In the end he made my 5-43 look like 5-150. and he just blew us away.

We did take something from that game, though – the realisation that we could bowl Australia out twice, something other teams had been unable to do.

The problem was, in that game we didn't take those 20 wickets quick enough. In the first innings, great, we got them in no time at all, but then we didn't get the runs and we were out of the game. Nevertheless, we'd stood up to them, put them on the back foot. We'd found a chink in their armour.

Not only that but a big unknown had been answered – how was Kevin Pietersen going to perform in a Test match? He scored 50 in both innings and we knew he was here to stay. He was going to take anybody on.

He wasn't bothered if it was Warne, McGrath, whoever, and he wasn't bothered what the Aussies threw at him. They'd tried to get KP with a bit of verbals during the one-dayers, but then after that they were wary and watched what they were saying.

There are people you don't wake up. Brian Lara was one, Steve Waugh another. You don't try to rattle them because if you do they'll just come out fighting that bit harder. It was a case of let sleeping dogs lie. I batted with Kevin in both innings at Lord's. When he got his first Test 50, I joined him when he was in the mid-30s, and there wasn't too much said to him. There was a little bit, mainly about him being a South African playing for England, but he was used to that – we were giving him that in our dressing room! They didn't come up with anything that we hadn't already told him ourselves!

Vaughany was keen that we should build on the positives and otherwise forget the game. It should also be noted that our togetherness remained the same, and that came from being a good group of solid men. We didn't have any prima donnas, anybody who was above their station. People were grounded. The characteristics of the players in that side was level-head-edness and everyone understanding their game.

There was definitely part of us leaving Lord's after that first Test match thinking, 'Oh fuck. We might not be as good as we thought we were.' But I had a strong belief we were not dead and buried, that we shouldn't be written off, as some people were saying. We'd taken 20 wickets and that always gives you a chance of winning games.

At the hotel afterwards I was waiting for my car to come round the front and this bloke, just some random dickhead, came up and had a go at Vaughany. The usual stuff, "You're all shit, England are useless. You should all be fucking sacked." I had a clenched fist – I wanted to knock him out. He knew, though, that if I hit him it would be a story. He was well out of order, having a dig at all of us, but mainly our captain. Thankfully, the security guard on the door of the hotel eased him away.

Unfortunately, that's what happens sometimes when you're in the public eye, but I must admit I was raging. Any other time I'd have laid him out but we could not afford to lose our tempers or our focus because we had work to do.

The last couple of years had been building to this. All that winning and togetherness had to count for something.

If not now, when?

16

SHAKE, BATTLE AND BOWL

"I don't know what was more surprising, that McGrath fell over or that Ricky said they'd bat"

I'd calmed down a little by the morning of the Edgbaston Test.

We were in a huddle on the pitch, Vaughan going through the last few instructions, when all of a sudden Geraint jumped up – "McGrath has fallen over!"

We all looked over at him and could immediately see from his face it was bad – he was like a ghost. At that moment, we all thought the same thing, 'He's not getting up. We're 25 minutes from the toss. He's out of the game.' He got carted off and I'm not going to lie, it gave us a lift. And for the Aussies it did exactly the opposite.

It was a massive moment for us. Obviously you don't want

to see a fellow professional get injured, and you want to play against the best, but at that moment we knew this was doing us a favour. What McGrath did to us at Lord's, all of a sudden in our heads it had gone. We always said if either McGrath or Warne didn't play we could get at them.

We then went into the toss. To put it mildly, Vaughany had a poor record in this area, and so were hoping against hope that he wouldn't mess it up again. We knew the wicket was flat and chances are the chief exec had said to the groundsman that he wanted five days of pure 'kerching'.

From the minute we saw that pitch we knew Vaughany had to win the toss. We were on at him all the time. "You've got to win it, Mick," I told him. "For Christ's sake, get it right."

In the dressing room, you know who's won the toss by which captain the interviewer goes to first and then, of course, we see the coin come down, and who does the interviewer go to? Ponting. The reaction was unanimous. "Fuck's sake, here we go. This is going to be a long day." And then Ricky said, "We'll have a bowl first." I don't know what was more surprising, that McGrath fell over or that Ricky said they'd bowl.

I can only think Ricky put us in because he thought there would be a bit in it first thing in the morning. Maybe he also thought there were a few scars among the batsmen when it came to facing their bowlers.

You could see he had a bit of a point, but we knew the wicket was flat, and the only person who could possibly justify Australia bowling first, Glenn McGrath, was in hospital.

If they'd gone out and batted, they couldn't have lost, and would still have been one up after Edgbaston, going into a series with only three games left. It completely backfired on them and did seem slightly arrogant. Whether there was method to the madness only Ricky knows, but it seemed that, after Lord's, he'd dismissed what we'd achieved over the previous 12 months, and instead reverted to thinking of us as just another England team that would roll over and let them tickle our belly.

But that kind of England team didn't exist anymore.

What Ricky had actually done was make a 'Nasser Hussain at Brisbane' call.

There was talk of team changes for us in the media, but Vaughany wanted to make sure this group stayed together, to the extent, he says, that he ignored phone calls from the selectors.

Whether that's true or not, I don't know. In the build-up to Edgbaston, his message was that we couldn't win if we were negative. We had to back ourselves to score runs quickly and back ourselves to knock them over. Otherwise, the rate they scored their runs and took their wickets meant we'd be overwhelmed if we didn't match them.

The England team embraced that attitude — and then some — and the English mentality of facing the red ball in a Test match changed that morning.

Trescothick at the start and Pietersen in the middle played that red ball in a way that no-one had ever seen before.

Trescothick, in particular, took a different, more forceful attitude, Pietersen was already hardwired that way. They didn't look to deflect it like Nasser and Athers and Nick Knight used to do, tickling it down to third man or not quite off the square. Those two looked to put it out the ground — they went hard at it.

After nine overs, we looked out from the dressing room balcony and the sight that greeted us was a joy to behold. Shane Warne was stood looking at the wicket, shaking his head. In fact he was shaking it so hard the only surprise was it didn't fall off. We knew exactly what he was thinking – 'Why the fuck are we bowling on this?'

All the good work they'd done at Lord's had gone straight out the window. That was when we realised we had a chance. The best seamer in Australia is on crutches and arguably the best cricketer ever to have played the game is standing in the middle shaking his head, looking at his captain thinking, 'What the fuck have we done, bowling first on here?'

Ricky didn't respond, but he must have known within five overs that he'd made a massive error.

Whether there was a power struggle between Ricky and Warne was hard to see from the outside, but we definitely felt there was something there. Rumour was the Aussie dressing room wasn't a happy camp, people had fallen out with each other, people didn't like each other, but, aside from this one occasion with Warne, which was more bemusement than a public show of dissent, never once did we see that on the pitch. That's a sign of a strong team, because it was clear, if there were rifts, when they went on the pitch it was all forgotten.

When you played against Australia you definitely played against 11 men but Trescothick, Flintoff and Pietersen took the game away from them that day.

In the middle session, Fred and KP were basically having a competition – who could hit the hardest, and who could hit the furthest? It was phenomenal. Having been put into bat, our line-up flayed the Australian attack to all parts, including Tres clubbing Shane Warne back over his head for six. Within six hours we watched the whole momentum of the series shift.

There was no way Australia could stem the tide. They didn't

have the containing bowlers to go to that we had. They didn't have a Hoggard, a Flintoff, an Ashley Giles. McGrath could attack and contain, but he wasn't there. Well, he was, but he was up on bricks.

An attacking spinner like Warne, meanwhile, is always likely to go for a few. There was nobody to shut up shop. Jason Gillespie might have been that man but he was scarred by the one-dayers when KP got stuck into him. Michael Kasprowicz came in, but he went for five an over and Brett Lee for more than six.

That batting performance on the first day was a joy to watch. We were constantly out of our seats cheering. I even missed my siesta! I was just sat watching the TV. I would have gone outside, but the viewing areas at international grounds were terrible when I was playing.

Edgbaston was dark, dingy and badly laid out so you'd end up sat on the floor. Lord's was great but once you got three or four big lads on it that was it, Trent Bridge the same. But as long as there's somebody out there watching, that's what matters. I wasn't a great watcher.

Generally, I would watch the new ball to see what it was doing because chances are I'd be out there same time the next day. Otherwise I'd have my three courses at dinner, settle down and try to get some kip. Some liked watching, others didn't.

Some would read the papers, have a chat out the back – it doesn't mean they weren't supporting. As long as people could see they had support on the balcony, I didn't see it as a problem. Some people did have a problem with it. They wanted everybody out there to watch. But the ability to switch on and switch off in cricket at the top level is one of the most important skills.

In the field you can be involved six hours a day, so you have to be able to switch off and take your mind away from the intensity of it all. If you're concentrating, focusing, involving yourself constantly for five days, eventually it will ruin you.

We eventually made 407 and when Australia then batted, the fun started straight away as Hayden smacked his first ball straight to Andrew Strauss at extra cover.

Vaughany has since changed this story to add some much-needed oomph to his after dinner speaking and claims Strauss was late coming on to the pitch and he just stuck him there rather than wait for him to get to slip.

If ever you hear that one, take it from me – did he bollocks. He put Strauss there especially for that shot. Australia ended up 99 behind on first innings and, with us wobbling second time round, Fred saved us with a quickfire 73.

That rabbit in the headlights was now a lion in the spotlight and, after missing out at Lord's, he was ready to do some roaring. With the Aussies chasing 282, and going along quite nicely at 47-0, Fred produced the defining over of the series.

Fast, swinging, aggressive, into the pitch, it had everything. After cleaning up Gillespie and Kasprowicz LBW in successive balls at the end of the Australian first innings, Fred was actually on a hat-trick when Vaughan brought him on to bowl.

He didn't get the three in a row, but he did account for Langer's off stump with a lightning fast second ball. That brought Ricky to the wicket and Fred gave him as torrid a time as I have ever seen on a Test match pitch, bowling ridiculously fast and seemingly moving the ball at will.

It sounds daft, but Ricky showed his class in getting that duck because no-one else would have survived four balls. Eventually, he couldn't get out the way of a searing leg-cutter and was caught behind. The look in Ricky's eyes was something I'd never seen before.

Not fear, but that of a man who appeared helpless to his fate. It was an astonishing piece of bowling matched by a truly incredible atmosphere. You could have run the National Grid on the electricity produced in those five minutes. This wasn't like Botham's Ashes – this wasn't Freddie's Ashes. But as the series went on, the big lad stood up every time something wasn't happening, whether it was with the ball or the bat.

My slower ball came to the party in that Test, an unexpected guest, and one which was usually fairly forgettable.

At the end of that third day, the momentum of the game was just starting to get away from us.

With seven wickets down and the Aussies still more than a hundred behind, we never thought the game would get anywhere near to what would ultimately happen but, with Warne and Clarke at the crease, that nagging doubt was still there.

We knew if they came back fresh in the morning it could be tricky.

That final over, I'd given Clarke a couple in the body hoping he'd tickle one down to fine leg so Warne would be on strike, but it hadn't happened.

By the third ball I was literally just thinking to myself, 'It's been a long day, we're all knackered. We'll come back tomorrow.' I never even dreamed of bowling a slower ball, but just as I turned to run in, I thought, 'Well, you've thrown everything else at him – yorkers, bouncers, straight balls for LBW, I've tried to hit him, what if...', and the slower ball just came into my mind.

Fred and Tres told me later that, because of my hand position, they could see it coming from the top of my mark and when they saw what was happening their immediate reaction was, "Oh no!" because my slow ball is that bad.

But this time, as the ball totally bamboozled Clarke, almost floated towards him, they went, "Oh no... yes!"

The next day, on one of the most important mornings of our cricketing lives, the tension in the dressing room was lifted in an unusual way.

That morning, the *Sunday Mirror* was reporting a kiss 'n' tell involving KP. Apparently, he liked shagging in the dark and she had to shout, "Kevin Pietersen, Kevin Pietersen, KEVIN PIETERSEN" throughout the whole thing.

Basically, Kev had got lucky with a girl.

He was about to get very unlucky with us.

When he walked in the changing room, we were waiting for him, the lights were switched off and everybody started shouting his name as loud as they could! That's what dressing rooms do. It's like being hit in the balls – it's hilarious for everybody except the person concerned. But that was the world Kev wanted to live in and he was front page news.

Most importantly though, he was a single bloke at the time, he had not hurt anybody and he was totally fine with it, grinning away at us all. If he had been upset about it, we would have all been there with an arm around his shoulder.

It certainly helped us relax ahead of a day that would eventually test our nerves to the absolute limit.

Two balls would have done it on that Sunday and it could then have been a long liquid lunch for the supporters in the ground. In fact, *it was* a long liquid lunch – except we had a bit of a fright before the first sip.

Warne was phenomenal with the bat throughout that series, and he continued his heroics from the previous night, putting on 45 with Brett Lee before standing on his stumps trying to evade a Flintoff bouncer.

That should have been it, one more wicket and we were done, but from then on it increasingly felt like the match had gone. As time went on, I just began to think, 'It's not going to happen.' There was a group of about 60 Aussies, yellow shirts, a touring party, and they were counting down and singing after every run. When they got down to 40, we were thinking, 'Shit, this is real. It's actually happening.' We shouldn't have been so surprised. Brett Lee is one of the greatest cricket characters the world has ever seen – always played with a smile on his face, always did everything flat out and he would take anything on.

When he came out to bat we knew he wasn't going to roll over. We were going to have to get him out. We hit him again and again. He was like a voodoo doll. He got pinned everywhere. Two or three runs he got without holding his bat, because he'd dropped it from getting hit on his body.

As the target got lower and lower, it was a horrible feeling.

If we lose this game, we lose 5-0.

After what they'd done to us at Lord's, and now them coming back from the dead at Edgbaston, there was no way we were recovering from that. Runs were ebbing away at an alarming rate and it felt like we weren't even going to get a chance.

And then it came, a tough one, to Simon, a top edge to third man off Michael Kasprowicz. Inside I was willing him to catch it but I'm glad he didn't now, not because I eventually got the wicket, but because of the drama of it going right to the end.

Simon lost the ball in the crowd but if he'd dropped it through lack of judgement, no-one could have blamed him. The tension was unlike anything I've ever experienced on a cricket pitch.

When I wasn't bowling and was standing at fine leg, I was shaking. Physically shaking. I did not want to be Simon Jones when that ball came flying through the air. Sod that. But with the ball in my hand bowling I was fine. It was just somebody at the other end I had to get out.

The problem was walking back to my mark. Then I could see the scoreboard and how many runs they needed to win, and that was terrifying. It seemed everyone felt the same. You could hear a pin drop when any of us ran into bowl.

It was like being at a tennis match or the golf. In between the action there was a bit of a murmur, but then it was as if somebody was holding a 'Silence!' placard up. Richie Benaud said it was pure theatre, and he was right. And, as an actor in the play, for me bowling was the best place to be.

With Brett Lee on strike and them needing four to win, Vaughany came up to me and asked if we should take out the deep point. I would have done it if it had been Kasprowicz, but not for Brett Lee. He was properly in, never looked like getting out so what we needed was one more chance at Kasper.

Next ball, out came a big booming full toss and I thought that was it – except Lee smacked it straight to deep point. The man was still there, it only went for a single, and Kasper was back on strike where I wanted him.

The thing that had let me down all day was my bouncer. It

was tiredness more than anything else. I wasn't driving my left arm through and my left side was pulling away, which meant the short ball was just dribbling down leg side. In the end I stopped bowling it. But eventually, with Australia needing just three to win, I knew I had to try it again.

As I ran in, all my focus was on getting it right, too much waywardness and the game was gone.

It didn't do much good, it still didn't come out right, the ball was veering down the legside. But it wasn't enough down the legside not to tuck Kasper up a little.

As he looked to fend it off, it got the glove, Geraint made a brilliant diving catch and the rest, as they say, is history.

The actual moment of victory was unreal.

The whole place erupted. I was the first person to shake Brett Lee's hand but I wasn't as camera savvy as Fred was! Whatever happened round that time, Freddie was the man.

He was the one whose gentlemanly image is preserved in time, even if I'd got to Brett first. "Amazing effort," I told him, and that was it. I wanted to say loads of things but in those situations, you can't. You've won, he's lost. You don't want to sound patronising. The time to wax lyrical is an hour later, when you've both got a beer in your hand, not on the pitch.

To me, after such a titanic battle, it was about celebrating but also trying to be as respectful as possible. I hugged Geraint who had just taken such a great catch after getting no small measure of stick off those Aussies in the crowd, because, of course, he grew up in Australia. We could barely hear ourselves speak because of the excitement and the noise, just reward for the people of Birmingham because that game could have finished in five minutes. Instead they'd seen 90 minutes of highly entertaining pressurised cricket. Afterwards, a lot of the Aussies came into the dressing room and we sat and shared a drink for a while.

Someone had to win, and someone had to lose, but there was a lot of appreciation of what we, the players of both sides, had achieved.

It was a theme that would run throughout the series. Ricky came in only at the end. Vaughany was the same. For a captain it's different, there's more to think about. It's not so easy to sit having a chat with the opposition.

You need to keep a bit of distance. Gilchrist spent a lot of time with Geraint, talking about all things wicket-keeping gloves, but then again wicket-keepers are a strange breed. In the end, I came away. I went home that afternoon. I always wanted to come home. I always felt that waking up the next day in my own bed was a lot better than driving five or six hours with a hangover and not getting back until seven at night.

Having a few days at home meant a lot because I knew in no time this whole mad circus would be starting up again. I wasn't the only one like that because the lads with families tended to disappear while the single lads, who didn't really have anything to go home for, went from hotel to hotel.

That means there wasn't the big team celebration as you might imagine after what people were already referring to as 'The Greatest Test Of All Time'.

It might well have been that, but there'd be a couple of contenders to come.

17

KNIFE EDGE

"'You fucking cheats,' he shouted across at us. 'Is this how you want to play, is it? He shouldn't even be on the field'"

I t was funny.
I'd been in to do some training at Newcastle United before the first Test and all the players were there, including Craig Bellamy and Lee Bowyer.

"Are you going to watch the cricket?" someone asked them. Bellamy shouted, "Nah, not interested in cricket – crap game," just taking the piss out of me. Bowyer was the same. "I'll be walking the dogs, I'm not watching that shit." I went back in after the second Test and Bowyer couldn't stop asking questions. Alan Shearer shouted up, "Were you not walking your dogs when that was on then?"

Scott Parker came across. He wasn't a cricket man either but he'd been watching.

"That Shane Warne, can you not just run down and hit it

before it bounces?" Funny as anything. But that, perhaps more than anything, made me realise what we were doing with this Ashes series. These lads who had no interest in cricket, but had started watching it because they knew me, had properly become involved.

That made me think. 'Hang on, if these lot are watching, everybody must be watching!' I wasn't wrong – 8.75million people watched that Sunday morning at Edgbaston on Channel 4, and overnight we were household names. Freddie was getting bigger, KP was huge, but by going back to Ashington I managed to keep my own life.

KP wasn't the only one who picked up press attention during that series. Before the Lord's Test, a tabloid tried to dig up some dirt on Simon, claiming he'd slept with a girl behind his fiancée's back, which Simon strenuously denied.

At times like that it felt like it wasn't just Australia who were trying to beat us, there were outside influences trying to do us over as well, people trying to have a dig and a pop and knock us off our perch. It didn't work because we stayed strong as a group and helped each other.

People ask if it overshadowed the experience the attention Fred, KP and Vaughany were getting compared to everybody else. Not at all. I loved it. Absolutely loved it. Happy days. I could come back to Ashington, sit in the Buffs, have some time with the family and let Pietersen, Vaughan and Flintoff have as much attention as they wanted. That kind of thing just wasn't me. I'd go to the cricket club, watch a bit of football, stay in with the family.

All the time in Ashington I was just Jimmy's lad. Nobody bothered me. Another Ashington-born England paceman, Mark

Wood, does the same thing now. Nobody bothers him because he's just one of us. If Kev wanted to go to these big nightclubs with paparazzi everywhere I was all for it. Because I didn't.

After Edgbaston, we really did start to think we could win the series. I remember being asked by Nasser if I believed we could win it, and I said we had to – we had to believe because that was what would get us through. If we didn't believe we could do it, we would get steamrollered.

If the series had captured the imagination before, now it went totally ballistic.

On the last day at Old Trafford, we thought a bomb had gone off. Me and Geraint were driving in from the hotel that morning and all we could see was people outside the ground. We were stuck in the traffic, trying to make other drivers see it was us so they'd let us through. When eventually we did reach the ground, we asked the gateman, "What's the matter? Has a bomb gone off?"

"They can't get in," he replied.

"What, there's something wrong with the gates?"

"No. It's full."

"What the... ?"

By this time we were late. It was half past nine and we were normally in the ground for nine o'clock. Rushing up to the dressing room, we changed quickly and got out for the warm-ups.

It was the oddest feeling, like playing at Manchester United or St James' Park, warming up in front of 20,000 people. Some of us were laughing – "This is what we wanted to be – footballers!" It was surreal, an atmosphere like none of us had ever experienced.

And that's the enormity of what that series was. The chat in the bars, in the newspapers, on the radio, wherever you went it was cricket, cricket, cricket. The crowds actually in the grounds were louder than usual because of the standard of cricket being played.

When Flintoff or Pietersen were going at the Aussies hammer and tongs, or when Warne or McGrath were having one of their spells, it was spellbinding. A crowd will always be lifted when they see greatness, and what they were seeing in the summer of 2005 was greatness.

McGrath had to play at Old Trafford despite not being fit. Unfortunately, if you're a fast bowler with ankle problems the one place you don't want to play is Manchester. The footholds are rock hard, it kills your feet. That was the first thing that went against him. The second thing was luck. First up, Gilchrist dropped Vaughan off his bowling. McGrath turned around, came in again, and promptly castled him. "No ball!" Vaughan went on to get a massive hundred. If we hadn't lost a day to the weather, we'd have won that match.

As it was, it came down to a last day showdown. We had to take 10 wickets. They had to survive. It was then that Ricky Ponting showed what he was made of. Whatever we threw at him he was an immovable object.

It was an innings that showed Ricky's true character. At the other end, though, we chipped away until it got to a point where we were thinking it was back on but nut then Simon got cramp, and he'd been a real spearhead for us in this game.

I'd bowled a decent long spell at the opposite end to him, and after that my race was run. I'd gone, my legs had gone, I literally had nothing left. But when Simon went off, Vaughany threw me the ball and I just had to get myself going again. The good news is batsmen get tired too.

All day we'd bowled some great balls to Ricky and, in the end, he got out to one of the worst ones going, off me, a long hop down leg side which he got a touch on as it went through to Geraint.

Ricky's departure got the adrenalin pumping again but by that last over I was beat. It didn't help that they put a countdown on the big screen reminding everyone of the equation – "Six balls, one wicket".

Every delivery where the last magic wicket wouldn't happen, it clicked down another number. It didn't add to the pressure but it was certainly off-putting, something else to consciously or sub-consciously register in the brain.

I might not be the brightest, but I could count to six on my own. Scoreboard or not, I knew what was going on. The truth is we'd got ourselves in a winning position but were now out on our feet. Hoggy had put in two massive spells earlier in the day, Fred had kept going on adrenalin alone, Gilo had bowled an awful lot of overs from one end and everyone else had gone through a massively intensive day in the field.

Mental tiredness can be overwhelming at times. It's bigger than physical tiredness. If you can overcome being mentally tired you can get even the weariest legs going again. But we were all out on our feet.

Birmingham and Manchester were back-to-back Tests and we'd been drained by Edgbaston. Even the energy we'd used celebrating – not drinking, just thinking about what that victory could mean in terms of the series – was part of the deficit we were now feeling.

We'd all travelled through those ups and downs, and then at

Old Trafford we were going through them again. The emotions constantly changing, the massive crowd on that final day – it hit us in the last hour that we were all dead and buried.

That last over I just tried too hard. I was desperate just to get some momentum into the crease, but the stuffing had been knocked out of me. I was absolutely knackered and, in the end, it wasn't to be. In the huddle afterwards, Vaughany was telling us, "Look at their balcony, celebrating. This supposedly great Australian side is celebrating getting a draw."

I hadn't picked up on it, although I had picked up on the way Brett Lee celebrated, pumping his fists. But I hadn't thought what Vaughany was thinking. Even though it was just words, it meant something.

Vaughany was also talking about where we could be going, what we could achieve. But inside I couldn't help thinking, 'Have we blown it? Is this our chance gone? Are decisions likely to go our way, as they did in this game, again? Is Simon going to be fit?'

All this was going through my mind as I was driving home and then when I was home it carried on.

Had we missed our chance to go 2-1 up in an Ashes series with two to play?

It was a whole load of 'what ifs'.

I was also worried about myself. It felt like all my energy had gone with the first game at Lord's and I couldn't reach those heights again.

There were passages where I did but not as many as I'd have liked. For me, the mental energy expended at Lord's had harmed the rest of the series. I was nowhere.

My head had gone, my legs had gone, my body was nowhere.

The emotions of Lord's took effect on me during that series

in a way that I didn't initially realise. A lot of stuffing had been kicked out of me.

Mental stress is an issue that affects us all.

I had people I could confide in when I was having a bad experience, and over time they could see the signs that maybe I was having one of those days. If I was quiet, they knew why – I was in a darkish place – and I appreciated that. I was the same with others. When other people were down, I would try to help. I'd ask myself what it was they needed.

At Manchester, I felt I could see something in Geraint. He was always quiet, he'd sit with us at dinner, not say anything all night, and them come in the dressing room the next morning and go, "Great craic that was lads!" He just took things in. This was different. I was really close to Geraint and could see he was going through a bit of a dodgy time, not anxiety or depression, more on the back of worries about his form with the gloves, and he was just going to stew in his room.

When any teammate was struggling, me and Fred would always try to gee them up. That time, we happened to be going to the dog racing at Belle Vue. Fred had a dog running and we were going to watch it.

There'd be a few of us, including my mates, my dad and my brothers. "Get another seat," I told Fred. "Geraint's coming."

Not that I'd told Geraint this yet. I went to his room. "You've got to come. You can't sit in here all night stewing on what's just happened today," I told him. He'd dropped a catch. "Come on, we'll go and watch this dog of Fred's. We'll be eating it by the end, because knowing Fred it will be hopeless." And, sure enough, it was. Geraint had a great night. He really got involved in both the racing and the company. Fred looked at me at one point, "Good idea to bring him along." Geraint didn't know a thing about dogs, he didn't have to. It was a release for him.

None of us are robots and we occasionally need to get away. We should always have an eye on our teammates, both for them and the team. When it comes to taking wickets, LBW is down to me, bowled is down to me. But that's as far as it gets. I need 10 other players to catch it. If a player has their head down, just leaving them isn't an option because it will make the team worse. You've got to look at the bigger picture and that 2005 group were very good at looking after their teammates.

A lot was made about England's bowlers going on and off the pitch in that series and it would eventually come to a volcanic head in the next match at Trent Bridge.

The Aussies had been whingeing about it from the word go. Personally, I thought it was rubbish. It riled the Aussies but I couldn't understand what they were rattled about. You could set your watch by Simon Jones – quarter past 11 he'd be off to the toilet. It was just nerves. He was a lad who got nervous. Not only that but every season we had analysts and sports scientists coming in. I don't know where they got them from half the time. One dietician came in and declared, "I back and believe everything I do. I won the Premier League with Chelsea last year." 'Hang on,' I thought. 'You tell people what to eat, you don't put the ball in the back of the net. You're not John Terry or Frank Lampard.' But we had loads of these people at the time. Sports science was big on hydration. We had to drink lots and lots. So what do you do when you drink? You go to the toilet. Ricky believed England were trying to pull a fast one. It had been a bugbear of his all series, so when he was run out by the substitute fielder at Trent Bridge it was always going to kick off.

As he waited for the decision to be confirmed out in the middle, he was already raging. "You fucking cheats," he shouted across at us. "Is this how you want to play, is it? He shouldn't even be on the field."

He was still going as he walked off and then served up a beautiful volley for Duncan Fletcher who'd interrupted making some toast in the dressing room – Duncan was Mr Toast – to come out on to the balcony to see what was happening. Duncan actually choosing that moment to smile for once didn't exactly help matters.

For us, to see Ricky rattled like that was brilliant. We'd got him, and through him we'd got them.

Truth is, Ricky didn't have a leg to stand on. In cricket you have a 12th man. On a touring party you're stuck with what you've got. I've done it myself a few times. I hated it. It's the worst job in the world, so I looked at it like I did decorating at home – if you mess it up and do a bad job you never get asked again.

On tour, the majority of time the 12th man will be the back-up batsman because he'll be the best fielder out of those who aren't playing. If you're at home, especially with the amount of cricket that goes in England, the person left out of the Test team will often go back to their county to play. If that's the case, you have to bring in a 12th man.

Normally, what happens is that teams without a fixture receive a request for two fielders. That county isn't going to send two fast bowlers down. They're going to send their best two fielders, and for Durham, the county concerned on this occasion, Gary Pratt fitted that bill. It was nothing new.

Paul Collingwood had done 12th man duties not long before, because he was the best fielder in the country. Why not? It's common sense. And chances are they're only going to be on the field for one or two overs unless someone gets seriously injured.

It should also be remembered that a bowler can only be off the pitch for two overs or eight minutes. After that you're not allowed to bowl for the equivalent length of time. It wasn't in England's interests to have bowlers off the field for long periods. If I went off I might change my shirt and socks. I hated damp socks. But that was while I was going to the toilet. Sometimes I've changed my socks at the side of the field, then I was back out.

It didn't help Ricky that he chose the worst possible moment to make his point. Simon Jones, who Gary Pratt was on for, was actually injured, to the extent he walked off the field and never came back.

He's not been on an international cricket field since. Ricky didn't realise this, and neither did the other Australians when Ricky's outburst spilt over into other people saying stuff. When I got Simon Katich LBW, he walked off having a go at everybody.

I know Simon from Durham and he's one of the good guys of the game, but he was a fiery character and when he walked off shouting about the injustice of it, that was him to a T.

We're human beings, and all human beings have emotions, and that was Ricky and Simon letting theirs out.

In fact, the emotion Ricky showed when he was run out by the 12th man was, for me, what made him one of the best who's played the game.

He was a gutsy and emotional character who was a winner, and he didn't believe what happened was right. He got frustrated. He hated getting out and, on this occasion, he'd been got out by someone who, in his eyes, shouldn't have been anywhere near an international cricket field. But the truth was we'd lost a bowler who couldn't participate in the rest of the game.

At the same time, we gained a fielder who could field inside the ring and not be a liability. As it happened, he ran the best player in the world out.

Ricky would get over this perceived wrong and carry on a glittering career but, for me, it was the end of Gary Pratt. It was a shame. I remember playing against Essex at Ilford and talking to Ronnie Irani, telling him what a good group of kids we had in the likes of Pratt and Nicky Peng. We chased a score and Pratt got 80 or 90, same with Peng.

For a while it was a case of who could hit the best shot, like when KP and Fred were batting at Edgbaston. I remember looking at Pratt thinking, 'This kid has got a chance.'

The thing is, during 2005 it seemed he wanted to be 12th man for England more than play cricket for Durham. The more it went to his head about how well he performed as a fielder, and then subsequently running Ricky Ponting out, all of a sudden he stopped being Gary Pratt the cricketer and became Gary Pratt the 12th man – and this extended to Durham.

It was a shame because the kid had ability – a left-handed batsman who played a lot of good shots. I wouldn't say he went 'big-time', but he lost the sense of what cricket is about. He was putting himself forward to be 12th man when he should have been playing. When he turned up on the bus for the victory parade, I couldn't help thinking, 'What the fuck are you doing on here?' He was 12th man, and there he is, front of the bus. I couldn't believe it. I was sitting at the back with my family. In five Test matches I'd taken nearly 20 wickets, and he's there with his hands round KP's shoulders. It wasn't like he was the only 12th man we'd had.

For me, it ended his career because he seemed to like what happened that summer too much. He even ended up on *The Weakest Link*! If he'd then gone back to Durham, got his head down, and worked, potentially he could have been there as number one to 11 and not just a hanger on.

His fielding was magnificent but in the end I think Durham looked at him and thought, 'What are you playing at son? Do you really want to play cricket?' His career just petered out. I couldn't understand it because he was a good lad and had a lot of ability.

From a personal point of view, Trent Bridge is the game I'm most proud of in that series.

My 3-93 in Australia's second innings there meant more to me than my 5-43 at Lord's, because it was in a winning cause – a cause which proved what we were as a group of men.

When the chips were down, we came out fighting for each other. When Simon went off injured, we were facing one of the greatest batting line-ups the game had ever seen with three seamers. That was a tough ask. But making them follow-on was the right thing to do.

From a drama point of view it made it even more special again!

Fred was brilliant during that Test match. You couldn't get the ball out of his hand when he was bowling and when he was batting, the first innings partnership between him and Geraint

Jones was the reason we won the Test match. As a pair, they complemented each other well. Fred was somebody Geraint felt comfortable with. He was more relaxed around him than anybody else.

At Trent Bridge it was all about not losing what we'd achieved at Edgbaston and Old Trafford. We had to make sure we were on the front foot and not let Australia up off the floor. McGrath didn't play again, which was a bonus. Instead they brought in Shaun Tait, similar to Brett Lee but not as skilful, and we felt that was to our advantage. Tait could bowl at 93mph but it could go anywhere (ring any bells?), and we tried to exploit that.

After a difficult series so far, Jason Gillespie had been ditched for this game. He seemed to lose a little bit of the zip that made him the great bowler he was. I'm not sure if that was the English conditions or the slower pitches, but the little bit of bounce he used to get, the spring off a good length that would find the edge, just wasn't there.

In the one-day series, the ball just sat up and KP really belted it, so when we came to thinking that we needed to score at three-and-a-half an over in the Tests, he began to emerge as one that potentially we should target, and we exploited that tactic really well.

The confidence factor then came into it, something I was used to myself. If you pitch it up you think you'll get driven, if you bowl short it sits up to be hit. The margin for error in your own mind is minute, thinking becomes blurred, and it's very difficult, at that point, to see what's going. I think that's where Jason was in that series. He looked broken as it went on. Like a few of the Aussies, he looked like he'd never been in such a position before. They didn't know what to do. They should have asked England

– we'd been doing it for years. The crowds also gave Gillespie a lot of stick but I never really knew what for.

At the end of my career, I went to play for Yorkshire because of Gillespie's presence at Headingley. The reason he's such a great coach is because he's such a good bloke. The brief time I had with him I could see he not only understood the game, but he understood how to talk to people in a good, calm, relaxed manner.

He knew how to get the best out of them. But obviously when things aren't going well as a cricketer, something he wasn't familiar with because of the great team that he played in, and the crowd are having a go, it's different.

I think the crowd sensed he was a bit down on his luck and they tried to play their part in keeping him down.

Aside from Warne and Lee, none of the Australian bowlers really stepped up to the mark. Kasper bowled a fuller length and needed the ball to swing, but it never really did during that summer, which made him easy to drive, the same with Tait.

It reversed more than it swung which suited our bowlers who were more about reverse than conventional swing. The conditions fitted us more because we had more adaptable and suitable bowlers, backed up by Giles, a man who never got the credit he deserved for his performances across that series.

People talk about Freddie's over against Ponting or my slower ball at Edgbaston, but, for me, the best wicket in that series was when Giles bowled Damien Martyn at Old Trafford – like Shane Warne's ball against Mike Gatting, only better – but nobody speaks about it.

Ashley was a massive part of that group. People always talk about England's bowling 'quartet' of me, Fred, Simon and

Hoggy but there was five bowlers in that side, and it irks me that Gilo does not get anywhere near enough credit for what he did for that England team – and his fellow bowlers.

Ashley never used to go for runs and his ability to stem the tide built massive pressure at the other end.

Hoggard could also stem the tide, as could Flintoff, but Ashley consistently did so. He picked the wickets up when things were going in his favour but, when things weren't going his way, he had the ability to go at less than two an over. The opposition weren't going anywhere but we still had attacking options.

Ashley was also great in the dressing room. He could be fiery – you could have an argument with him – but he was very straight, a good team person who didn't suffer fools. He was a father figure. He had a very sensible head, he had knowledge, not just about the game but life in general. He was a calming influence, the same as Strauss and Trescothick. We needed that. There was me, Hoggy, Simon and Fred bouncing off ceilings. If it hadn't have been for Ashley, we could have caused some serious damage.

After such great service as a player, Ashley got shit on by England when, having been the one-day coach for two years, he went for the job as head coach.

My understanding is that as soon as he said he could get the best out of Kevin Pietersen, a big line went through his name. Kevin had an ally in Ashley, but the ECB didn't want Kevin anymore.

Our lack of a fourth seamer in the Australian second innings allowed them to get a few more than we hoped and we ended up with a squeaky bum target of 129.

We'd got off to a great start and at 32-0 all looked to be going swimmingly. I was thinking we had it in the bag but, just then, the public address system burst into life. "Change of bowling at the Pavilion End – Shane Warne." As soon as Warne's name was mentioned, it was like the air was let out the crowd.

There was one big sigh. We knew, and the crowd knew, what it meant to our chances, confirmed when he got Tres straight away.

Brett Lee also launched a spell of bowling which was just terrific, deadly accurate and at supersonic speed. Brett had already got one over on me in that game, hitting me for the biggest six ever. When he hit it, Shaun Tait at the other end shouted, "Run!" No great need, mate. It was massive. I looked at Brett and smiled. "Fair play, that's big." When he bowled that spell in the second innings, with Warne at the other end, and with Fred and Kevin fighting for our lives, it was exciting, thrilling, frightening, everything rolled into one.

It was two teams going hard at each other, with their best two performers in the series – and biggest personalities – at the top of their game. They were doing everything in their power not to let England win. Bat and ball, throughout the series, if it wasn't for those two we could have won much easier, because they were brilliant.

We steadily lost wickets until, at 116-7, I found myself sitting with my pads on. Out in the middle were Giles and Hoggard, and I would much rather have been where they were than where I was. The ones before me, Strauss, Flintoff, Trescothick, Bell, Pietersen, Vaughan, Geraint, they'd had their go.

I'd still got to have mine. This could potentially come down to me. Hoggard and Giles were in a place where they could control what was going on. I had no control, and when you haven't got any control, which happened a lot of times in that series, it's absolutely terrifying.

Out on Trent Bridge's poky little balcony it was so tense.

Magical: The 2004 West Indies tour was the start of a truly awesome period for English cricket

All guns blazing: We wanted Australia to feel the heat from the very first ball of the 2005 Ashes. I hit Justin Langer (above) and captain Ricky Ponting (bottom left) in an opening spell that set the tone for the series. Although I celebrated my first Test five-for (below right), we could not win the match as Glenn McGrath proved to be too good. But the challenge had been set. And accepted

The greatest Test? At Edgbaston it looked like the Aussies had stolen it with an amazing batting display but Michael Kasprowicz gloved behind and Geraint Jones (with me, below) clung on. We had won the Test by two runs. The entire nation was waking up to the fact something special was happening

Attack, attack, attack: Simon Jones (top), Matthew Hoggard (below left), Freddie (below right) and Ashley Giles (bottom right), made up England's bowling attack for the 2005 Ashes and we complimented each other perfectly. Bottom left, fans were locked out at Old Trafford on the last day – English cricket had never seen anything like it

Glory: Above, Shane Warne and Glenn McGrath are bowling legends who pushed us all the way, (top right) KP's astonishing 158 saw us get the draw we needed at the Oval, (right and below), we partied hard in the dressing room, at Trafalgar Square and 10 Downing Street

Palace party: Gilo's kids, Anders and his sister Tilly, (centre back view) dance with my Emily (face on) and Abbie at Buckingham Palace after an invite from Her Majesty

A living nightmare: Smiles were in short supply on the 2006-07 Ashes Tour. My infamous first ball in the first Test (top), got us off to a bad start and it went rapidly downhill from there

A mixed bag: After the Ashes failure in Australia, I knew my international career was on the wane but I still enjoyed moments to savour like jumping into my brother Ben's arms after winning the County Championship in 2008 at Canterbury

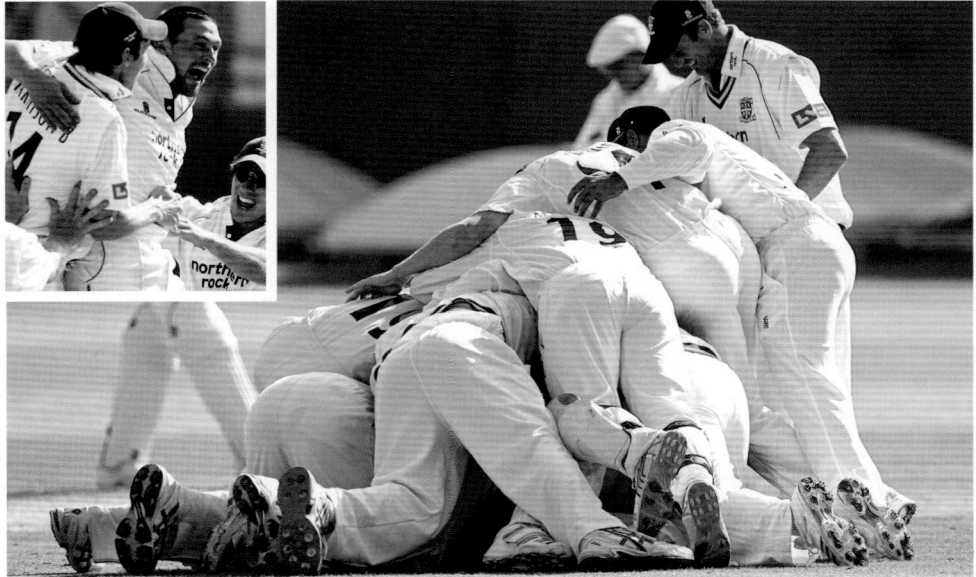

As one door closes... Above, I celebrate Stuart Clark's wicket – my last in international cricket, (top right), me and Fred celebrate another home Ashes win, (below right), same seats, same mate, same picture as 2005, (below left), me and Hayley in the Oval dressing room – she's my best friend and I owe her everything

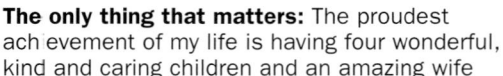

The only thing that matters: The proudest achievement of my life is having four wonderful, kind and caring children and an amazing wife

Despite the target being tantalisingly close, England were far from over the line, as horribly emphasised when I looked up, only to see Simon trying to get his pads on over his medical boot. Superstitions come in at that point.

Sometimes when things weren't going well, I wouldn't go to the toilet or try to stay in the same spot. On that day, I sat in the corner hoping and praying I wasn't going to get a chance to go in. Hoggy had gone out before me. He tried not to show he was nervous, but you could see it by his body language and demeanour. Brett Lee bowled a ball and it just missed his stumps and Hoggy was laughing. Hoggy was daft, but he knew that sometimes daft is exactly what's needed to ease the tension. Playing the fool and acting the fool was one of his special traits, but he had a fiery determination.

Eventually, with the game on a knife edge and the tension ratcheted up once again in this ridiculous series, Brett bowled a big full toss and Hoggy just about managed to get it through the covers and over the rope for four. Hoggy had some horrendous pieces of wood so to see that was amazing.

When Ashley then hit the winning runs off Warne, it was the best shot I have ever seen by any batsman – because that was what got us over the line to win the Ashes. Also, it was always the other four bowlers who took the headlines so seeing Gilo get some of the credit was amazing. Nobody seemed to realise that Gilo was an integral part of that bowling attack, one who allowed the rest of us to do our work. He came back in and punched the air. He deserved that moment in the limelight.

Hoggy, don't forget, had also hit a cover drive off Brett Lee bowling at 90mph. This was something we all needed a moment or two to absorb. When he came back in, none of us could speak to him for 20 minutes, we were so amazed. All we could say was, "Where the hell did you get from?" Usually he couldn't get it off the square!

The explosion of emotion on the balcony, the jumping, the shouting, the hugging, the punches on shoulders came from not just relief, but belief.

When Giles got that two and we won, the belief really was there that we'd got this. The momentum was ours. The Ashes were ours to lose rather than Australia's to win. I think that was why, surprisingly enough, the actual post-match celebration was muted.

There wasn't some massive drink-up like people might imagine. We knew the job hadn't been done. The urn was there, and we could see it, but one slip and it was going back home with them. That's why we were so very focused on being at our best at the Oval.

We would take them on as a group.

18

NICE THREADS

"He was just starting on Suspicious Minds when someone turned the microphone off"

Leading into the Oval, we were thinking, 'Right, five days of rain and here we go'.

As it turned out the only clouds were in my head.

Three or four days before the game, those familiar feelings started building up. Twenty-four hours to go, the anxiety kicked in big time and the depression too. I couldn't think straight. I couldn't sleep. My stomach was turning over, I couldn't eat. I was hoping it was nerves, the reality was I was going through another bad episode. I wasn't in a very good place. In fact, maybe I shouldn't have played in that game.

If I'd known in advance I was going to feel as bad as I did I might have had to be man enough to say, "I don't think I can play here. I'm struggling and I don't want to cost us."

Instead I didn't tell anybody. I didn't dare. If I'd said anything I might have been advised not to play, and despite everything I was desperate to get on that pitch, one to play for England, and two because playing usually made me better.

I didn't let on to anybody how I was feeling, not even Fred. I kept it in. Instead people put my quietness down to tiredness, the end of the series, and all that had gone with it. Actually I was churning like no-one would ever believe. I was all over the shop from a mental point of view. I was having negative thoughts. Doubts were coming into my mind. Again, I started telling myself it was the occasion. It wasn't. It was me.

If I thought the game starting would offer magical relief, I was sadly mistaken.

I really wasn't in a very good place and struggled all day. It might have cost us, but luckily we were batting first and thanks to an unbelievable Strauss century, made under incredible pressure, I got through it without having to step on the pitch.

On the second day, however, it told – I didn't bowl a ball above 82mph. I was ill. My head and insides were a mess, like they were fighting a battle with some unknown force, and I was just a bit part player with no control over the outcome.

I didn't want to bowl, I didn't want to let go of the ball. My mind was just a quicksand of negativity sucking me down inside. I think Vaughany felt he couldn't trust me – Hoggard and Fred bowled a hell of a lot. But on the third day, after Hayden and Langer had both got tons, I came back fired up. I'd had a better night and the lowness had begun to lift.

The feelings never went away fully, but I was back up to 85-88mph and finally got the breakthrough by bowling Langer. My mind was back on the game rather than on my troubles. I again began to think of what had happened as being nerves about what we were doing rather than anything else. I was kidding myself, but whatever was happening, I could take heart from the thought that again my problems hadn't done for me, that I'd never let them defeat me.

Even with the improvement, though, I was nothing more than a minor figure in that game. The spotlight fell well and truly on someone else – KP.

When Kevin was on, there wasn't a better sight in English cricket, but that second innings knock at the Oval was ridiculous. Two slog sweeps he played off Warne early on, when England were five down, told you so much about the newcomer.

Bear in mind that at 126-5 we were staring defeat in the face. Not many English-born players would have done that. They'd have just tried to hang in there. The rest of the England dressing room can count themselves among them.

We were thinking, 'What are you doing? Just hit him for one!' But that was the old English mentality. Kevin didn't have that. KP thought, 'Five down, I'm going to take it to them.' He believed in himself so much. People ask what it was about Kevin that made him special.

I always believe that not being English was a huge part of it. The English way and the English manner is negative. We are a country of cautiousness, but because he was an outsider he wasn't hamstrung by it.

The four hours he was in the middle was one of the gutsiest things I've ever seen. People say he took a chance. No, that took balls, and I've not seen many Englishmen play like that, from bygone days or whenever. The closest we've seen was Ian Botham, but in 1981 against Australia at Headingley, he played like that because he was batting with the tail.

Kevin was playing like that when he was with the top six. If he'd got out batting like that in those circumstances, he might never have played again. People would have held it against him because of his nationality (he said he was English, but we all laugh at that!). That, for me, was Kevin's great strength, that he had a different mindset.

Talk about being in positions and not wanting to move in case it made things worse. When we were four wickets down, then five, I really did not want to move. I was staying where I was, lying on the floor watching the telly. All of a sudden everything went crazy. The whole game just got faster and faster. Brett Lee was bowling incredibly fast and KP just kept swinging. It was hilarious. Even to this day, though, I still think KP was shitting himself when Brett was bowling those bouncers.

His beans were going and he just couldn't stop himself swinging at them. The faster Brett was bowling, the faster Kevin was hitting. He never looked to get out the way, he just wanted to hit him out of the ground. That hour in the middle of that final day when he went at Lee was yet another massive moment in what made up an incredible series.

It was ironic that Warne should be the one who dropped him, a regulation catch to slip on 15, because he was one of the few Australians in that series who really stood up.

If anybody else had dropped him, they'd have been getting a bit of blame but nobody could blame Shane in that instance. England would have been over the line long before the Oval if he'd not been there. If he'd stepped on that ball at Edgbaston and not McGrath, we'd have been out of sight. The word 'great' gets used too much, but rightly so in his case.

Eventually, Kevin was bowled by McGrath for 158, having taken enough time out the game, alongside Giles, to ensure the

Aussies couldn't reach a target. Our last wicket to fall should, for me, have been where the game finished, but still the umpires insisted that we all go back on for an Australian innings that was clearly only going to last a matter of balls before they offered them the light in the descending murk.

I was chucked the new ball and I apologised to Langer and Hayden. I told them they'd be getting no trouble from me. "Look," I said. "Every one of these will go over your heads here." Hayden and Langer knew this was just going through the motions and nodded their agreement.

There was no point confronting the umpires about it. What's done was done. Nothing was going to change it. My plan was to get the umpires to act on the light by bowling bouncers. Four balls later we were off.

Then, for me, it was the biggest anti-climax that you will ever see.

Vaughany went into the umpires' room and he came back in punching the air. "That's it. It's over!" We were all over the Oval dressing room dancing around in a circle, but all the country could see was two umpires out in the middle theatrically flicking a bail off. I thought it was embarrassing. The umpires had grabbed their chance to be in the spotlight. It made it about them. There were 25 different people who had played in that series. They deserved more respect than that because of what they had just put on for world cricket.

To have it taken away from them by others who wanted to be in the limelight was just ridiculous. That huddle we had in the dressing room should have been out in front of 25,000 people. That was the most upsetting thing. We didn't get the chance to shake Langer and Hayden's hand as they walked off, and to celebrate in the middle.

Instead, it was egotistical umpires deciding they were going to have their little moment.

Vaughany didn't make a speech. In that huddle he just talked briefly about us doing what we'd wanted to do, realising the goals we'd set out to achieve. He knew that if he stopped the celebration to make a big statement, to say what didn't need to be said, or say what everybody knew, he was just slowing down what had to happen, because the emotion needed to come out.

Eventually, we did get out on to the pitch to receive the urn. The celebrations kicked in, the Champagne was flying, the cigars were out, we were having a great time, and then someone came over from the mayor of London's office, saying we were going on a celebratory bus trip round the capital the next morning.

There'd been rumours all day about it. I just laughed at him. I couldn't stop. "You're joking! The state we could potentially be in!" To me, it had 'massive fuck-up' written all over it. "Well, you're going to have to take us as we are. We can't be clean shaven, suited and booted, stone cold sober," I said.

The mayor, Ken Livingstone, probably knew fuck-all about cricket but thought it would be good for a bit of feelgood factor – get them on a bus, take them round, and listen to them say how nice the politicians are.

It was bullshit.

Still, there was some time to kill before we appeared in our very own episode of *On The Buses*. After a lap of honour where, as well as them cheering us, we could show our appreciation of a public which had urged us on all summer, we sat in the dressing room and drank with the Aussies, just as we had at Edgbaston, Old Trafford and Trent Bridge.

At half past 10 on that last night, half our lads were in their dressing room, and half of theirs in ours. Two teams together, two teams that had just put on a spectacle for the cricketing world, but you'd be hard pressed to know which was the winning side.

It was just two groups of players sitting together with great respect for each other. I remember talking to Ricky about golf! Well, the cricket had finished, I suppose!

I also spent time with Lee, Katich, Gillespie and Kasper, basically the lads I'd got to know through county cricket. It was an incredible few hours, time just for us, the people who'd been at the very epicentre of this most incredible of experiences, to sit and reflect. We talked about anything but cricket – what golf courses they'd played on while they were here, what football matches they'd seen. In 2009, when they played at Durham I took half the Australian team to a match at Newcastle. Those are the kind of conversations you have. We're human beings as well as cricketers.

That dressing room was a good place to be, and when the Aussie bus came at 11 I couldn't have been more disappointed. I could have sat there all night in my whites. If it had all finished there, that would have been great.

All through that series I didn't meet any bad Australians.

They played a tough game, but they played a respectful game. If one of ours scored a hundred, there was a clap and a handshake, a respectful acknowledgement to the game. Yes, there were words said, and the gamesmanship that came with them, but we all did that. They could have seen the series differently, complained, particularly about the umpires. I don't know what Damien Martyn had done to the ICC umpiring panel but he got some shockers. Steve Bucknor, what was he doing? He gave him out twice LBW when the deflections weren't even little – they were massive.

Billy Bowden, meanwhile, was such an insecure character that if he gave one not out, and then you talked about how close it was, there was a very good chance you'd get the next one.

That might not sound great, but at the time those umpires were there to be got at. Is that right? Is it wrong? Neither – it's sport. You do whatever you can to get the correct result for you, to get your team on the front foot, and the final decision is up to the umpires. No-one has made them do anything.

It's their decision. They don't tell me how to bowl the ball any more than I tell them how to run the game but if there's a chance of helping me get the next wicket, then I'll take it.

When we got back to the hotel, all the lads were wanting to go out to a club. Great, if that's what you want to do. But I didn't, and neither did Fred. We stayed in the bar. My brothers, my dad, my kids, Hayley, were all there. Same with Fred. All our friends were there, like Neil Fairbrother, and Piers Morgan was there as well.

Even so, somebody managed to get a couple of pictures which found their way into the papers the next day. I didn't particularly like that. We had deliberately decided to stay inside out the way. Once you're out in public that's different. In the hotel it was supposed to just be guests of the team.

As the night went on, the lads started coming back, drifting in and out of the bar. People went to bed, but nobody could sleep. Tres came in with the papers at about five o'clock – every single one carried a front page picture of us celebrating on the Oval pitch. In the end, about seven, I was beginning to nod off.

Fred, however, was still going strong, throwing shoes around, the odd headlock, generally being Fred. I thought, 'I'm going to have to get away'. I went upstairs and tried to have half an hour, because I knew we had to be back down for 9.30. It was about nine that

I received word from the top brass that I had to go and get Fred.

I thought there'd be no way of waking him. I needn't have worried, he was still sitting in the bar – cigar, pina colada, glass of Champagne. He'd got his feet up, totally chilled and relaxed.

Honestly, I wanted to leave him. All I could think was, 'Why are we doing this?' I just wanted to pull a seat up and join him. I wanted to say, "Look, we're not going anywhere." After what we'd been through as a team, I just wanted to sit there. I didn't want to be paraded.

We managed to get Fred upstairs to his room and Rachael got him dressed. The rest of the lads were mingling round reception, kids were flying around, wives, girlfriends, mums and dads were all congratulating each other, and rightly so – they went through it as much as we did.

When Andrew Strauss got a hundred at Old Trafford, the camera went on to where the families were. His wife, Ruth, was on her feet clapping, as was Hayley, Rachael Flintoff, Geraint's partner, Jen, Hayley Trescothick and Nichola Vaughan.

They're involved as well, massively. Good days, bad days, we're going back to them. Good days, bad days, we take it out on them. That's why they had to be on the bus. There was talk about it being just the players. No. There was talk of putting the women's team on with the men. No. Nothing against the England women's cricket team but I want my wife on the bus, not somebody else.

Before we got on the open-top bus, we took a coach to Mansion House, the official residence of the mayor.

Fred had just started to drop off at exactly the time when he needed to wake up. Hoggy and Simon were the same. All three were like bears with sore heads. Vaughany was saying to me, "Keep Fred out of the way. In fact, keep all the bowlers out of the way." But it wasn't as simple as that. As we staggered into Mansion House, Ken Livingstone came up to see Fred. He had the full mayoral regalia on – red coat, daft hat with a big feather, head to foot in all the kit.

Fred looked him up and down. "What the fuck have you come as?" he asked, diplomatically. Somebody pointed out to him that this was the mayor of London, the one who'd be providing free Champagne on the bus. "Pleased to meet you," said Fred.

When you see the famous footage of Fred slipping on the steps as we're coming out of Mansion House, and he points with his finger, that's at Ken Livingstone. What you can't hear is him saying, "Nice threads."

We got on the open-top bus and started touring the streets of London. In all honesty, as we set off, I didn't think anybody was going to turn up, but as word was getting back to us about the size of the crowds down the route, I decided this was a moment I wanted with my wife and my kids.

They wanted all the lads at the front but I sat with Hayley, Emily and Abbie at the back. My celebration was with my friends and my family, not with the rest of the lads. I'd just done that. I wanted this to be something different. I'd celebrated like an idiot during the night and now this was something we, as a family, were never going to forget.

Even though I didn't think the bus tour was appropriate at that time, I knew that, as a family, it was going to blow us away. I wanted to take it all in with them. Abbie was asking, "Daddy, what are all these people doing here?"

"You'll find out in years to come," I said.

It was brilliant. People were up lampposts, hanging out of windows. We knew we'd achieved something, but didn't realise how big this thing was. When you're caught up in the bubble, you don't understand what's going on outside of it.

It was massive, mega, all the way to Trafalgar Square where, we discovered, we were expected to go on stage to be interviewed. "No! I don't want to be interviewed. I can't speak!" I was standing next to Hoggy and Ashley Giles. We were all thinking the same thing – 'Just Kev, Fred and Vaughan – don't ask the rest of us anything!' Fred, naturally, was straight in there. When the microphone came to him, he thought this was his chance to be Elvis in front of a ready made crowd of 50,000.

He was just starting on Suspicious Minds when someone turned the microphone off.

The bus trip, this great public spectacle, would have hurt me if I was Australian. That series was played so well by both teams that to disrespect one of them so badly was awful. It wasn't something we needed and having played seven or eight weeks of unbelievable toe-to-toe cricket, to rub their noses in it when they hadn't even left the country I thought was poor. I really did. Fair enough, we hadn't won the Ashes for 20 years, and we were going to celebrate, but the bus trip was uncalled for.

There were two teams playing on that pitch. Two teams who'd produced a series like no other, one that will never be repeated. So for one of them to then have this shoved in their face, I thought was terrible.

As it happened, it hurt them so much they went and got their game together and rubbed our noses in it big time next time we met.

I enjoyed the bus trip because I was sharing something with my wife and family, but I didn't enjoy what it stood for.

Underneath, as we were going round Downing Street, Mansion House and Lord's I didn't feel comfortable because I couldn't help thinking it wasn't really for us. It was for other people in other ways, other people were benefiting from us. It would have been better to have left it a few days. When it was announced we'd be receiving honours for our performance, that felt like an achievement. We were getting rewarded for what we'd done. The bus trip, though, we weren't getting rewarded, we were getting paraded. There's a significant difference and it didn't sit very well.

We were invited to Downing Street, but we were there for nothing more than a photo opportunity with Tony Blair.

They couldn't get us in and out of there quick enough. They wanted us off the bus, in, out, bang. That was it. We weren't there to celebrate, we were being used. We had other ideas. If we were going to be invited to Number 10 then we wanted a couple of drinks and a look round. Even then, the politics didn't stop. I was sat on a swing in the garden when the sports minister, Tessa Jowell, collared me.

She was on about the Zimbabwe trip the year before and whether the government should have pulled us out. It was the last thing I needed at the time. I was about 14 hours drunk. I was sat on the swings, Hoggy was half asleep on the swing next to me, Fred was half asleep on the slide and Simon had decided he wanted a go on the trampoline. It's hardly *Question Time* is it?

One thing that didn't happen was somebody weeing in the garden. That was somebody in a political publicity machine asking, "How do we make this travel a bit further?" Stirring up a story about a, conveniently unidentified, England cricketer taking a piss in the Prime Minister's garden was one way of doing it.

It was originally just orange juice and water at Downing Street, but Vaughany always says he got some scruffy little teenager to go and sort us out some beer.

That, of course, was Euan, Tony Blair's lad. By the time we got the lids off, we were leaving anyway. I did get the chance to speak to Tony, but I've no idea what was said. I do, though, remember Hoggy calling him a knob. That was the grand finale of the visit. We were standing outside the door of Number 10 for the big photo opportunity in front of a line of snappers about a hundred yards long. Out came Tony Blair. He shook hands with Vaughany, looked at KP's hair in amazement and then positioned himself next to Hoggy. Now the person you don't want to stand next to, sober or drunk, when he's in one of his moods, is Hoggard. Tony piped up, in a smiley way, "I wonder what all these photographers are doing here?"

Hoggy just turned and came out with it. "For a picture of you, you knob!"

We didn't know whether to laugh or cry. There's a picture of Tony Blair where he looks like he's got a hot chip in his mouth. His jaw is hanging open. Back on the bus, we said to Hoggy, "What did you say that for?"

"Well," he replied. "Because he is."

The people at Number 10 must have been thinking, 'Who are these lot?' But if you ask a coachload of blokes who've been drinking for 14 hours round to your house, that's what you're going to get.

The final stop was at Lord's. It was just more meeting and greeting, but by then we were all bushed – there's a great picture of about six of us asleep on a bench.

From there a lot of the lads were off on trains home, but a few of us had to go back on a coach to get our kit from the hotel. On the way we'd been asked to sign souvenir shirts, but in no time Fred fell asleep on the back seat – and he takes some waking up.

Trust me, I've had to do it many times! It was the first time he'd been to sleep since before the final day's play had started. He was gone for all money. I slapped him a few times, nothing. Slapped him a bit harder, nothing. I was just reaching for the emergency hammer when somebody handed me the marker pen for the signing. I got the pen, looked at it, and then looked at Freddie's face.

A few people were egging me on a bit so I just started drawing. I thought it would be OK. Across his cheeks, I wrote, 'Ashes Winner 2005', before drawing some glasses on and colouring in his chin.

Then I wrote 'TWAT' on his forehead, and 'CUNT' down his nose.

So far, so good.

But when we got off the bus, all of a sudden there was a cameraman there. He had a girl with him, who, we later found out, was from the *Daily Sport*. She was going to run up to one of us, bare her breasts and the snapper would get the picture.

Seeing Fred's newly applied adornments, however, the photographer abandoned that plan and thought, 'Kerching!'

In the end, because Fred was a columnist for *The Sun*, they bought the image to keep it out of the papers, before using it a few days later when he did his feel-good piece about the celebrations.

I've apologised many times since, and he's got me back on loads of occasions. He's pulled all the handles off my bags once – five bags, trying to get them from terminal to terminal. Other times he's cut the legs off my trousers – one 32-inch, the other 36. To be fair, I've done the same to him. Pinching his dress shirts so he has to come down to a dinner naked but for a tie and a blazer. By way of retaliation, he'd put big buckets of iced water above my door.

This, though, I could see had the potential to be a monumental fuck-up. It was too late, but as soon as I saw the photographer I chucked my blazer over Fred's head and pushed him into the hotel lobby. From there, I steered him into the lift and took him upstairs to Rachael. She opened the door, took one look at him, turned to me and asked, in a fairly restrained manner all things considered, "Harmy, what have you done to him?"

Apparently, he went in the bathroom and spent five minutes wiping the mirror before he realised it was on his face. Fred got me back by telling his own version of the story on Jonathan Ross. "He's a bit dyslexic," he told Jonathan. "He wrote 'TWIT' on my forehead and 'CAN'T' on my nose." I thought, 'Yes, very good Andrew.'

Arguably, we're still celebrating that victory now, because it was a monumental series that changed English cricket forever, not only putting it on a standing it had never enjoyed before, but displaying a blueprint for success, a blueprint for togetherness.

Even now, when I talk about the 2005 side with Neil Fairbrother, he says how we were different with each other than we were with other people. There was a deep connection. That group needed everyone, it didn't rely on just one or two people. Everyone knew their job and everyone did their job. We were allowed to be who we were, and nobody took any liberties.

The spirit of the group made us what we were. Vaughany wasn't bothered if Trescothick got a hundred, Trescothick wasn't bothered if Strauss got a hundred, none of the five bowlers could care who got the wickets – "Let's just get them and get off."

It's always easier when you're winning, and that's what we had, a winning group. There weren't people trying to protect their places. Instead, we were enjoying each other's company, enjoying each other's success. We worked hard for each other and when you do that as a team you're halfway there. At the same time, whenever we needed our big players to stand up, more often than not they did. Everybody produced a bit of magic. Even Colly, with his 10 runs at the Oval, used up 50 balls and 70 minutes at a pivotal moment when we were in the shit.

Straussy's one-handed diving catch of Gilchrist at Trent Bridge was another one – we just had something special in us when it mattered. To have come out on the winning side makes me proud, but just to have been involved in that side makes me equally so.

Never did I forget, though, the earlier guys – Butcher, Stewart, Thorpe, Nasser and Gough – who'd helped us reach the pinnacle. They were so pleased for us when we won in 2005.

There was no sense of bitterness in the success we were having – these cheeky little players who came into the dressing room and chucked their stuff everywhere, getting pissed, missing curfews.

They'd been through so many hard times against Australia and now, finally, we'd beaten them. If I was one of those five, seeing us walking round the Oval with the Ashes, I'd have been thinking, 'I helped that group. I was part of it.'

I hope they did, because it wouldn't have happened without them. They took us from the bad old days of the '90s to winning the Ashes.

Thank you.

19

DOWNHILL

"He looked at me. 'I'm struggling a bit.' And then the whole lot came tumbling out"

In our joy and jubilation at winning the Ashes, there was one thing none of us could have ever appreciated – the West Indies tour was the start of something special, and the Oval was the end of it.

The team of 2005 would never play together again.

Within weeks of scaling the heights in London, we were on our backsides in Multan. Michael Vaughan's knee had sent him home early, Simon Jones never made it on to the plane and we'd just capitulated to Pakistan in our second innings in a way that made a mockery of all we'd achieved.

The only saving grace was that me and Fred had inter-connecting rooms. We used to get a lot of stick off the other lads for doing this, but I hated being away from home so needed someone around me all of the time, and he hated sleeping in the dark, so we'd leave my toilet light on and it would give him just enough light to get by. The others thought we were odd but, for me, it was like touring with a big brother, like being with family. The only time people were jealous of it was in Multan. The hotel was like *Carry On Up The Khyber*. It wasn't finished and there was a row of tiles from the front door to reception to the lift, corridors and rooms.

At check-in, the receptionist asked, "Do you want hot water or air conditioning?" The other players weren't desperately pleased at the choice, but me and Fred high-fived one another. "We'll have one of each."

Sharing in this way was something we did all over the world. Once I was writing my column for a Sunday paper with the great old journalist, Reggie Hayter, and all of a sudden the connecting door opened. Fred, without realising I was with someone, shouted, "Hi honey, I'm home!" Reg nearly fell of his chair! But that's how it was. We were like brothers. We argued all the time, more on whose turn it was to get something from the fridge or what we were going to watch on the telly, than anything else. We used to wrestle occasionally. I bit him once. He had me in a headlock – I was turning blue. The only thing I could do was bite him on the arm. The mark was there for days.

With the on-field stuff not going great in Pakistan, and the off-field entertainment options not being huge, amusement had to be found in other ways, such as the press and players' quiz night. Me and Fred weren't really big on quizzes, the Renaissance artists of 17th century Belgium were never really our thing, but there were a few beers knocking around, so down we went, late of course.

Bumble was giving out the prizes at the end, and after taking the piss out of us for about 10 minutes, he gave us a booby prize. It was two wailing alarm clocks shaped like mosques, one green, one blue, and when they went off they belted out the sound of the call to prayer.

"Thanks David, that's great," we said, all the time thinking, 'What are we going to do with these?' As we were on our way back to our rooms, we saw Bumble go into the restaurant with Paul Allott.

"Right," we said, his 10-minute piss-take still ringing in our ears. "We'll have him."

We got into his room, set the blue one for 4am and put it under his bed. Then we set the other for 5am and put it behind the telly. Next morning, it became apparent they'd gone off as planned. Bumble came stamping into our room. "You pair of twats!" Already we were pissing ourselves. "My room's also got an inter-connecting door, only in my case it's got a Pakistani businessman on the other side." This set us off even more, but he didn't seem to share the humour.

"It took me ages to find those bloody alarm clocks," he spluttered. "The first one, I thought it were the telly. I was pressing all the buttons, trying to turn it off when it wasn't even on in the first place. The man next door was braying on the wall going mad. By the time I'd found it and got back into bed, the other one was going off. This bloke was going spare. I've had him at my door this morning trying to start a fight because he had no sleep."

Me and Fred were crying with laughter when he told us what had happened.

Some way removed from the heroics of the summer, Pakistan saw us lose both the Test and one-day series. At least me and Fred had a slightly shorter tour than the others as we'd spent the first 10 days in the slightly homelier surroundings of Sydney after being picked for the World XI to play Australia in a one-off Test. Graeme Smith was the captain.

"Forget what you thought about me when you played against me," he told the rest of us. "Judge me when you play with me." He was spot on, because he was a twat to play against.

As person, though, Graeme was a great, fantastic man and a great leader. KP, however, who'd been picked for the one-day stuff, couldn't agree. He'd had a falling out with the South African captain over his defection to us.

At that time, it's totally fair to say they hated each other. The night before the game we were sitting with Graeme having dinner in the MCG dining hall. He'd just left his seat for a moment when Kev came in. Pointing at the empty seat, Fred shouted up, "Here, Kev! Come and sit here!" Graeme didn't see what had happened until he came back. Fred did the intro-ductions. "Kev, Graeme – Graeme, Kev."

"Fred, you dick," I said, but actually it was quite good. It broke the ice between them a little bit and nowadays they are really close and get on famously.

Shoaib Akhtar was 12th man. The day of the game he came into the dressing room looking sorry for himself. He was wanting to go back to the hotel, saying he didn't feel very well.

What he meant was he had a hangover. He was moaning and moaning. He was clearly going to be hopeless if he had to play, prompting Fred to say, "Look Shoaib, there's no point looking like Tarzan and bowling like Jane."

It was a good line, but what Fred had forgotten was that, three weeks later, we were heading straight into the backyard of the Rawalpindi Express. He bowled the speed of light for a month.

He knocked Fred's stumps over and ran down the wicket beating his chest and doing a Tarzan impression.

The World XI game was never going to work as a contest. The Aussies were a team. We were just people thrown together for 10 days. Inzamam had a terrible decision, given out LBW when it wouldn't have hit another set.

When he came back into the dressing room, we were all, "Hard luck Inzy, bad decision." He just smiled. He wasn't bothered, and he wasn't the only one. It was 10 days in Sydney, a few grand in the pocket, and off we go. It was a shambles, an exhibition match.

Back home, the highlight of the summer was the match against Pakistan at Old Trafford when I took 11-76, the best figures on the ground since Jim Laker took 19 wickets when crushing the Aussies in 1956.

With the bat in my hand, however, I was joined by an unusual partner at the crease. Stark naked he was – and before you ask, it wasn't Fred, he was out injured for this game. It's the one and only incident I ever had with a streaker. I'd describe him, but I don't remember much about his face.

He came haring on, stinking of drink, he jumped over the stumps at one end and then came and stood with me at the other. He didn't say anything, so I thought I'd break the awkwardness. "All right?" I said. "You could have brought us a pint."

Still nothing, which surprised me – he had a few seconds before a meathead in a high-vis came and rugby tackled him to the ground. You have to hand it to him, it's a brave man who takes his clothes off in Manchester in July.

Something rather more serious and with somewhat deeper repercussions happened during that Pakistan series. After the one-day game against Pakistan in Bristol, Tres came to my room.

I wondered what he wanted because, while I respected him hugely, we weren't close. Also, he lived not far from Bristol so he wasn't staying in the hotel anyway. He came in, and just sat on the sofa for a few minutes. "Tres," I said. "What's up?"

He looked at me. "I'm struggling a bit." And then the whole lot came tumbling out. Tres had disappeared early on the India tour and it had been obvious to the lads that he was in a bad place mentally, but I'd never realised quite how much he'd suffered down the years.

It turned out that when I was pouring my heart out in notebooks in South Africa in 2004, scared stiff of the feelings of desperation that were ripping me apart, he was doing exactly the same.

When I was gazing at photos of my children, wondering what they'd look like when I got home, and if they'd even recognise me, so was he. When I was sinking into an abyss in the home summer of 2004, exactly the same had happened to him in 2005.

We'd never had that buddiness to exchange any thoughts, to take some heart that we weren't alone – two successful sportsmen being ripped apart by what lurked between the ears. Tres had kept his problems better hidden than me, but he'd come to me now because he knew I had similar issues. He needed to sit and talk to someone who understood. Not someone who'd utter platitudes, pat him on the head and send him on his way, but someone who could comprehend every pain he was going through, and someone who knew easy solutions would never be forthcoming.

We sat and talked. He was visibly upset, talking about how low he felt, the issues he'd suffered over that winter, the loneliness, the fear of being alone, the guilt of being away from his family when they needed him. He spoke of how it made him feel physically ill, how the feelings would consume him with a fear like he'd never felt before, how anxiety would overwhelm him and how hard it was to find an escape. Like me, he was realising his ambition, doing the best job in the world, but there were times when he reached for his whites and he might as well have been reaching for a prison uniform. Our jailer was the relentless stream of bleakness in our minds.

Lack of stability, a sense of not being in control of our own destinies, affected us both. As cricketers, where we were and when we were there was entirely out of our hands. When we went to India after Pakistan, for instance, I didn't want to do the one-dayers, because Isabel was being born and Hayley had gone through a tough pregnancy. I wanted to be there at the birth. I didn't want to take any chances. I told Vaughany before they picked the India touring squad I didn't want to be part of the one-dayers – "Fine mate, it'll be all right" – and then when the squad was announced, I'm in it.

"Mick, what's going on?" I asked. "Don't worry, mate, we'll sort it," he promised. "We won't pick you – we'll let you go."

Before the first Test, though, Vaughany got injured and went home. The good thing was that Fred was put in charge, and he knew how I felt about the one-dayers. He knew what was going on. However, when, towards the end of the Test series, the team management had a meeting about the limited overs stuff, Fred came to see me.

"Harmy, we've got a problem here."

"What's the matter. What is it?"

"Fletch thinks you're here for the whole tour, including the one-dayers." I stormed across to see Fletcher. "I've spoken to Grav," he told me. "And he knows nothing about it."

In the end, we had to get Vaughany on the phone – and Grav completely backtracked on everything he'd told me, saying there had never been any consideration of me missing the one-dayers. By that time, my body was hanging off and my shins were sore. I stayed for the first three games and went home.

Knowing Tres's mental issues – and with other players suffering injuries of a more physical nature – during the summer of 2006, the team was looking less and less like the one which had performed heroics just a year earlier.

Vaughany's ongoing knee issues meant he was an absentee while Fred missed a lot of the action with an ankle injury. Ashley Giles was another long-term casualty, this time with a hip problem. Simon Jones, meanwhile, was going through a hellish time trying to get back to what he was in 2005. I felt for him – he'd seen more of the surgeon's knife than the cricket pitch.

With the Ashes round the corner, it was clear this would be a very different prospect to last time. The togetherness, the confidence, the never-say-die spirit had disappeared down a maze of hospital corridors and into umpteen operating theatres, never to be found again.

In the absence of Fred, Andrew Strauss took over against Pakistan, again doing a decent job. It would come down to a straight choice between them as to who led the team in Australia.

There was definitely a sense of some people wanting Strauss and some wanting Flintoff. Obviously, I wanted Fred. I thought he was a good choice, big stature, big character. When he finally got the nod, some elements of the media people started putting it round that the only reason he'd been chosen was because the selectors thought he would get the best out of me. That's bollocks.

He was made captain because England felt they needed a big man, a passionate man, to front the team in Australia.

The powers-that-be saw what Fred had done to the Aussies in England and the big talismanic figure he was, and that's what they wanted him to be in Australia. But it wasn't just, "He's our big figure, he's our hero, let's stick him out there as captain." There was a lot more to it than that. Fred had captained many teams in his career and had a very good cricket brain.

A lot of the success England had enjoyed had come as a direct result of Fred's thinking. The problem was Fred wanted to beat Australia by himself. He thought he was invincible – 'I'll hit them for six. I'll bowl them out. I'll be the big man for England.'

Unfortunately for him, the team behind him wasn't good enough, and over the weeks to come there would be tests and Tests that none of us could have ever considered.

20

THE BRISBANE BALL

*"He catches the ball. I look at him, he looks at me.
He doesn't know what to do any more than I do"*

The Gabba, Brisbane - Thursday, November 23, 2006

I'm stood at the top of my mark.

Before me, in brilliant sunshine, is the Gabba, and I'm feeling the heat. Not so much the heat of the sun, rather the heat of expectation. The hype leading up to this moment has been a never ending storm of craziness, and I'm right in the eye. The ball is in my hand. It's up to me to bowl the first delivery of an Ashes series that's been talked up, pontificated over and bullshitted about since I bowled the final ball of the last one.

That day seems a long way away now.

That person seems a long way away now.

I walked out to bowl those four balls at the Oval a certain Ashes winner. Now I've never felt less certain about anything.

I didn't have a problem with any of this until about 12 hours ago. Then, suddenly, last night, alone in my hotel room, it hit me – 'I'm not sure I'm ready here.' I couldn't stop thinking about how terrible my preparation had been. My side went on the morning of the last warm-up game in Adelaide and I had to pull out.

For someone who needs to play to keep ticking over, it was the last thing I needed. It knocked me back. I couldn't miss a week and then rock up, everything hunky-dory for the next game. The biggest Test match since the Oval in 2005 was just around the corner, and I was fighting to be fit. In fact, at that point, I wasn't thinking so much about missing the next game, I was thinking more along the lines of, 'That's it, Ashes over.' I'd hardly bowled. There was a part of me which said, 'I'll do it, I'll just turn up', but in the back of my mind I knew I was under-prepared, big time. We are normally undercooked as bowlers on tour anyway, but I was even more so. This was all sitting, nagging, at the back of my mind. Even then, though, I'd slept all right, and actually got up this morning feeling OK.

I was nervous, yes, but that's only to be expected – that comes with any Test match – but when we walked out on to the pitch I was fine. We were all pumped up. "Come on," said Fred. "Let's do this!" We'd waited a long time for this thing to arrive – "Let's get this show on the road!" Fred tosses me the ball...

Make no mistake, Australia is a great place to go.

Go to the Academy or on an A-tour and you only see the best of it, but the Ashes tour is a hard one because you get stick wherever you go. And not just from the crowds or people in the street, but organised stick.

We got drug-tested at 6am on the first day we were there. Jet-lagged, five or six of us had gone for a very early run down to the Sydney Opera House. We ran back up the hill, into breakfast, and there's the drugs people. That was no coincidence. They were obviously trying to rattle us from the word go.

There was only half a dozen of us up, but the rule is that once they've done one they have to do the whole lot. All of a sudden the lads who weren't so badly jet-lagged and were trying to sleep were getting woken up, people banging on their doors. I'd been there four years previously, so I knew what Australia was like. I had first-hand experience – and it was telling me we've got three more months of this.

Next day, after finishing practice, a few of us got changed and headed out for something to eat. We ended up in a restaurant in a mall, half a dozen of us – Gilo, Tres, Strauss, Fred, Hoggy, and me. All the time we were there we could see photographers clicking away outside. Next day, front page of the papers, there we were. Six England players eating lunch in a restaurant – fascinating. The scrutiny was constant, and I felt, even that early in the trip, that Tres was finding the whole experience particularly hard to handle, like people were getting at him. To me, it was part of the catalyst for Tres ending up on a very dark road indeed.

Not long after, we had a warm-up game against a Prime Minister's XI at Canberra and Tres sat in front of me on the bus on the way back to Sydney. Shaun Tait was bowling at the speed of light and Tres lasted just six balls. "I couldn't see it," he told me. He didn't mean he'd been beaten for pace, he meant he literally couldn't see the ball, like his brain wouldn't focus on it. We were talking quietly and he looked upset. I knew then he wasn't going to last. I remember thinking, 'What are we going to do without Tres?' Immediately, I felt bad. I knew that wasn't the right thing to be thinking. I should have been thinking more about what a bad way he was in.

It all finally unravelled a few days later when we played New South Wales at the Sydney Cricket Ground. Tres had already left the pitch after lunch for a toilet break and then I did the same.

As I did so, I could see someone waving by the dressing room, as if to indicate something unusual or an emergency was happening. When I walked in, I could see Tres was upset – more than upset, utterly distraught. He was sitting, with his head in his hands, in his England whites, sobbing his heart out.

He'd gone. I got upset for him because I knew exactly what he was going through, and I knew also that I could do nothing about it. I'd been in his shoes. I'd sat in that position he was in. At that point, no matter what anybody says or does, it doesn't get through. It doesn't register. It's just you and a big hole. Your whole life is disintegrating and there's nothing you can do about it. I couldn't say anything to him, the doctor couldn't do anything for him.

The only thing I had to offer was to sit next to him for a couple of minutes and put my arm on his shoulder. "I know what you're going through, mate," I told him.

Outside I could still hear the game going on. I patted him on the back. "I can feel your pain." But I knew nothing I could say or do was going to help this situation. Tres was taken out of the main dressing room and into the adjoining physio's room where Fletcher had been lying in the dark because he had a migraine. I said to the doctor, "The only thing that can help right now is for him to go home. You can't keep him here – he has to go home."

There was a bit of a discussion about his wife coming across.

I was sat there shaking my head. "He's gone. He's got to go. Not for England, not for anyone else – for his sanity he has to go home." That was what disappointed me. People were contemplating other courses of action. I can understand them doing that from a team point of view, but they knew this guy had a mental health issue, they knew he'd had a struggle. It was staring them in the face – he had to go home. And thankfully that's what he did.

To actually see Marcus disappear down that hole was horrendous. People say it's only a game, and it is, I agree with that, but not to the people in the dressing room, especially on an Ashes trip.

I fully believe Marcus would have been trying his hardest to find a way of staying on that tour. I have no doubt in that whatsoever. But seeing and knowing what he was going through, I'd have been the same – "I'm not going, I'm not going. I'm strong-minded, it's not going to beat me." But it had beaten him. At that point, it had won. He had to go.

Given time, Tres would see it was his international career that was ending, not his world. He could go home, have four months rest, and then start playing cricket again for Somerset. He didn't have to contemplate going on tours with England again, making overseas trips. He could still have a good life, a good career, and that's what he's done, and I'm over the moon. What he's done is a massive inspiration for people with mental health issues.

Yes, it beat him that afternoon in Sydney, but it hasn't beaten him in the long-term.

As I run in, I can't escape the enormity of the situation. I feel not just 25,000 pairs of eyes on me in the stadium but those of friends, family, everyone I know, at home. This can't be just any other ball. I've got to bowl that million

dollar fast ball that everybody wants, that everybody has been pumping me up for.

This is what my brain is telling me, but there's no communication with the body. I realise too late that I'm trying too hard, so hard that all the basics have gone out the window. I'm at the crease, and I'm here way before I should be. I'm pulling my left side out too soon. The timings are all wrong, the mechanics are a mess. The ball is coming out the side of my hand, my direction has totally gone, this is not going to be good. It's slewing off course, veering now.

It's not going to Geraint, it's going wider and wider, it's going to Fred at second slip.

He catches the ball. I look at him, he looks at me.

He doesn't know what to do any more than I do.

In the end he doesn't say anything, he just claps as the ball begins its journey round the field and back to myself. A few of the lads are smiling and laughing, trying to make a joke of it. Hoggy has just finished running in from fine leg — "Yes, great start!" He can't understand why the ball has ended up at slip and nobody's cheering.

I know myself why nobody is cheering. It's because I've just bowled the worst opening ball in the history of Ashes cricket.

After Brisbane, my own battle was to come back from a ball that, despite all I've achieved, would, in the eyes of some, define my career.

I can't deny it's one of the things I'll always be best remembered for. Do I mind talking about it? No. Is there anything good to come out of it? No. Is there anything bad to come out of it? Even more no. It's one ball out of the whole trip. One ball when I tried too hard. When people say that ball set the tone for the series, that's bollocks. These are the same people who said I set the tone in England when I hit three batsmen at Lord's on that opening morning – we got beat by an innings and a 100-odd runs. That ball in Brisbane didn't set the tone. We weren't good enough to beat Australia whether that ball happened or not.

After I let that ball go, I knew two certain things – the first was that I was stood in the middle of a cricket ground with nowhere to hide, with 25,000 laughing at me and, secondly, I had to turn around, go back to my mark and do it again. And again. And again.

At that specific moment I wanted the ground to open up and let me drop into it, but that is the life of a bowler for you. Play a bad shot as a batsman, nick one off, and you're gone. Bowl a bad ball and you've got to turn round and do it again. You've got to keep doing it and doing it, and you've got to stew on it as well.

Initially I was just annoyed with myself. 'I should have eased my way into it,' I told myself. 'Found a way to get the ball down the other end, and built on it from there.' But I also know there's times when you get nervous, there's times when you forget where you are. You forget what you are, and who you are. And I think that's what happened.

The physical side effect is to lose control, but when I try to think back over it again, I can't because, mentally, it's all a blur. It's a weird feeling, the strangest sensation and, at the time, I didn't know whether to laugh or cry.

I managed to get through the rest of the over and even bowled a couple of good balls in amongst the shit, and then I had to go and stand on the boundary. People think I copped a lot of abuse stood out there at fine leg but I didn't hear a thing. Hayley could have been standing there shouting her support, my mum and dad, brothers and sisters, it wouldn't have mattered because I was shell-shocked more than anything. I remember that after six hours anguishing on the side of the field, I went back to the hotel. My mum and dad were there, the kids, Hayley, and we went down to the pool for a swim.

We messed about for a while as I tried to take my mind off what had happened and then headed back to the room. I called room service and put the TV on, making sure it wasn't an Australian channel – they were showing my ball again and again on loop.

Eventually we settled on Sky News, the UK version and there it was again. "England start embarrassingly in Australia," the announcer said, as they trawled over the day's events.

From there, they went straight into another story – "Two soldiers have been killed in Afghanistan." I couldn't believe what I was seeing. "What is this world coming to?" I asked Hayley. "Two soldiers have died, and they're talking about a ball in a cricket match."

Yes, cricket is news, but so is somebody's life.

Suddenly, everything was in perspective. That ball, the day I'd had, it all got context. I crawled into bed, but I couldn't sleep because I was thinking of those soldiers. I got up at one point and started cuddling the kids and I was thinking of how wrong it was that a cricket ball was more important than two lives.

I knew we were in for a rough ride in Australia, it was obvious we were no match for them, and I also knew that it was this night, and what I had heard of these poor soldiers, that would get me through. They have given their lives for their country. I was playing cricket – I'm only bowling a fucking ball.

We eventually lost by 277 runs in Brisbane. By the end of play on the fourth day we were five down chasing what seemed like a thousand runs. The game wasn't so much gone as three miles down in the Pacific Ocean. That night I went out to meet some family and friends. Neil Fairbrother was with me and we sat and had a lovely conversation with Richie Benaud before we left the hotel at about half past 10, just as Duncan Fletcher was coming in.

After what had happened to me during the game, I was thinking it was probably my last day on the trip. "They can't pick me again after that," I told Neil. "I'm going to bat tomorrow and then I'll be going home." But the plane ticket home never came, and when I look back at it, what happened afterwards was probably one of my greatest achievements.

Whether I should have stayed in the team or not, whether I was picked because Flintoff looked after me or not, I played every minute from that Brisbane ball on. Some people might not have got to the end of that first day. The South African trip in 2004 came to the fore in offering a safety net. Knowing how bad I was feeling in South Africa meant I could say to myself, 'If I can get through that I can get through anything.'

I understand that ball was a big thing in cricket.

I've seen Brett Lee, Morne Morkel, bowl wider balls than mine was but that was in the middle of a game – the situation I was in, everyone had been waiting and waiting for that game for months and, for me, it's something that will always be there too. That ball affected the way I started my first bowling spell every game after that. It was a mental bruise which would reappear every time. It sat in my head to the point where it became almost part of the routine. First ball of a game – top of my mark – Brisbane ball – off we go. Even now, if I started bowling, that ball would be there. It was a reference my brain felt obliged to make. It didn't then affect my performance on the field, because I also remembered that newsreel. I was playing cricket. It wasn't the be all and end all. It is for some people, they're obsessed by it.

Perhaps they're the ones who fall by the wayside. There's a reason I got more than a 100 England caps in all forms and took the amount of wickets I did – because I wasn't obsessed by it.

One thing that did bug me was when Fletcher, after he'd left the England set-up, claimed Flintoff threw me the ball first-up at Brisbane because I was his mate. I didn't quite understand that because I always bowled the first ball in England. But Duncan would say a lot after he left the England job.

A lot more than he ever said when he was in it actually.

Hoggy had a different way of referencing that delivery.

Next season, we were playing Yorkshire at Durham. He came out to bat while I was bowling and proceeded to take guard two yards outside leg stump with a big stupid grin on his face.

I ran up and, a bit like the delivery that hit Langer at Lord's, the ball was just back of a length and bounced on him.

It hit him flush on the glove and broke his thumb. I looked at him sheepishly as if to say, 'Are you all right?' He carried on batting. The next ball I aimed for the stumps. The way he was now, nursing a broken thumb, if it was on target he was out.

I thought I'd bowled him and was away celebrating, only to discover it had gone over the stumps by an inch. "Fuck me," I said to him. "How has that missed?"

He looked at me. "I don't know," he said. "I had my eyes closed."

21

DUNCAN DISORDERLY

"I just thought, 'Fuck it, I'm not standing for this.'
I let him have it big time. 'You're joking,' I told him.
'I batted at number nine when I'm not a number
nine, faced more balls than both wicket-keepers
combined, and now you're blaming my batting for
what's happened?'"

In my mind, it couldn't get any worse. So when they asked me if I wanted to play, felt able to play, in Adelaide, I said yes. As it turned out, I felt I bowled as well as I've ever bowled in my career. On a slow, dead wicket, I bowled good line, good length, and yet never got a wicket. If I'd bowled those areas in England, I'd have had a hatful.

We got off to a great start. Colly got a great double hundred and KP batted brilliantly for 158.

By the end of day two our mindset was that Brisbane had been like Lord's – we could put it to the back of our minds and get on and win this match. Having racked up 551-6 declared, at the very least we felt there was no way we could lose. The wicket was flat, dead, and no-one was spinning it either. Which makes what happened in our second innings something I still don't understand to this day. We just became totally bogged down. The run rate was two an over, if we'd upped it to 2.5 or three, they were out of the game.

We panicked, I think. There wasn't an instruction to go and bat like that. Even though McGrath and Warne bowled well, there was no reason for it on a flat wicket. But we lost a couple of wickets in the middle of the afternoon and it just seemed to knock our thought process. Added to that, the tail had lost its ability to score quick runs. All of a sudden we'd gone from scoring 550 in our first innings, and thinking there was only two possible outcomes in the game – win or draw – to them chasing 170 on a flat one.

They say Shane Warne always believed Australia could win, but I'm not sure even Warney thought they could be victorious from the position they were in. In fact, Australia didn't win it. England lost it.

Afterwards, in the dressing room, we were gone. There were a lot of similarities to Edgbaston. If we win, the momentum is ours and Australia start panicking. They win and they take the series 5-0. That's exactly what happened after Adelaide.

Confidence, demeanour, body language, everything, collapsed – as we sat in that dressing room, we knew we were not coming back from this. Everywhere I looked, there was disbelief. The batting unit that got us into the game arguably put us under pressure at the back end of it. At the same time, our bowling was toothless.

It wasn't like one could blame the other. It was the complete disintegration of the team. We were all saying the same thing – "How on earth did that just happen?" Those who were too struck dumb to talk were thinking the same thing.

We went up to Perth as low as we could possibly be. Factions were forming in the dressing room, people were withdrawing into their own groups and finding their own space. The blame game had started, the discussion as to whether Fred should ever have been captain was on.

There was a bit of whispering in the background, although people wouldn't say it around me because, as one of Fred's biggest mates and allies, they knew potentially what would happen.

Whereas in 2005, everyone in the group was together, now there were two here, three here, four there, and that doesn't help the team and the cause.

Because the families were there, getting the lads back together was very difficult. I'm all for having the families on tour. No-one is a bigger supporter of it than me. But it killed us in Australia in 2006 because, after those two bad defeats, it stopped the unity we needed.

The families came out just before the first Test and looking back I think that was a mistake. It's unusual for the families to be out that long but the players had insisted on it because it was such a lengthy trip. That Ashes tour was ridiculous because, yet again, we were going from Ashes to one-dayers to World Cup. The success of 2005 had made the playing group more powerful, allowing us to dictate the things we wanted, and the families was one of them. There's two ways to look at this situation. The families aren't there and the lads start taking it out on each other and making it worse. Or the team is brought closer together, the ones who are struggling for confidence start to feel better, and it's a help.

Here, I don't think having the families there helped because there was no going out for dinner and talking about the game, no popping into each other's hotel rooms down the corridor.

It was for the same reason I didn't spend as much time with Fred on that trip as I was used to. That was the only tour where we'd not had inter-connecting rooms so I wasn't having dinner with him every night, looking through the door and making sure that he was OK, just having a bit of conversation through the door – "What are you watching?" "Spoke to anybody?" "How's Rachael?" "Kids all right?"

If he was struggling, if he was down, that support mechanism from a mate wasn't there. That didn't mean I couldn't see the change in him as it went on. I could see, day by day, his head going down. He was struggling. He wanted to be this invincible man who took Australia on and won the Ashes for England – and the whole thing was falling down around him. I could have kept asking if he was OK, but he was always going to say, "Yes, I'm fine." He's a big lad, and he wanted to portray that he was strong. He *is* strong. He's one of the most resilient characters I ever played cricket with. But everybody has a breaking point.

If it hadn't been Perth after Adelaide they might have left me out, but because Perth is fast and bouncy, and it was a game we had to win, I played, and I did all right, taking 4-48 in the first innings. With the game in the balance, it was then that Adam Gilchrist came out and just erupted, smashing us all around the WACA to record the second fastest Test match century in history. It was some of the cleanest hitting I've ever seen.

As a bowler, it's an impossible situation. When somebody is in the zone like that, you're nothing more than a spectator. I was bowling it in a good place at speed and he was hitting it 10 rows back. Monty Panesar got the same treatment as I did.

He was throwing it higher, throwing it flatter, throwing it everywhere. It didn't matter – Gilchrist just kept belting it. It was amazing to watch.

There's not many times I've stood on the boundary, 6ft 5in, thinking, 'I'm not even in a catching position'. He wasn't hitting it close to being a catch, he was hitting it that far and that well. He ended up with 102 from 59 balls and that was it, Ashes gone. The series had barely started and it was all finished. In the space of 14 days' play we'd gone from Ashes heroes to down and outs staring down the barrel of 5-0.

You put on a brave face in those circumstances, make noises about clawing back some respectability with a couple of wins in the remaining matches but, in truth, you know it's gone. It doesn't rain in Australia so we're not going to grab a draw, and where a win comes from I do not know. We've scored 550, got beat, bowled Australia out for 200 and got beat.

Melbourne could only be damage limitation. We batted poorly but then had them 84-5 only for Hayden and Symonds to take the game away from us.

They stepped up to make sure England weren't going to get back in the series. The boot wasn't just well and truly on the other foot, it was standing on our necks.

Once the partnership started building and building, the confidence just drained out of us. We were rock bottom, and from there they just blew us away. We didn't even last three days. We'd stopped just losing and had become embarrassing. What do you say to the thousands of England fans who'd flown over to see that? I can only hope they had a better time on the beach than they did at the MCG.

The only memorable moment was Warne getting his 700th Test wicket. It was a privilege to be playing in the same game, as it was when McGrath got his 500th at Lord's in 2005.

They are two very special players – 1,200 Test wickets between them says it all. It shows why Australia were the greatest side in the world for so many years. Warne, for me, was the best who ever played the game, not only as a cricketer, but as a man.

Whatever the showman on the field, the chirping, the chippiness, always having something to say, I always saw him clap hundreds, shake someone's hand for doing well, always showing respect.

Even if he was looking down a barrel, he always acknowledged if someone had done well against him. Not only did he live his life hard and to the full, and play the game better and different to anyone else before or since, he respected the sport and the individuals in it.

He didn't think twice about telling you where to go or giving you a volley if he thought it was the right thing to do, but if somebody got a hundred or five wickets, as he walked past there'd be a shake of the hand, a "Well done, mate!" and that, for me, makes him even better.

I remember being interviewed at the end of the first day at Lord's in 2005, and he walked past – "Great bowling, Harmy."

He congratulated Fred on his hundred at Trent Bridge and did the same with KP at the Oval. He never did it for the cameras, he did it because it was how he was. Put him 22-yards away down a cricket pitch and he was a different man. He was tough to face. Boy, he was tough to face! He thought he had you every ball – and often he did with me!

When people said, "You've got to play the ball not the man", it was very difficult with Warne. It's difficult to ignore the man when the man won't shut up!

When you played against him, the dialogue was almost as good as the bowling. "Great leave, Harmy!" he'd say as you lunged forward and the ball missed your bat by a millimetre. "That's the fifth you've left like that this over." The dialogue and the bowling couldn't be separated, they were one and the same. All I could do was marvel at this ridiculous personality, this insane bundle of energy, with the aura to go with it.

Going into Sydney 4-0 down in an Ashes series was an all too familiar feeling for a few of us. Last time the Australians had taken their eye off the ball and let us sneak in for an unlikely win. That was never going to happen in this series. They were going to make sure we suffered for what had happened in England, and what better way than a whitewash? They wanted to rub our noses in it, and they did. And I would have been exactly the same in their shoes. At least we lasted into the fourth day while getting battered into submission.

To say it had been a tough tour would be an understatement. This time it was the Australians doing the lap of honour, the big celebrations.

All we could do was watch, a once proud group reduced to a shadow of its former self. In 2005, Australia had encountered us at our peak. The shame is that we couldn't sustain it for a long period. Instead, that team disintegrated. It was gone like a handful of dust. Vaughany's body packed up, but losing him wasn't as big a loss as losing Tres.

Vaughany's guidance was very good but he didn't score the volume of runs that we needed at the time. The way Tres got us off to starts, he put the opposition on the back foot every time. That great weapon had gone.

Once Vaughany wasn't going to make it, there was a lot made of whether Strauss or Flintoff should have captained the group, and, because we were losing, that never went away.

As someone who was there, I can give the definitive answer on this. Whoever it was – Andrew Flintoff, Andrew Strauss, Nasser Hussain, Mike Brearley, whoever you want – it wouldn't have made a blind bit of difference. Where we were at the end of that series had nothing to do with who had the captaincy, and everything to do with the fact the team wasn't good enough.

First ball going to second slip, Monty being left out at Brisbane, the non-stop media analysis, none of it was a factor in us getting beat 5-0. The fact is the blokes who made up that trip weren't good enough to beat Australia, who were a fantastic side, and hurting badly from what happened in 2005.

Fred was aware there were people in the camp who didn't want him as captain, and that didn't help. There was nothing openly said. It was more like as the tour went on the team became more distant from each other.

There wasn't that closeness there had been in the West Indies, and that can lead to a disconnect in the group.

If anyone was going round saying, "We've got the wrong captain here", all they were doing was confirming they were very weak characters, blaming something that wouldn't have made any difference – Andrew Flintoff or Andrew Strauss, we were getting beat 5-0. One thing I can guarantee is Strauss himself never acted against Fred. He just wasn't that sort of character. Strauss was too good a man to be resentful. It's not how he is or who he is. I didn't see any resentment between the two, whoever was captain at any time.

And what was Fred supposed to have said by the way? If you get offered the England job, you take it.

Sadly, what little support I had been able to offer Fred was now coming to an end.

After the Perth Test match, I'd announced my retirement from one-day cricket. In the past year, I'd spent more than 300 nights in hotel rooms. And what for? When it came to the one-day stuff, I was basically touring the world as a glorified drinks carrier, only being turned out when it was a fast and bouncy pitch or somebody needed roughing up.

I'd told myself many times that it wasn't forever, and what I was doing from a financial point of view was making it worth it, but none of that weighed the scale down more than the other side, which was that I simply wanted to be there more for my loved-ones.

My family life was worth more to me than an extra 10 grand here, 15 grand there.

If I was playing, it might have made a difference, but being on tour and not playing was the nightmare scenario for me. It left me vulnerable to the demons in my head. With nothing to occupy me, in they'd pour.

By myself I was history. My mind was very good at wandering into places where it didn't need to be, back to family, feeling lonely, separate, detached, wherever it may be. It was never about my self-worth, whether I belonged. I was never questioning whether I was good enough.

I was just questioning where I was, what I was doing, what my kids were doing, Hayley, my brothers, my mam and dad, my mates. It sounds daft but on a Sunday night there used to be a games night at the Buffs – darts, pool, that kind of thing – and my mind would wander. I'd be lying on my own staring at the world going by and feeling as if my own world had ended, and in my head I could see them there having a good time. I never thought about any of it when I was playing cricket. That was my ultimate release. I had been through this the last time I went on an Ashes tour.

Five Test matches, endless one-dayers, and then on to a World Cup where I was never going to be anything but a spectator, all the time wishing I was at home in Ashington. Even now people say to me, "But you were in some fantastic parts of the world, staying in fantastic hotels, representing your country, being around all these players. I'd have given anything to do that." They're right. On the surface, I sound like a spoiled brat. But ask yourself, if you had small children, a wife, a close family, if that was where your entire life existed, real life, not something in a holiday brochure, then wouldn't you miss it?

International sport is an amazing thing, an amazing life. As a trainee bricklayer from Ashington, I can't believe I've just written that I'd happily turn my back on an extra 10 grand here, 15 grand there, and I don't want that to sound arrogant, but when you're missing people, when you're a bit part player in your own children growing up, then money on top of money doesn't mean anything.

That scenario – Ashes, one-dayers, World Cup – was what was lined up again here, and I'm sorry but I wasn't going to be around for the last two-thirds of that arrangement. If I'd broken a leg I would have come home. I don't see the difference when it comes to mental health.

Before I left Australia, I had an appraisal with Duncan, something he was never comfortable doing.

In fact, I know for a fact he hated it.

He wasn't a great individual people person. A sit down one-on-one was not his kind of thing. But a couple of players had sued for unfair dismissal at counties and the ECB had brought them in to cover their backs. "You should have been better prepared with your bowling," he told me. 'Fair enough,' I thought, but then he started going on about my batting, and at that point I just blew up.

The way I saw it, by the time I next played for England there was no way he was going to be coach, so I just thought, 'Fuck it, I'm not standing for this.' I let him have it big time. "You're joking," I told him. "I batted at number nine when I'm not a number nine, faced more balls than both wicket-keepers combined, and now you're blaming my batting for what's happened?"

I didn't think that was right. We'd lost because we just weren't good enough. It was as simple as that.

The players who were established were having a bad time and the ones who were coming into the team needed the more experienced players to front up. I'd have had a lot more respect for him if he'd said, "You should have played in that warm-up game at Adelaide and that's why you were underdone for Brisbane." But to have a go at my batting was actually quite bizarre. I shouldn't have had a go back because it was disrespectful, but it had been a difficult tour, the pressure the Australians had heaped on us had been relentless, and we'd gone through the trauma of seeing the mental decline of a great player and colleague like Tres.

We all knew full well the tour should have turned out better, and we all knew full well it hadn't. Do you then need the grand finale of the coach chipping at you about something that wasn't even your role in the first place?

But that was Duncan all over. He never had tried to establish a relationship with me. I had dinner with him once in eight years. There was me, Fred and KP in Pakistan in a hotel restaurant, no-one else in there. Fletcher came walking in and while he knew we were there, he was looking where to sit.

We couldn't believe it – "He's going to sit by himself!" We got him across and we had three-and-a-half hours talking to a man who'd had one hell of a life.

He'd been in the Rhodesian army, a very tough man, before making his way, establishing Zimbabwe as a Test cricket nation, taking some significant scalps along the way. It was one of the best nights I've had. We were all thinking the same thing, 'Why has he never shown this side of himself to us before?'

Next morning, having had such a great time, we got on the bus and Duncan was sat there on the first seat. "Morning Fletch," I said but I barely got a nod back in return. I was gutted. I genuinely thought I'd broken the ice with him. But now, nothing. I went to the back of the bus. "Did you see that?" I said to Fred. "I got exactly the same," he replied. But we'd seen the same thing happen in South Africa.

There were a couple of times, when we were around his mates at barbecues or enjoying days out on boats, where you could see he was a completely different man. He was warm, he let his hair down. Then next day it was back to this big stoney-faced bloke behind the sunglasses. I have no idea what that was about.

We wouldn't have abused a friendship with him, but he didn't want to let us in. That was the way he felt was best to coach his group. Everybody has to be different, I suppose.

Fletcher had a group within the group, and I didn't fit into it. He was very big on team management meetings. It wasn't so much that he had his favourites, but he definitely had people he'd go to for advice. I was never part of that. When I did go to the management meetings, I always ended up thinking, 'It doesn't matter what I say. He's got Collingwood, Trescothick, Vaughan, Strauss – whatever I say, it's not going anywhere.'

He worked with the people he wanted to work with, and those he didn't want to work with he got the relevant people, such as Troy Cooley and Matt Maynard, to work with them instead.

I didn't have any resentment at not being part of his group. I didn't have any desire to be part of it. It was an irrelevance for me. If I felt I did need to say something, I'd do it another time one on one. Is it a good thing or a bad thing that I didn't have that relationship with Duncan? I don't care.

All I needed to know was that he trusted me enough that he picked me as many times as he did to play for England. I'm thankful for that. I enjoyed playing under Duncan because it was the best I'd played, but I wasn't playing for him, I was playing for England – he was just the coach. If I disagreed with what he said I'd make the point, but at the end of the day it never stopped me going out there and doing what he wanted.

My attitude was always, 'If that's what he wants me to do, and thinks is best for the group, then I'll go out there and do it to the best of my ability.' If it doesn't work, I can say afterwards why I thought it wasn't the best plan.

Looking back now, I'm gutted how the last conversation I had with Duncan on a professional basis ended. I'm not somebody who holds a massive grudge.

If somebody I don't particularly get on with comes into my space, I'll just try to avoid them. Duncan was different. I had a lot of respect for him. When it comes to other coaches who learn everything from a book, they should at least do it from a book written by Duncan Fletcher. If he wrote a coaching manual, I'd read it back to front. But did we get on? We got on as much as a player and a coach needs to get on.

I'd love it to have been different, but Duncan wasn't like that. And then when he disappeared from the England set-up, he disappeared full-stop. He didn't get another job in county cricket, or in the media, so there was no chance to get to know him in a different way, no opportunity to bump into him once in a while and talk about these great times we went through, and I think that's sad.

As much as it didn't end well between us, I've got a lot to thank Duncan Fletcher for. He got the best out of me, as he did with Flintoff and Pietersen. You might argue that he got us at the peak of our careers – but he helped to get us to that peak.

I speak about Duncan in a warmer way than Fred does, and when I do he gives me a bit of a look! But I didn't experience the inside issues that Fred did. Fred had a trickier relationship with Duncan because he captained under him. I'd never seen that side to him.

Fred and Duncan's relationship became untenable after the Test matches in Australia. When I said goodbye to Fred, I felt for him big time. His family was going home and some of his biggest friends – me, Geraint, Hoggy – were leaving as well.

All of a sudden he was left with a team where his close mates weren't there anymore, and that was the breaking point where he started finding solace in a drink. During the one-dayers, everything got on top of Fred and he self-destructed. But the pressure that was on his shoulders, I think anybody would have done the same.

When he was replaced by Peter Moores, Fletcher suddenly became a lot chattier in his autobiography. A lot of it was about Fred's drinking in Australia, wondering out loud what sort of state he would have been in without the responsibility of the captaincy.

Fletcher's thinking was that if he hadn't been captain he'd have been doing it more. I didn't like it when he said that. That wasn't right, because, when it came to the drinking, I don't think it really mattered if Fred was captain or not. If anything, the captaincy made it worse. It was because he was the leader and, therefore, taking the team's performance to heart, that he was in the position of reaching for a bottle. Maybe we should turn this the other way round. If Fletcher had worked harder to establish a relationship between him and Fred, and not been so unapproachable, then maybe he would have been in a position where he could have sat down with Fred and said, "Come on, what's going on?" and looked after his captain a bit more.

The blame for the breakdown would eventually be laid solely at Fred's door, but the insecurities of Fletcher didn't help Fred one bit. Fletcher was OK when we were winning, but he had an ego and when we started losing he'd suddenly sink into the background. Coach and captain have got to stick together.

A coach might not like his captain, but he has to back him.

Some people have asked me if it might have been different for Fred if I'd been around? Possibly, because I would have been alongside him. I would have been there for him, like he had for me before. Then again, I might have just been alongside him at the bar.

As Fred felt the pressure, it suited people in the England hierarchy for him to be seen as having lost all sense of responsibility. It suited the narrative for it to appear that whatever was going on was largely his fault, that he wasn't behaving in a manner suited to being England captain. There was a lot of talk on that trip that somebody inside the camp, not the players, but from the ECB, was giving stories to the papers.

It was said the credit card bill from some of the hierarchy was through the roof in entertaining journalists, keeping people sweet and happy. Whether that was true or not you just don't know. But for me there's no smoke without fire.

It just got worse and worse for Fred, culminating in the pedalo incident in St Lucia during the 2007 World Cup in the Caribbean where he was vice-captain.

Fred barely even put a foot in that pedalo. It was reported that he nearly drowned – the water was ankle deep and all that happened was a security guard told him to get off it. It was blown out of all proportion. I'd spoken to Fred a couple of days before. He'd had a hard time in Australia, and, as the tour, and now World Cup, went on and on, inside his head he was finding it hard to cope. "I'm struggling," he told me. "I feel alone. There's no-one to share anything with. I'm not enjoying the trip, it's not the same. I can't wait to get home."

When the pedalo incident was then all over the Sunday papers, I sent him a text – "Long way to pedal home!" – as mates do, to lighten the mood. I got a predictable reply back! But I soon saw that this was turning into no laughing matter.

The management had decided they wanted to make a very public example of Fred by parading him in front of the media. I couldn't believe what I was seeing. There he was, Andrew Flintoff, the man who had done so much for the England team, and gone no small way to enhancing the reputation of the coaching staff, being hung out to dry in front of the assembled media. Duncan was with him but Fred was very much on his own.

He'd been deliberately isolated, positioned there for maximum humiliation. I was embarrassed to be an England cricketer when I saw that. As a coach, as much as you might want to throttle him, as much as you might want to fine him, or take the vice-captaincy off him, he's still your player. Duncan Fletcher had a duty to protect Andrew Flintoff.

Even if he didn't want to, and it was killing him to do it, he should have protected him. But he didn't. He just sat there. Impassive. That same nothing face. I was upset watching it on TV. It was awful to watch. There's my best mate, someone I think of as family, sitting there, and he's on his own. Fletcher's sitting next to him, but he's on his own. And that's not right.

That pissed me off big time. The best cricketer England had seen for 25 years, made to feel an inch high. It was disgraceful.

Fair enough, hang the man out to dry in the team environment, but not in front of the public, and the fact he had to sit there in front of the media just made it worse. Again, these were people he'd trusted, people he'd given a lot to down the years, and now they were all queuing up to shaft him. That hurt him as well.

Why Fletcher felt the need to act in this manner, I don't know. It stank of bitterness and revenge. It wasn't about a single incident with a pedalo, he'd just come to the conclusion that the pedalo was the moment to act and get him away from the captaincy roles.

Afterwards, I tried to ring Fred but he wasn't picking up. He'd locked himself in his room and wasn't talking to anybody. The hotel weren't putting anybody through either. I felt helpless, to the extent that I genuinely was going to fly out to St Lucia to see him. It had to be me because if anybody from the family had gone it would have been a massive story.

As a mate, I just wanted to go and see if he was all right and make sure he was as good as he could be in the circumstances. I didn't want him to be in a hole by himself, even if I could totally understand why he wanted to shut himself away from the world. This wasn't just about one man having too much to drink and making a fool of himself. It was about a man at a low ebb, using alcohol to blur the world collapsing around him. It's a shame no-one had the intelligence to see that. A Geordie with no qualifications could have told them if they'd asked.

Fred didn't exist on an island – well, he did at that point, but you know what I mean. There were things happening behind the scenes, other people trying to manoeuvre themselves into Fred's position by making themselves look better in Fletcher's eyes. There had been a few players out on the pedalo night. When, the next morning, Fletcher asked them to write down what time they came in on a whiteboard in the team room, there were two or three who knew what the fine threshold was and basically said a different time.

That, to me, is out of order, if you don't put the real time, you are hanging the others out to dry. You're shafting your teammates. And that's a no, no. If I'd been in that meeting and Fletcher had asked me to put a time, I'd have refused. Not because I didn't want him to know, but because by then it was too late. That doesn't detract from the fact that Fred shouldn't have done it. He knew that. But should he have been treated the way he was? No.

In any sport, when it comes to the social side, there's a fine balance between enjoying yourself and going too far, but the vast majority of the time all the lads want to do is have a couple of drinks and relax.

Yes, we're cricketers, but we're living a life as well. There's only so many cheeseburgers or chicken burgers you can have from a room service menu. Sports people go out to have some sanity. If they didn't, with the intensity and scrutiny, they would crumble. Sadly, with modern social media, now they literally can't do anything.

I'm not saying we should create a massive drinking culture, but there are times when it's good to relax. A few of us got it in the neck when we stayed and had a drink in the Australian dressing room after the defeat in Adelaide, but people need to wind down.

I'm a grown man, if I want to go and talk to someone on the opposition team, I will. It's a game of cricket, not a war. I'll be as tough as anyone on the pitch, but does that have to continue off it? The Aussies had experienced exactly the same thing in 2005. Then it was their critics saying they were a soft touch, that they'd got too friendly with England.

That was bollocks – they weren't. It wasn't about being friendly. It was about two teams playing in a fantastic series that England won by two wickets and two runs.

It takes two teams to create a game and if they want to relax together afterwards, then so what? If somebody wants to drink, let them drink. If they don't, fine. But don't portray a sportsperson as bad because they like letting their hair down and want to enjoy themselves.

Looking back on it, Fred took one for the team that winter because if Andrew Strauss had been captain we'd still have lost 5-0 and it would have been him getting all the stick instead.

Instead, Fred suffered professionally and personally, allowing an unblemished Strauss to take the role at a later date. In the same way that Andrew Flintoff wasn't a bad captain in 2006-07 – he just didn't have a very good team – when Andrew Strauss went there and won in 2010-11, it wasn't because he was a great tactician, his side were better than Australia's.

Fred would later admit he suffered mental health issues on that trip. He has since come out and spoken honestly and openly about it, and I respect him so much for that. Fred's a man's man, and they're the people who can find it the hardest to open up.

But if a pair of daft northern idiots like me and him can talk about mental health, then there's hope for all of us. More men should realise how sympathetic and responsive other men can be.

22

TARGETS

"One day after play, Kirk Russell decided I needed an ice bath. Great, now we had something to keep the beers chilled. He'd be asking me to get in and there'd already be 40-odd cans of Heineken in there"

"Come on you bastard, let go! Let go of the bastard thing!"
If I thought playing at home against the West Indies in May and June 2007 would be a doddle compared to the nightmare of Australia the winter before, I was sadly mistaken.

There were times in my career where I couldn't let go of the ball, and this was one of them.

I'd be looking at the clock, dreading training, dreading the game. It was the yips, a mental block which stops a player releasing the delivery at the right time. Darts players suffer the same issue, and it afflicts golfers with the putter.

It put me in a dark place – was there no end to the ways my mind could trip me up? I didn't want to be on that pitch,

I wanted to go back to my room and shut myself off. At Old Trafford, I was all over the shop. I didn't know what I was doing.

I was looking at the sky in the field, anything so as not to make contact with the captain – 'Please don't bring me on.' I spoke to Neil Fairbrother and he got me to meet Karl Morris, a sports psychologist.

"Look, I'm at the cricket tomorrow," said Karl. "I'm in one of the boxes, and when you turn round on the way back to your mark I don't want to see your arms going, rehearsing, practicing over and over in your mind, because you are mentally killing yourself. I want you to turn round, pick a point on the sightscreen, walk back, and stare at it. Don't think about what you should be doing with the ball, your arms, your feet, just look at that sightscreen and think of nothing." I don't know what it says about me, but the thing I focused on was not the sightscreen but a big yellow advertising board for Wolf Blass wine. I bowled beautifully. I didn't know if it was the alcohol that had got me through the day or Karl Morris's advice. At the end of the day, I went up to the box to thank him. "Feeling better?" he asked me.

I thought about it. "I need a glass of wine."

I missed the entire home India Test series with a hernia injury, before heading off to Sri Lanka and then New Zealand, a trip most notable for the official opening of The Harmison Arms.

I'd first taken my dartboard to Pakistan a few years earlier and it had proved a hit, so much so that when it came to the follow-on tour to India I ditched my one-day pads to fit it in my luggage. Compared to the dartboard, the pads were non-essentials.

Sometimes you have to make sacrifices. However, by the time the one-dayers came round there were no other Gunn & Moore sponsored players in the team, so I was stuck to borrow any pads. I didn't get a game but a sponsor expects you to wear their gear in practice because there are still photographers and film crews around. I was getting calls from G&M saying, "Why aren't you wearing your blue pads in the nets?"

"Because I took a dartboard," I told them. Honesty isn't always the best policy. They weren't best pleased!

In Sri Lanka, the dartboard really came into its own. There were more and more people wanting to come and play. It became a routine. Every night, the lads would come to my room and we'd ring down for room service.

One day after play, Kirk Russell decided I needed an ice bath. Great, now we had something to keep the beers chilled. He'd be asking me to get in and there'd already be 40-odd cans of Heineken in there.

Swanny came up with the tag of the Harmison Arms, and it has to be said all we were lacking was a bag of peanuts and a jukebox – Swanny and James Anderson would provide the musical accompaniment as they both had guitars. It wasn't always darts. I'd take a load of DVDs on tour with me, films, sitcoms such as *Only Fools And Horses* and *The Office*, so people would come and watch those.

Plus I had the biggest collection of sweets you'd ever seen. I used to go to Costco before we went away and fill a suitcase full of chocolate bars and Haribo. Some players would walk in, dip their hand in, and just go back to their room. Others would stay for a chat. One man who'd nip in and out was Hoggard.

He had the room next to mine in Galle, and one night, while

the rest of us were playing, we could hear some odd noises coming through the walls. Now odd noises were nothing new from Hoggard – he was the sort of man who revelled in doing such things down your ear at volume – but these were particularly odd, a combination of shrieks and howls.

I thought I'd go and investigate. Poking my head round the door, I could see him sat throwing peanuts off the balcony. I went back to my room. "What's he doing?" asked the lads. "Oh nothing," I said. "Just talking to the monkeys."

Calling it 'The Harmison Arms' makes it sound like it was more about drinking than it was. For me, it was just about having people around me to stop my mind wandering to other areas. I needed people around me to survive and creating a 'pub' in my room every night was one way to do it.

If they didn't come to me, I'd go to them. I'd look for corridors where doors were open, pop in, see how people were going. The difficult part was from 11 o'clock onwards when people went to bed. Then it was back to struggling in darkness. The Harmison Arms could be expensive, though. After one stay, the room bill came to a thousand pounds.

The second part of that winter took us to New Zealand, and prior to the first Test I made a naive mistake that would cost me big time. My wisdom teeth were killing me on that trip, and the day before the first Test match in Hamilton I thought enough was enough and went to the dentist.

I'm shit-scared of dentists and have been since I was 13 when I had my first filling, but I had to get them removed, they were killing. I totally underestimated the effect it would have on me. I was groggy afterwards, having your wisdom teeth knocks you about a bit, and I knew from day one I shouldn't have put myself up for selection. That was my own stupidity for not wanting to miss games, and it cost me. Immediately, people were questioning me. I had a poor game and it cost me in terms of confidence and making myself an easier target for people who wanted to have a pop. To them it was evidence of my inconsistency.

Boycott, in particular, had a go – and I had a go right back. Boycott had come out with the usual bullshit – "Harmison shouldn't be playing, doesn't like playing, doesn't want to play, only likes playing in England" – the usual crap.

I had a column in a national newspaper at the time and when they asked me what I wanted to say, my response was simple – "Nail the bastard." It had been my fault that I'd gone on the field feeling like that, but none of what he was saying was true. I never made excuses for my performances, excuses are for weak people, and I didn't make any this time. But I did point out that whenever I crossed that boundary rope and played for England I never gave anything less than 100 percent. Playing for my country meant everything to me and for him to suggest I was shirking was an insult.

After I'd said my piece in the paper, I bumped into him. He tried to be all pally. "I respect you more for having a go back," he told me. "I couldn't give a fuck, Geoffrey," I told him. "I've got no interest in what you think. I've got no respect for you. I just haven't. None whatsoever."

And I haven't, even now. The way he's spoken about Alastair Cook at times during his career is a disgrace. As a broadcaster, the first 10 seconds of what Boycott says is very good, the rest of it's garbage. As a cricketer, his record speaks for itself, but the personal attacks on people are beyond the pale. I can't bring myself to have any respect for somebody like that. People say, "Well, that's how he is."

Well, if that's how he is, fuck him.

He gives nothing to the game of cricket in this country. He's so negative. Is he bitter? Is he jealous? He's got nothing to be bitter or jealous about – he was an unbelievable cricketer. His record speaks for itself. It's a shame, he's one of the greatest players ever in our game, and I walked away from him thinking, 'What a complete idiot.'

While we were in New Zealand, Hoggy made a comment to Vaughany about feeling weighed down during the Test in Hamilton – he had troubles at home and they were really getting to him.

He was walking back to his mark and he said to Vaughany, "I don't think I can do it – I'm going to do a Tres." He never played for England again.

It reminded me why, as far as people's perception of me was concerned, it had to be homesickness that I had. I still had to disguise the fact I was clinically depressed so I was happy when people were saying I just missed Ashington rather than anything else, because I knew it hid an underlying problem.

I talked to Hoggy about how he was feeling. He's a very emotional person. He portrays himself as having this big, dumb insolence, a strong bravado, but deep down there's a softy in there. I offered to babysit for him. "I'll look after Ernie so you two can get out together," I offered him one night. And that's what I did. I sat in their room watching the telly and the kid never stirred. I knew from my own experience how tough it was with small children, so to help them have a little release was something I thought worth doing. And leaving a little one with me was quite something! As Hayley points out, I've not changed a nappy yet.

Whether Matthew not playing again was down to saying what he did, I can't be sure. But people came in and cemented their place, and he never got it back. I was dropped at the same time and it took me a year to get my place back.

The next Test at Wellington, I did an interview for Sky on the outfield with Nasser. He was pushing me, questioning my desire, playing up on the idea that my performance in Hamilton showed that I was lazy, that there were games when I just didn't turn up to the party.

I didn't mind that, he was just doing his job, but he must have known I wasn't just going to roll over to that line of questioning.

Away from the cameras, I'd had another massive argument with him at Lord's when we playing Pakistan in 2006. Again, he was questioning my desire. "Why don't you give it everything, Harmy. Why do you come into series undercooked? Why does it look like you don't want it?" I went for him. "You don't know what you're talking about. Nobody works harder than me to be in the best place I can be to play for England. I've always given everything for England."

We were standing there pointing at each other, shouting. An official came over and said, "The game's about to start, you'd better take this on to the Nursery Ground." So that's what we did. We went off, had a chat, shook hands and walked away. That was the thing about Nasser, he didn't hold grudges, not towards me anyway. He respected passion in someone, and that's what he got from me.

There was some light relief in New Zealand and it came from Philip Mustard, who'd broken through from Durham into the England set-up.

We were in a minibus, half past eight in the morning, on our way to training when the news came on the radio. "Jesse Ryder, the New Zealand opener, has been arrested after a bar-room altercation in the early hours of the morning."

Peter Moores, the former Sussex coach who'd come in to replace Fletcher, turned it up. I was actually driving the bus that day but, even from the front, I could hear a voice pipe up from the back and I recognised it straight away. It was the Colonel. "That's strange," he said, when he heard about Ryder. "He was all right when I left him at half past four." Moores looked up from his morning paper, looked at me and gave a look that said, 'Did he really just say that?' He looked back down again, shook his head, and carried on with his paper. Me? I was pissing myself, it was so funny. But that was the Colonel, absolutely priceless. No-one understood a word he said, and when you did understand it, you couldn't help but wet yourself.

The Colonel should have played for England a lot more, but I'm not sure his lifestyle helped him. He couldn't play at one point because he got gout! The night before the Friends Provident Final in 2007, he was sitting in the bar, well on his way. At half 11 he ordered another bottle of wine. This is the biggest game Durham have ever had – and he's the opening batsman.

"Colonel, go to bed!"

"No, I'll be all right."

Next day he went out and smashed 49 off 25 balls. And he needed to be like that. That was his character. If he'd gone against it, it wouldn't have worked. You have to let people be sometimes.

Vaughany finally gave up the ongoing war against his knee injury in 2008. With Strauss in poor form with the bat, the ECB felt it was time for a new era – and the person to bring it in was deemed to be that man again – Kevin Pietersen.

I think Peter Moores knew deep down from the start that this wasn't going to be one of life's great relationships.

Peter's methods were always about working hard – run more miles than anyone else, hit more balls than anybody else – whereas Kevin was a more radical thinker. I liked Moores as a character. Certainly, his man-management was better than Duncan's – for a start, he actually talked to you. But the way he wanted to coach England was the same as the way he did Sussex, and while at Sussex he had two or three players who stood out, the rest of them were workmanlike.

With England he had 11 standout individuals. The whole thing of work, work, work, doesn't wash with international players. It stifles them and tires them out.

International cricket is more draining in the mind than arguably any other sport because of the emotion that goes into it and the length of the game.

When you then try to work physically harder, on top of constantly being bombarded with information, before and after games, it's hard. I felt knackered just thinking about some of the stuff that was going on, let alone going out and performing.

He was holding back players by constantly trying to get them to concentrate on things they didn't need to concentrate on. He was taking energy out of players instead of putting it into them, pushing them into doing things when they didn't need it.

He would make players have long nets whereas someone like KP might have 10 balls and if he felt good he'd walk out. Vaughany was the same. On the other hand, KP would bat for an hour if he felt he needed to.

With me, I didn't like bowling the day before a game, I liked bowling a long spell two days before, but those personal choices by senior players were being overridden.

Peter's stuff was all about holding people's hands, trying to get every ounce of ability out of players who weren't quite good enough to play at the next level, because that's what made Sussex great.

To try to do that with England was a mistake. Peter's ideas on cricket and how to get a team performing didn't suit either international cricket or Kevin Pietersen, and that's where the relationship broke down.

When you're dealing with egos, attitudes, people who've performed at the highest level, and you come in and change things drastically, which Peter did, then you are going to get resentment, especially if it then doesn't work. You've got to get your senior players on board.

Peter could have taken an easier option by offering the captaincy to Paul Collingwood or a couple of others, but I think he was trying to get Kevin on-side by offering it to him. Kevin, though, was thinking the opposite way – if I can get the captaincy, I can get rid of Peter.

Peter was also fighting a bit of, "Who is he? He hasn't played international cricket." It didn't matter to me one bit that he hadn't been an international cricketer himself, but if you don't get off to a good start then dressing rooms are like a flock of sheep. The senior player, the big player, the big voice, says something and everybody else goes with it. I've seen it myself. A young player goes into the England dressing room and it's been a tough day's play, and Flintoff or Vaughan or Pietersen says, "We were unlucky there lads," that young player then starts saying it himself. No we weren't – we were fucking awful. That's what dressing rooms are like.

There was another conflict going on in the background. Kevin courted the IPL. If he got the captaincy, he could then bang the IPL drum with the ECB. The ECB, though, thought the captaincy was a good way to lure him away.

For me, Kevin's rise to the top was good news. He rang me up before his first match in charge, the last Test of the South Africa series in 2008. "I'm captain now," he said. "I want you playing, and I want you bowling the first over at the Oval."

I thought that was great captaincy, especially after what happened at Brisbane. I did open the bowling, and Cook dropped a catch off me at gully off my first ball.

When the one-dayers came round and Ryan Sidebottom got injured, Kevin wanted me to come out of one-day retirement. I met him and Peter Moores at Durham and told them I wasn't interested. I had no heart for all the travelling involved.

Going off around the world wasn't something I wanted to do at that time. Durham were doing well and I was happy with my life. But they carried on asking and, in the end, I said I'd do it.

It's one of my biggest regrets that I didn't just say, "I'll come and help you until Ryan gets fit." I hadn't realised at the time but the million dollar Stanford game was coming up, so it looked as if I was just coming back for that. I should have just said I'd play to the end of the summer.

Alan Stanford was this big brash American guy who had money. No sense, but money. The ECB decided his offer of a one-off $20million T20 game in Antigua between the West Indies and England was a way of fending off the IPL's overtures to our best players. This shows how warped their thinking was at the time – "Let's allow a dodgy American, who several other international cricket boards have told to get lost, to fly into Lord's and stand on a stage next to Sir Ian Botham and Sir Vivian Richards with a million quid in a box, because that will be much more seemly than letting our best players earn a few quid, play alongside the world's best, and massively improve their skills in the IPL."

None of what happened with that game was the players' doing. It made me laugh that at press conferences, reporters were asking us some tough questions about getting into bed with Stanford, who'd made his money from less than straight-forward banking deals.

I wanted to say, "You're asking the wrong people. We're just employed to be here, like you're employed by *The Sun, The Mirror, The Times*. We're only in this press conference because the people that pay our wages sent us here. If you've got an issue with it, go and ask the people who made the decision."

I couldn't stop laughing at it.

I didn't know what the ECB were trying to achieve from a longevity point of view with Stanford. The IPL was established. It was only going to get bigger and bigger and better and better. So get in with them. Just let the players go and play in the IPL and then we wouldn't have this farce. Get over the fact we messed up by not getting in with them at the start, get over the fact that because of that they don't like us, let's get in with them now. But instead we had Stanford. It was his bat, his ball, his field, and we were going to do it his way.

The whole thing was embarrassing. At one point during one of the warm-up games we were sitting in the dressing room watching the cricket live on TV when the camera panned to Stanford to find him sitting with the players' wives.

He had Matt Prior's wife on his lap and his arm around Alastair Cook's girlfriend. "What the fuck is he doing?" we were saying. "What the fuck is going on? How is he getting in there?"

The entire group looked uncomfortable and, to be honest, a couple of guys were on for going over and laying him out there and then.

Whenever he came into our dressing room, we'd all leave. Someone on the balcony outside would issue a warning – "He's doing a lap of the ground." That was it, we were out the back before he got anywhere near the dressing room. But that was Stanford, sleazy and low-rent.

You could see it a mile off. The only people who couldn't were the ECB because their vision was blurred with dollar signs. When the British media send the front-of-paper journalists out as well as the sports reporters, you get the sense that something isn't right. When news journalists are asking questions, alarm bells are ringing.

But then again, now we were in this situation, we thought we might as well try to win it. If we did, it was happy days, money in the bank. We talked about how the pot would be shared, because it was 15 blokes and only 11 spots in the team. I felt uneasy as I'd just come out of retirement and so sat on the fence. I copped out of making a decision because it could easily have been levelled at me that I was only there for the money.

It hardly mattered. In the end we got hammered, and the majority of me is glad. It didn't feel like a competitive fixture and it wasn't played like one. We should never have played under the banner of England. It should have been a separate entity away from the national side, a team called the Three Lions perhaps.

As employees of the England and Wales Cricket Board, we fulfilled the fixture, but it didn't have the same feeling as an England international.

Afterwards, Stanford persuaded a lot of the West Indies guys to invest in his bank. But the American, as so many suspected, was nothing but a cheap fraud. Those West Indies guys lost the lot. In the end, with Stanford going to prison and all the disgrace that surrounded him, it felt like we'd swerved one. The only thing that I'm happy about is that we got beat, and that we got a free holiday with the kids.

Going on to India, I was starkly reminded why I had quit one-day cricket in the first place.

In the first of seven one-dayers they got 300-and-plenty on a small ground at Rajkot. I knew exactly what was coming, for the second match we'd bring another slow bowler in and despite everyone going round the park, the one to make way would be me.

The reason why I'd retired from one-day internationals was because I hated not playing, especially going on trips and not playing.

It made my mental health a thousand times worse and when Kevin told me I was being left out, I totally lost it. "The reason I came out of retirement was to play," I told him. "Not to go back to carrying drinks." I stormed up to the dressing room and got my bag. I was so fucked off. The very reason I gave up one-day international cricket had just happened to me. I walked out the ground, got the nearest tuk-tuk, and got it to take me back to the hotel.

It was a total breach of security to do that but I didn't care. The security guy had a go at me, and then Kevin and Moores had a go at me. I still wasn't in the mood to take it. "The exact reason I sat with you two at Durham and told you I didn't want to play is because of this exact moment," I told them. "You both know how important playing is to me. How did you think I was going to react?"

There were some harsh things said. Next morning at breakfast I was sitting on my own when KP came in. He was about to sit somewhere else. "Where are you going?" I said to him. "Sit there." He was looking sheepishly at me as if to say, "We just had a big barney last night."

"That was last night," I said to him. "It's gone."

My cricketing troubles were again put into perspective when, after the fifth one-dayer, India was subjected to a sickening terrorist attack on Mumbai.

Me, Fred and KP were watching the terrible events unfold on TV in our hotel in Bangalore. It was a scene of utter carnage and chaos. There were bodies lying in the road in front of the famous Taj Palace hotel, and the building itself was ablaze. Gun shots could be heard as the terrorists went through the rooms killing guests. 'Chilling' doesn't even begin to describe it – this was the same hotel we'd stayed in two weeks before. Those rooms where people were being slain in as they cowered in corners were the same ones we'd stayed in.

I could imagine in my head where people, desperate, terrified, would be trying to hide. I could see the layout – bed, wardrobe, bathroom, shower. Someone was in there now, either already dead or trying to hide themselves, their family, their children, and realising the hopelessness of the situation.

The gunmen had rampaged through the restaurants where we'd eaten and set fire to the gym where we trained. People we knew – the manager, chefs, all kinds of people, would undoubtedly be dead. What had happened to the staff who'd served us when we were up on the roof in the bar having a drink and something to eat? We were getting word that the big tall chef in the Japanese restaurant we liked, who would cook our dinner in front of us, was dead. All across Mumbai, terrorists were killing people with random brutality. I felt sick. We all did. We couldn't move from in front of the TV for the sheer shock of it all.

With the security situation so tense, we obviously thought we'd be out of India on the next plane. But the ECB had other ideas. The message coming from the top brass was that the tour should go on, otherwise they would be liable to a compensation claim from the Indians. If anything epitomises the gulf between the suits at Lord's and the players, it is that. Unbelievable.

We were high profile targets, and all they could think about was money. In the end, the ECB realised this wasn't perhaps the best course of action and we flew out to a holding camp in Abu Dhabi and then back home before the first Test while security experts assessed the situation. While we were there,

KP reiterated that if it was deemed that we should go back, it would be left to individual decisions. The papers portrayed it as being in the hands of me and Fred – "If Harmison and Flintoff go, they'll all go – if they don't, others will pull out." I put my trust in Reg Dickason, our security expert, who was still in India finding out what was happening.

When he came to Abu Dhabi, I had a good chat with him on my own. I asked him outright, "Is it all right to be going back?" When he looked me in the eyes and said, "Yes, it'll be fine," that's all I needed to hear. I trusted Reg implicitly. From that point on, it was a simple decision for me – we go. But I didn't want my decision to influence others – the old flock of sheep thing – because at the time I was a very senior player. I didn't want to cloud the decisions of Cook, Prior and some of the other younger ones who did have a rabbit in the headlights look about them. I kept schtum and let them make their own minds up.

The first time I knew Fred was going back was when he said so in the team meeting. I wasn't surprised, because he'd got the same information as me, and again trusted Reg. KP was always going back.

Leading by example was one reason, the IPL another. He knew India would be a big part of his future and wanted to show them some loyalty.

It was scary going back, but India is cricket crazy and we felt that if we didn't go back the misery and the mourning would just go on a little bit longer. We knew that going back would be good for them, almost part of the healing process. It's for that reason that the defeat in Chennai – the two Tests were moved from Ahmedabad and Mumbai to Chennai and

Mohali – was the only Test loss in my career that I wasn't massively bothered about.

I'm not sure even a scriptwriter could have come up with what happened – Sachin Tendulkar, the great Indian hero, walking off having hit a hundred and the winning runs at the same time.

He was in tears, thanking us in the dressing room. What it meant to him, the great son of Mumbai, was everything, and that's why he was so grateful we'd gone back. It was like it was written in the stars that it should pan out like that.

For him to come into our dressing room and thank us was very moving, very humbling. There was a lump in the throat to see one of the greatest players of all time like that.

He'd just taken a hundred off us and his team had beaten us, and now he was in our dressing room thanking us. I didn't know whether to lamp him or cuddle him! It was a weird time, but I'm so pleased we went back. It was nothing in the grand scheme of things, but it was something for them to celebrate, to be happy about.

That was more than a game of cricket, it was a healing process and I left Chennai feeling proud to have played in that game.

A tough time for the team had ended with smiles on our faces, despite having lost. As we sat in that dressing room, what we didn't, in fact couldn't, know was that for England, the tough times had not ended. They had barely even started.

23

WE NEED TO TALK ABOUT KEVIN

"There were things going on that were unprofessional. A fake Twitter account was set up to mock Kevin and whether that was Broad, Swann or whoever, it was totally out of order"

I thought Kevin was a good captain.

If you take away some of the bravado, his decision-making was excellent, he had ideas about how he wanted to captain and he backed them all the way.

He wasn't just a maverick in the way he played, he was a maverick in the way he thought as well. For me, Kevin would have been a very good captain over a long period. He could have moulded a team in his way, thinking differently, but a lot of that comes down to the person you work with.

The captain is the man in charge but the coach is the one who guides, and if you're not prepared to be guided by that person, then there's a problem.

You need that combination between captain and coach to make things work. Captain and coach don't have to be the same, but they have to understand that the environment they set and bring to the group is the most important thing. It was blatantly obvious that Moores and Pietersen weren't on the same wavelength. I think Kevin would have been a good captain with Duncan Fletcher but, again, he was a larger-than-life character who the ECB didn't really want. An in-form Strauss was their man. So when they first got a chance, they nailed him.

At the end of that India series, I was sitting in the bar of the hotel with bowling coach Otis Gibson, batting coach Andy Flower, and Fred.

When I went to the toilet I saw KP sat all alone in the dining room, just sitting there contemplating his thoughts. I felt sorry for him. A lot had gone on with that tour, the terrorist attacks for one. I went over to see how he was. It was then he mentioned he couldn't work with Moores anymore.

He wasn't slagging him off, he just saw it as a dynamic that wasn't happening. The two of them had different ideas of how they wanted the game played. They were poles apart. It was a professional disagreement.

"The ECB have asked for a rundown of the tour," he revealed. "They want the whole nuts and bolts of what I'm thinking."

"Tell the truth," I told him. "Because, if you don't, you're going to end up with Moores again, and if you can't work together, we suffer. You can't let things fester, if you can't work with him you've got to say so. You don't believe in what he believes in."

I went back to sit with the lads in the bar. "Kev's next door," I told them. "He's got the weight of the world on his shoulders, he's really unhappy and he reckons it's just working."

Andy Flower then said, "If he fucks Peter Moores over, I'll never work for the ECB again." It was an off-the-cuff comment, which didn't really get a response from anybody at the time, and nobody really thought any more about it.

It was like me saying, "If Peter Moores fucks Kevin Pietersen over, I'll never talk to Peter Moores again", because he's a player and I'm a player and he's my mate. But considering Flower would be the next England coach, it did indicate that he was no great fan of Pietersen.

I don't know if it's like Sunderland/Newcastle or Man Utd/ Man City, but there might have been a little bit of a South Africa/ Zimbabwe thing going on with Pietersen and Flower.

The very first week of that Indian trip, we were in the nets. There were three – a seam bowling net, a spin bowling net and a throw-down net. Kevin had his seam, then his spin, and was now going into the throw-down net, which Andy was running.

This was early in Andy's England career, and the first time he'd ever thrown to Kevin, and Kevin just dismissed him – "No, no, not you." He got Phil Neale in instead. A lot of us thought that was out of order, but Kevin could sometimes be like that, where his mouth was three seconds faster than his brain. When he was in the moment, and he was concentrating, things could come out.

If I was Andy Flower in that situation, part of the coaching team, I would have thought, one, 'What am I doing here?' and two, 'Who is this bloke to embarrass me in public?' – because there were a lot of people who'd seen it. That comment from Andy Flower in the bar probably came as a result of that. He was letting some early light in on a relationship that would rarely be settled down the years.

Kevin did what he was asked and sent the ECB an email with full details of the tour as he saw it.

Of course, that email then got leaked to the media – the ECB was feeding the media a line, just as it had done with Fred. All of a sudden, as with Fred at the World Cup, there was this big hullaballoo. Pietersen's reputation was tarnished, presented as a man with a vendetta against Moores, while Moores was hung out to dry as a backward-thinking journeyman who couldn't work with the big talent.

In the meantime, Strauss was back scoring runs and, all of a sudden, Flower was in prime position to get the England job. Kevin was just another captain sold down the river. The ECB wanted rid of him as captain. They wanted Strauss, and the only way they could do that was by hanging Kevin, with Peter as collateral damage. I didn't believe that was the right way to behave, even though I didn't think Moores was right to coach the international team at that time. Kevin did a lot of good things for the ECB and to sack him was disrespectful.

Pietersen was weakened in the England set-up from that point on, and that didn't help when Swann, Prior, Anderson and Broad became the big players in the dressing room, none of whom had any relationship with Kev. As others came into the dressing room, they listened to those four – it's sheep again – and picked up on the negative KP vibe.

One of Kevin's big bugbears was that, when he first came into the England dressing room, he respected the senior players – Flintoff, Harmison, Vaughan, Strauss, Trescothick. "I respected the people in here," he'd say. "Some of the young players now haven't got the same respect I had." It was hard to disagree, and that's why the likes of me, Vaughany and Flintoff would stick up for him on and off the pitch. In Kevin's eyes, as a senior player, he'd been separated. Dressing room banter was going too far. That's always the case when there's something malicious underneath.

There were things going on that were unprofessional. A fake Twitter account was set up to mock Kevin and, whether that was Broad, Swann or whoever, it was totally out of order. There's no smoke without fire, and for Kevin to have been that upset, there must have been some influence in that Twitter account coming from within.

Quite why other players would do that to someone on their own team, I don't know. Never in a dressing room should there be someone hung out to dry, because all of a sudden you're playing 10 against 12. If there's more than one, then you are in the shit.

Kev was calculated. Agreed, he said some stupid things, he said some nasty things. One of the reasons I got on with him was that I took no notice of it. I wasn't bothered. It was just hot air, venting his frustrations. I let it go in one ear and out the other. If he'd done well, but we as a group had a bad day, for example, then that was it, in his eyes we were shit. But by doing that he was just getting rid of tension.

People either preferred not to realise that, or exploited it for their own means. This is in the dressing room of the national cricket team. What they should have been concentrating on is winning games.

If ever I had an issue with Kevin, it was sorted out very, very quickly, and that was because of the personalities we were.

Straight-talkers – people who shot from the hip. There were numerous times I tried to knock his head off. Bowling, that is, not literally. In Perth, for instance, when we were 2-0 down in the

Ashes, we were bowling in the nets with some old dog-end balls and Kevin had upset Hoggard by taking the piss and slogging him. KP's argument was that this was how he intended to bat. Hoggy's argument was that he was showing no respect. Me, Hoggy, and Jon Lewis went to the bag.

"Right, new balls!"

KP was having none of it, but we were insistent. "No, no. If you're going to bat like that, we're having new balls."

Fletcher was trying not to look so as not to get involved. Me and KP were two strong-minded characters, but no-one was as strong as Hoggard. When he wanted to do something, he did it. He ran up first ball with the new cherry and bowled Kevin a bouncer. Lewis, same again, bouncer. 'I've got to stay in the bowlers' union!' I thought. So same again, bouncer.

Kevin was not happy. "What the fuck's going on?"

"Well, Kev," I said. "We'll go back to the old balls if you bat properly. If you don't we'll bowl with these things. So what are we going to do?"

In the end, he gave up and we got the old balls back out.

Talking behind others' backs wasn't our thing. If a younger player sees that, they start thinking that's the norm. That can never be right – that player who's been marginalised, be it Kevin or anybody, has got feelings too.

I remember when Kevin's wife Jessica came over to India for the first time, she was sat at the back of the team bus, a good northern girl.

Me and Fred were like, "What the fuck are you doing with a dick like him?" Me and Fred would have a go at KP all the time, but in a funny way, in a good way. KP could be portrayed as being a bit precious, but he wasn't at all. When I played he was part of the group. No-one was in a corner on their own. By the end of Kevin's career it was blatantly clear they weren't together. There was that lot – and Kevin.

Swanny and Kevin had never got on, dating back to their time at Nottinghamshire. It's hard to say whether they were too different or too the same. Either way, Swanny was very influential in the England dressing room at the point it went tits-up with Kevin because he had Broad, Anderson, and Prior on his side.

From 2004, when he came in, through to 2006, when that team started to break up, Kevin had people in the England dressing room who understood him. We were a more mature side. That had gone.

As well as finding himself pushed aside, Kevin also didn't like some of the things he saw going on in the dressing room. An example was players being made to apologise in front of the group if they'd dropped a catch or mis-fielded a ball. I can't see how that's anything other than humiliating.

This whole situation, with people having a go at players mis-fielding, really ramped up towards the end of my time with England. Ryan Sidebottom shouted at me in Sri Lanka after I dived over one at gully. I lost it. I went up to him. "I don't do it on purpose. Don't ever do that to me again."

I very rarely had a go at anyone when they dropped a catch off me. If anything, I'd go the other way. I'd tap them on the back because I knew they hadn't meant to do it.

At Durham, Gordon Muchall dropped one at slip – straight down. "All right, Muchy," I said. "You'll get the next one." Two overs later, a catch – again, straight down. "Muchy, I hope it doesn't come to you a third time!" I laughed, and I did that not because I didn't care, but because I knew if I had a go at him there was even less chance of him catching the next one. No-one drops them on purpose.

After I'd left the team, I did sense, as a fan and a pundit, there was a lot more pressure when it came to fielding. If that was what was happening, Kevin was right to highlight it because that doesn't help the harmony of the group. It would never have happened in my time because one of the big characters in that dressing room would have stood up and said, "You're bang out of order." In fact, if that was going on, I'm surprised England won any cricket matches at that time, because you can't have that going on when you're on the park.

When the management joined in the victimisation, that was what did for Kevin.

To compile a dossier behind his back, as they did on the 2013-14 Ashes tour, was a disgrace. Fair enough, they might keep an eye on the situation but to have a dossier, that shows intent. It shows they wanted to do what they did a long time before they did it. They were basically just biding their time until the right moment – a moment which worked for them, made them look good and had maximum publicity.

I can't imagine for one minute there were 16 dossiers. I don't imagine there was one against Graeme Swann, Jimmy Anderson, Stuart Broad. We have a culture in English sport where we look for the easy way out, whether that's in football, rugby, cricket, whatever. We look to blame instead of taking responsibility, and that comes from the environment that's been set down the years.

What was the point of sacking Kevin in such a public manner? There was no need at all. There's a selection panel. They should just have told him, "Go and play in the IPL and if a spot comes back in the England team, and you're making runs, we'll pick you.

If not, then we're probably not going to pick you again."

Instead, the ECB let their own egos and agendas come into it. I honestly don't know what they were trying to achieve by doing what they did. It actually backfired on them, because a lot of people came out on KP's side, and he already had plenty of people in his corner anyway.

Having said that, there are times in dressing rooms when it's better that your best player, no matter how good he is, is not there.

Bear in mind that it was Alastair Cook who brought Kevin back after he was accused of secretly texting information about the England team and, in particular, then captain Andrew Strauss, to the South Africans in 2012.

Something must have happened for that ally to go by the end of the Ashes in 2014. Flower wasn't an ally, nor Broad, Anderson, Swann or Prior. There was only one senior man in that group who wanted him there, and that was Cook.

Fortunately for Kevin he was the most important one – the captain. But sometimes you get to a point as a leader, a manager, or a captain, where you think that no matter how good you are, this team will perform better as a group without you. A player could be 10 percent better than everyone else, but if they're not there is everyone else going to play five percent better?

In the end Alastair thought the younger players would be better off without Kevin Pietersen in the dressing room. Instead of doing that simply within the existing framework, there were people at the ECB who then made a simple decision very difficult and created a nightmare for Cook and the England management. There was an agenda from the ECB hierarchy to embarrass Kevin Pietersen, to ridicule him but that made the whole thing worse.

I always felt that Kevin was 10 percent better than anything we had, and that when he became on the same level as everybody else, England would move him on because they didn't want the big brand Pietersen to overshadow everything. They wanted a team environment. They didn't want mavericks. English cricket has always had a problem with mavericks. The ECB doesn't like people who have got their own opinions. They are very controlling, which I'm not a fan of. But people want to look after themselves. They want to preserve their jobs.

The ECB had a problem with Kevin Pietersen from the start. From early on they, like a lot of other people, thought Kevin was a disruptive influence, but I never saw him like that. When people said he was rude and abrupt, I thought that was nonsense. That was just him as a person. He was South African. Their way of speaking is different to ours – they say what they think. I've played with a lot of South Africans and they're all like that.

Kevin could be seen as being divisive in the dressing room, but only because he was a product of the time. Kevin was a larger-than-life character who was brilliant at his job. If there was a sponsorship deal or money to be made on the back of that, he was there. I didn't have a problem with that because I wasn't like that. It never really interested me. It wasn't something I felt comfortable about.

When we went to India in 2006, Vaughany and Flintoff did a shampoo advert which had them singing in the showers. "No matter how much money you paid me," I told them. "There's no way I'm doing that!" They were the brunt of jokes for the next six weeks, but they were getting paid ridiculous money.

By then, there were a lot more streetwise people in the dressing room, not working-class so much, but just realistic lads who, justifiably, wanted to make as much as they could, while they could.

The trouble was, while after 2005 cricket became a lot more

of a commercial entity, and some people saw the big dollar and the big cash, there were only so many endorsements to go round.

With Flintoff and Pietersen getting all the headlines, they were the main contenders and, inevitably, rivalry rose to the surface. Kevin was like Goughy. He liked the commercial side. He liked to be out there and for people to see him. He loved to be in the limelight, the nightclubs, all that stuff. Fred was a little bit different. He wasn't as much of a showman as KP. But they were, to some extent, battling for the same ground. There wasn't massively bad blood between KP and Fred. Instead there was a little bit of jealousy – not as much from Fred's side to KP, more the other way round – but it never got out of hand.

As the fuss over the Ashes died down, they got on better because they were no longer chasing the same thing.

KP was also probably pissed off that he seemed to be the brunt of every Fred joke. He copped it more often than not. KP could give it back but he wasn't particularly good at it, not like Fred was. Fred was a one-off, and it shows now on TV where he works on a show, *A League Of Their Own*, where you have to be quick-witted – that was what he had in the dressing room. But at the same time, Kevin knew that if he got in trouble, Fred would be by his side. And I don't think Kevin had too many people like that over the course of his career. Now I think Fred would do anything for Kev. The two of them get on better now than they did when they played. Fred always understood, like I did, that KP was misunderstood.

For the ECB, brand Pietersen was not the brand they wanted. They put up with brand Flintoff, because it didn't have the IPL push to it that brand Pietersen had.

Perhaps they've learned their lesson. Ben Stokes is a good

example. They could have easily hung him out to dry for some of the things he's done – punching lockers, getting sent home for being drunk – but they've identified he's the best we've got and worked with him.

They need to do that. England cannot afford to drive its best players away.

To me, how it ended with KP was sour, and that's why I'd love to see him sign for a county, get to a major final at Lord's and have one last big day.

I think the supporters of the English game would welcome the chance to give him the send-off he deserves.

24

DINOSAUR

"I could still theoretically play for England, but the reality was my lifestyle and my body were starting to let me down"

By the time we toured the West Indies, the place I'd made my name in such spectacular style four years before, I was aware my international career was petering out.

By now I was on my fifth captain, with Strauss, as predicted, taking the reins. But that didn't mean I wasn't as passionate as I ever had been about pulling on an England shirt, which meant yet another scapegoating pushed me over the edge big style.

I'd played in the first Test in Jamaica, in which we'd been blown away in our second innings for 51, and then left out for the second Test – batters don't get runs, but bowlers get dropped – only for that game to be abandoned after 10 balls.

They say there's 365 beaches in Antigua, one for every day of the year. They were wrong. The Sir Vivian Richards Stadium was the 366th. It was basically a sandpit.

The bowlers couldn't run in without risking a broken ankle. A replacement match was hastily organised for the old Recreation

Ground, and I was brought back because the pitch there was bouncier and the ball would go through quicker. We so very nearly won but we just couldn't get their last wicket, although it wasn't for a lack of trying.

Next up was Barbados, which was the bounciest pitch going, and then on the morning of the match I found out again I'd been left out. In the pavilion, I pointed a finger at Strauss. "Why the fuck am I not playing?"

He tried to explain, but I was so angry none of it was going in. "Every fucking time something goes wrong with this team, it's always me who pays the price. It's never anyone else. 'Let's get rid of Harmy, that'll solve it.' This pitch is ideally suited for me. Why aren't I in the team?"

On a normal tour, that conversation would have been with the coach. You don't go to the captain because he's got to prepare, toss the coin, concentrate on his batting and focus the team. But on that tour Andy Flower was only an interim coach. Strauss was the head man, Flower didn't have the full and final say quite yet.

If I was left out, I'd ask anyone why I wasn't playing. I did to Vaughany a couple of times, but not in the way I did on this occasion to Strauss. Looking back on it now, I regret it a lot.

When I see myself in my mind, I think 'What a dick!' – more from the fact of who I was doing it to than anything else. I'd grown up with Andrew through the Academy and on into the England team – I'd been close to him for eight years. I was right to ask questions, I just did it the wrong way. None of that crossed my mind. But that was me, that was my character.

You live or die by how you are. I know Andrew was disappointed and hurt. I just wish Andy Flower had been named coach before. Then, if some idiot from Newcastle, some Geordie, who has been dropped, and who's quite strong-minded, wants some answers, he'd have been there to deal with it.

Even if I had underperformed in the previous match, it didn't mean I wasn't going to be the match-winner next time out. But I'd got used to the pattern – if there was somebody going to be left out it was going to be me.

When Strauss had his way with the side, he wanted to play three seamers and a spinner. He probably didn't trust me to play as the third seamer. Maybe he was right. I had days when I could be devastating and knock teams over, like with Pakistan at Old Trafford, and there could also be days where I'd bowl 15 overs for 80 and put a lot of pressure on my team.

Thankfully, there were lighter times in that series. When we got to St Lucia during the one-dayers, we couldn't go out. This was 'pedalo island'. Fred couldn't go anywhere, didn't want to go anywhere, as everybody was wanting to see him because of what had happened before, so we were confined to barracks and would often send out for food, the dish of choice generally being a big bucket of chicken that would feed a family of six.

I love Free and Bad Company so we had that on full blast and were singing at the top of our voices. Dimitri Mascarenhas and Owais Shah were sharing the room next door and could hear the commotion and the noise. In they came to see what was going on. Dimi couldn't believe the amount of food there was.

He asked for a piece of chicken and so I threw one at him. Well, that was it. There was food going everywhere. We were plastered in chicken, coleslaw, the lot. A grown man trying to get into a pedalo was small fry by comparison.

Don't get the wrong idea, we could still be raucous in public too. After one game, we were all in a bar, taking turns getting up on stools singing and Monty wouldn't do it. The crowd were all chanting, "Monty, Monty, give us a song!" He wasn't having any of it. I kept saying to him, "Just get up and sing. Do one of their songs. Just get up and start it. They'll take over!"

In the end, the only way he'd do it was if I stood up next to him. He cleared his throat, got himself prepared – and started singing the national anthem. It was priceless. The crowd was erupting.

When the end came with England the next summer, it did feel like the changing of the guard.

I played the last two games of the Ashes series and that was it. Fred was the same. By this time he was like a stricken battleship, barely mobile but still occasionally firing its guns. Fred decided it was time to be tied up permanently in port, and I knew I had to do the same.

On the final sunny day at the Oval, the longer it went on, the more I was thinking, 'I've had enough.'

In truth, that had started during the first innings, when Stuart Broad took five wickets in no time at all to set us up for a brilliant win.

I remember talking to him on the field because he was getting excited. "Keep your head, this can still go away from us," I warned him, but I could see what a great bowler he was going to be for England for years to come.

At the other end was Jimmy Anderson. All me and Fred could do was watch these two from mid-on and mid-off. I was looking at him, he was looking at me. We were both thinking the same thing, 'I can't go on with this.'

Professionalism was changing, I was old school. If I went on tour, I'd be just someone to be wheeled out when someone got injured. I looked at Fred, and it occurred to me that the only person I had anything in common with was leaving at the end of the game. 'What's the point?' I thought. 'I'm a dinosaur. I'll finish this game and walk off.'

At the end, me and Fred were walking round the ground for ages and we stayed on the pitch for a long time. He wanted to be with his mate because he knew he'd gone, and I wanted to be with my mate because I knew I'd gone as well.

"That's it," I said. "That's me done." We were the last ones off the pitch. There was no emotion whatsoever. I'd run my race. The emotion for me was sitting in the dressing room afterwards and looking round at Jimmy Anderson, Stuart Broad, Alastair Cook, fantastic players who would take the team to the next level. I felt so happy.

Like 2005, me and Fred had our photo taken in the dressing room, same photo, same position, except now we were four years older, four years wiser.

We talked about what this team would achieve, and how great it was going to be. At the same time we were talking about how enough was enough. Going back to 1996 when we first pulled on an England shirt in Pakistan together, and now, in 2009, finishing at the Oval together, it all just felt right.

I spent time with my family in the dressing room, with Troy Cooley, and then went into the Australian dressing room, talking to Brad Haddin and Ben Hilfenhaus about people we'd played with. At 11 o'clock, when the Aussies left, me, Fred, and Graham Onions left and went back to the hotel.

Later, we sat in the hotel bar in our whites until four in the morning. This time a lot of the other players stuck around. To me it felt like the celebration we should have had in 2005, but then photo-opportunities for people outside the game came first.

When Andrew Strauss was asked at the end of the Test, "What are the celebrations going to be like?" he replied, "Muted." And that was a reaction to 2005. In 2009, we propped a bar up and had a few pints, and that, for me, was perfect.

Andy Flower spoke to me and I was honest with him. "I can go to South Africa and Bangladesh on the winter tour if you want," I told him. "But I'm not sure I can get through it."

Basically, I was retiring without actually saying so. I never saw the point unless I literally had nothing left to give. I could still theoretically play for England, but the reality was my lifestyle and my body were starting to let me down. If you go away in the winter, you have to be available to play in the summer again. You have to be part of the whole thing. Also, I hated not playing, and if I went to South Africa, chances are I'd barely get a game. I hated being on England tours and being 12th man.

For the money, I could probably have gone on another couple of tours, but the fact that I wasn't going to play meant the financial side didn't matter. I never played cricket for money. It was about playing and winning. The money was great. I'm not going to bullshit people and say that side of it isn't welcome. But I never made a decision about whether I was fit or unfit, injured or not injured, that had any financial implications. I just wanted to play – the rest of it would look after itself. Even now when I talk to younger players, I say, "Back your ability, the money will look after itself."

Before the squad was announced, Flower rang out of courtesy and said he wasn't going to pick me. He basically asked me if I wanted to get in first – if I wanted to announce I was going to retire. "Thanks very much," I told him. "But I'm not going to. If you ever need me I'll be there."

I didn't really think I'd ever play international cricket again but if I went away and played for Durham, got 50 or 60 wickets and England had an injury crisis, were 1-1 going to the Oval with Jimmy or Broad injured and I was taking wickets for fun, I'd still want to be in a position where someone could ring up and ask if I wanted to play.

And, knowing me, I'd have said yes. If you retire it makes things like that a much bigger deal. I still wanted to be a viable option.

25

SHOT

*"By the end, me and Paul Collingwood didn't get on.
He had a different outlook. He did things his way, I did
things mine"*

Durham Second XI v Scotland A - Chester-le-Street, May 2, 2013

I'm standing at the top of my mark.

It's a freezing cold day in Chester-le-Street and I'm playing for
Durham seconds against Scotland A.

*Even the one man and his dog hasn't shown up for this one. As I run in I
feel every day of my 34 years. The body isn't what it used to be. If I was
a car I'd be in the scrapyard not the forecourt. Everything feels a struggle,
everything aches, and as I approach the crease – aaghh - I feel my hamstring
go. I know straight away that this is it. When I walk off this pitch in 30
seconds time, it will be forever. Behind me are 211 first-class matches.
Ahead of me is, well, who knows?*

*It's no great shock, no great surprise. I've been feeling like a dinosaur for
some time. Recently, I was standing at slip and there were two young lads next*

to me – Paul Coughlin and Ryan Buckley. I was just messing about, talking bollocks. "Buckley," I asked. "When were you born?" It was something stupid, in the mid-'90s. "For Christ's sake, that was when I made my debut on this ground."

"Coughers, when were you born?" Again, it was in the '90s. "I played before you were even born!"

So this day has been long overdue. Maybe four years overdue. If I'm honest, I should have retired after the Ashes in 2009, walked off at the Oval against Australia and never played again. Sounds a bit better than Scotland A.

There's no great emotion in this moment. I've walked off pitches with an injury many times before and this feels like just another.

Bag packed, I get in my car and drive home.

And that, as they say, is that.

From 2009 onwards, I lost focus and the drive to get fit because, even though I hadn't retired from international cricket, I knew I wasn't going to stand on the big stage again.

I couldn't go back into county cricket and consistently perform in front of empty stands and enjoy it. By the end it must have been embarrassing for some people to watch.

Whereas bits of me had always hurt, everything hurt now. It was taking me longer to get out of bed in the morning, and I had to take more tablets just to get through the day. In the meantime, I was looking round the dressing room and thinking how my mentality was different. A more professional attitude was apparent, the gap was getting bigger.

It did not help that the season before I packed it all in, Paul Collingwood, the Durham captain, had farmed me out to Yorkshire behind my back. The first time I knew anything was happening was when I got a phone call from Michael Vaughan, asking if I'd like to join them. But I wasn't stupid, I knew the move would have been orchestrated by Colly.

I told Vaughany not to say anything because I'd see Colly the next day. Next morning, I had it out with him. "You should have told me first," I told him. "That's what's fucked me off."

By the end, me and Paul Collingwood didn't get on.

He had a different outlook. He did things his way, I did things mine and although I had huge respect for him – we shared a dressing room for 20 years after all – we had some massive professional differences. It seemed to me that, while the rest of us would be blamed and disciplined, he got away with a ridiculous amount of stuff. Nobody could party better than Colly, he was the life and soul of everything, but he never seemed to get caught.

Not only that, but we drank in different circles, we were different people. A lot of the time the only time we saw each other on tours was on the plane from Newcastle to London and then the one back again.

As the years have passed, me and Colly have got on a lot better. We had quite a frosty relationship at the end of my career but, for me, that's all gone – life's too short.

When you're retired in your mid-30s, to say you're not going to bother with someone is daft. We had a common goal. Some of the best catches I have ever seen were by him off my bowling, not just for England but for Durham – ct Collingwood, b Harmison, there was at least one a game.

Fletcher loved him – but that wasn't why he got picked for England. Paul Collingwood was a great cricketer for his country. There were county cricketers with more talent but when it came to the mentality of getting the best out of himself, and being a fighter, he was in the top three in the world and you have to respect him for that.

Since I retired, we've ended up doing Sky punditry together. The first time it happened, he made a joke. "Me and you on Sky together is the most we've spoken in about 10 years!"

I was at Loch Lomond with him recently for a golf day and I was helping him write a press release about being captain of Durham and signing a one-year contract. There were people there saying, "Hang on! You two didn't really get on!" and we didn't.

We had a different outlook on the game, but that's gone. I'd like to think my relationship with him now is a good one. He's the captain of the club I love and worked tirelessly for across 18 years. Anything that happened in the past was professional differences. We're grown men. We should be able to say, "Whatever happened, happened. That was your opinion, this was mine. We never agreed, but it's gone."

I've shared a lot of good times with people, but whether they're going to be a long-term part of my life or a passing drink and a shake of the hand, you never know. I've got no agenda with anybody. I believe you let bygones go.

By the time I went to Yorkshire, I was playing on reputation not ability. The young lads there must have been thinking, 'Who is this? He used to be number one bowler in the world and now he can't bowl a hoop downhill.'

I didn't so much feel embarrassed as start thinking, 'What am I doing here?' It hit me how, from a reputation and personal point of view, I should have left the game when I was in a much better place. The body was always going to pack up but more than anything, it was the performances that disappointed me. Wide down the leg side, wide down the off side, visually it must have looked like watching an old heavyweight boxer who shouldn't have been in the ring.

Yorkshire also had these figure-hugging shirts and I was about two stone overweight. I had to bowl with my jumper on every day because I didn't want anyone to see my belly hanging out!

One thing does stand out from my time at Yorkshire, though. At the Rose Bowl, at Hampshire, on a pitch that was doing all sorts, I sat in awe and watched a young man score a double hundred. I rang Neil Fairbrother while the game was going on. "I'm watching an unbelievable player," I told him. "Forget Lions and the Academy, this lad is good enough to play for England now." Step forward Joe Root.

Back at Durham in 2013, I found myself at a club where I was never going to play. I was contracted, but Colly didn't want me around.

I met up with him, Durham chief executive David Harker and Geoff Cook. "You've got an expensive problem," I told them. "Because I'm not going anywhere. I've got one year left on my contract, I'll get myself fit to play and if you don't pick me fair enough."

When I then tore my hamstring in the Scotland game, that was it. "I'm going," I told Colly. "You don't want me in this dressing room because you're not going to pick me, and you don't need me in this dressing room because people know there's a divide. If they're not in the team, they'd rather come over to me and whinge about the management than address why they're not performing, get their heads down and work at it. It's probably better if I'm not here so I'm not coming back," I told him.

And I didn't. I haven't properly been back to this day.

As England players, one thing me and Colly did share was the misconception of the Durham members that we didn't want to play for our county.

They couldn't have been more wrong if they'd tried. Going back to Durham meant everything to me. In fact, one of my biggest bugbears with central contracts was that I wasn't allowed to play as much for Durham as I wanted to, and needed to.

Duncan Fletcher got a lot of criticism for not letting me bowl enough, because giving me a week off was effectively like sending me back to the beginning again.

The problem was the ECB had to manage the counties so if Harmison plays for Durham, then Trescothick has to play for Somerset, Vaughan for Yorkshire, Flintoff for Lancashire, etc.

If it happened for one county, they'd all be expecting it. A lot of it was politics. Not only that, but other players were in Fletcher's ear saying they didn't want to play for their counties between internationals because they were having a break or they'd promised the wife they were going away for a few days.

I used to get criticised a lot for being undercooked as a bowler, but a lot of the time I got no say in it.

I loved my time at the club so much that favourite memory as a cricketer – I'd put it above even winning the Ashes in 2005 – came in a Durham shirt, when we won the Championship on the last day of the season at Canterbury in 2008.

It was a crazy match, not helped by me spending half the game with a broken wrist after Geraint Jones belted one at me when I was fielding at gully. Callum Thorp had run through their top order but then there was a lull and it looked like they might hang on for a draw. The coaching staff were getting more and more agitated and in the end, I told the physio to strap me up so I could go on. He refused. "I'm going to go on," I told him. "Even if it's just to stand there."

In the end, they relented, and on I went. 'Sod it,' I thought, 'I'm going to have a bowl.'

When you get down past number six, the intimidation factor starts to kick in.

They're not bothered that you've got a broken arm and it's going 70 miles an hour. To them, you're 6ft 5in, running down the hill at Canterbury, and they're in the line of fire.

On a fast and bouncy pitch there are some people you don't want to face. I'm one of them.

I wasn't bothered about the pain in my wrist and the fact it was going all over the shop, I was doing a job for the team. I took the last two wickets in consecutive balls and the sight of Martin Saggers' stumps being flattened to seal the win is one that remains with me now.

It had been 12 years since I'd first pulled on a Durham shirt, and now here we were, county champions. An awful lot of people had worked tremendously hard to bring Durham to this point and it was an emotional moment for them all. It was also reward for Dale Blenkenstein, one of the game's good guys, always trying to win games and the best captain I ever played for.

Durham had bucked the trend. When they started out, cricket in this area was elitist, but they turned their back on that and cast their net wide. They got Ben Stokes from Cockermouth, myself, my brother Ben and now Mark Wood from Ashington, Shotley Bridge for Paul Collingwood, Gateshead Fell for Graham Onions.

These weren't affluent areas. They were mining towns, pit

villages. Geoff Cook identified these kids from little towns and gave them a life in professional cricket. Some had three years, some had 10, I had 20.

I like to think that when Colly finally finishes playing cricket we'll both have something to do with Durham's future, and try to help them get back on the right foot after they were so heavily penalised by the ECB at the end of 2016 – penalised, as far as I could see, for doing everything the ECB had asked them to do, developing a Test ground, fitting floodlights and becoming a major venue.

The ECB encouraged Durham to do all that and has now punished them for getting into debt doing so. Perhaps if the ECB hadn't given Durham Test matches in May, the club might have got better crowds and, in 2016, they gave us a Test in the same week the England football team played at Sunderland.

That, to me, suggests that, when it came to Durham and international cricket, people at the ECB were either disorganised or didn't care.

Ian Botham has been named as the new chairman and nothing against Beefy, but I think that can only work so long as he's got some financial experts in alongside him. I see Beefy as the figurehead rather than the spearhead of Durham's recovery. One thing's for sure, with the talent we have in this area, Durham will be back.

26

CRICKET'S PROBLEM

*"When I saw Trott interviewed after coming home, I
thought, 'Wow, he's not poorly, he's weak'"*

It might seem strange to address cricket's problem by first
talking about a footballer, but there you go.

I first met Gary Speed at a golf day he'd organised
up the road at Morpeth. At that point he lived not far from
Ashington and, over the years, with going into Newcastle to
train as well, I got to know him well. As a professional he was
unreal. Sometimes we'd do the gym sessions as partners and
what I saw was a very strong man, someone with an aura about
him, a glow. Like Alan Shearer, he had the stature of greatness.
For me, to be that close to watching Gary train was like being in
the Durham dressing room at 17 watching David Boon walking
past.

On November 27, 2011, all that changed. I couldn't believe

what I was hearing – Gary had been found hanged in the garage of his home in Cheshire. There's not many times I've shed tears, but I did at that time.

Just hours before, Steve Harper and Alan Shearer had been watching Newcastle play at Old Trafford. When I spoke to Alan and Harps about it, they could barely speak. The Newcastle coach John Carver was the same.

Mention Speedo to people who were that close to him and they literally can't talk. I totally understand why. On a football team, like cricket, players are with the same people every day, training with them, travelling, eating. They stay in that circle because it's hard to trust people from outside. There was a good core at Newcastle of players who stuck together. To them, Gary was a family member. My first thoughts were with Gary's family, but for the people at Newcastle, to lose one of their own like that was tragic.

One thing everyone who knew Gary was sure of was that he'd never shown any sign of anything being wrong, and that just shows how bottling something up can have grave consequences. Gary had moved on from his playing career when he died, but his death illustrates why it's so important that all sportspeople keep an eye on their teammates.

As the years went on, those I shared a dressing room with knew, if I'd gone quiet, that I was having one of my bad days. At the same time, if I saw someone having a bad time, I'd be worrying. I'd be thinking, 'What is it? Are they just having an off day? Or is it something more?' As teammates, you have to look after each other.

Cricket has moved on from when I started and is now one of the most open sports when it comes to mental health issues.

Football maybe is a different environment to come out and say you're experiencing issues. It's a bit more rough and ready, working-class, up and at 'em, a place for strong men. When you look at people's sexuality, I'm not sure I'd be relishing what the first person to come out as gay in modern football is going to get when it comes to the stick off the terraces. But I think, be it with sexuality or mental health, a player would be fine in the dressing room. They'd get some stick, but it would be to make them feel OK, not to have a go. It would be much worse to tiptoe around it and for it to feel awkward. That's how dressing rooms are. You take the mick out of each other but it's all about being in a team, it's a part of everyone feeling involved and accepted.

That's why I wonder if dressing rooms where people talk three or four different languages can ever truly be united.

The fact that sportspeople are increasingly talking about mental health can only be a positive and there are organisations out there, like Opening Up Cricket, that are doing amazing work in helping those who need help and support.

In cricket, we've had not only Marcus Trescothick, but Michael Yardy, who approached me in India during the 2006 ICC Trophy.

His issues very much revolved around being away from home and the feelings it was causing him. "Yards," I said to him. "You're describing me there!" He was talking about packing in, not playing international cricket if this was what was going to happen. I tried to talk him through my mechanisms to get through each day. I told him my door would always be open because I know the desperation of needing someone to talk to. "Don't fight this on your own," I told him. "People close to you might not understand what's happening to you, but you've got to at least put it out there."

Michael got through to the end of the trip and decided he wasn't going to play anymore at that level. He got help and it's done him the world of good. Michael's a man's man, a tough man. But when you're in an environment like an England tour and you're in the sub-continent, you're all in the same boat.

Whether people think it's soft to go and knock on someone's door and talk about it, I don't know. But for me, you're more of a man if you tell someone.

Monty Panesar is another who's spoken about his issues. I didn't see Monty happening at all. Outwardly, he appeared a quiet man who kept himself to himself. Seeing him suffer was a surprise. It seemed to me that Monty's problems began when he moved away from familiar surroundings at Northamptonshire.

Sometimes the grass isn't always greener on the other side and when you add in not having family around, and the support network you're familiar with, then it can all add up. A support network in any walk of life is massive, but for cricket it's huge.

To be able to go back to a settled structure after you've been away, be it for a day or longer, means so much. If you leave that behind, and you're on your own, sometimes the bright lights can gobble you up.

When I saw Monty going through what he did, it was heartbreaking. He was a good guy, one who should still be playing county cricket with a top team. But the mind is a mysterious thing and once it gets a grip of you and knocks your confidence, it's a very difficult thing to escape from. Monty seems to have struggled to do that.

When it comes to Jonathan Trott's illness, it's not that I

question it, but I'd like to know deep down what the problem is.

The statements he's made, the things he's said, and the language he's used, makes me wonder if he just pulled the ladder up because the game got too hard.

When he came back early from Australia after being bombarded by Mitchell Johnson and used the word 'nutcase,' while talking about what had happened, I found that puzzling. For me someone who's got mental health problems doesn't use that terminology.

When I saw Trott interviewed after coming home, I thought, 'Wow, he's not poorly, he's weak.' A mental health issue would be spoken about in a completely different way to how he was doing it.

He was describing someone who was mentally not very strong, not mentally poorly. The words he was using and the way he was describing it made me think he just didn't fancy it. I hope it was mistranslation, but I will always have a nagging doubt in the back of my mind that Trott left the tour because he thought it was tough, rather than because he was ill. It didn't sit right with me.

I'd played against Trott before they picked him for his debut against Australia in 2009. I didn't question his overall ability, but I did question his ability to play the short ball in Test cricket.

Durham played against Warwickshire and Graham Onions bowled from one end and me from the other, and we were aggressive. Trott ran away from the short ball, he backed off from it. It was talked about on the Durham bus on the way back.

When he was called up to play in that last Test I couldn't help feeling that, against the Aussie quicks, including Johnson, on a fast Oval pitch, this could be interesting. In the end, he got runs, which was brilliant, but eventually he did get found out.

I want to believe that Trott was poorly, that how he explained it came out wrong, but he seems to have tied cricket and mental health together, whereas mental illness happens whatever. That's what makes me think it's a mental toughness issue, not mental health.

I'm not trying to have a go at him. In fact, when I heard he was coming back from Australia, I wondered if I should get in touch and see if there was anything I could do.

I hope he has genuinely come through a mental illness and made it to the other side because that's an amazing achievement and I know what that feels like. I just feel a little bit of clarity was lacking.

Either way, the most important point is this: there is help out there, whether you're a professional cricketer, a part-time cricketer or just a member of the public who has picked this book up. Don't be afraid to ask for it – the stigma attached to cricket's problem keeps improving by the day, and that is something I'm delighted about.

27

WHO AM I?

"Finishing as a cricketer is like carrying heavy shopping out of the supermarket and not knowing where your car is"

The state I'm in at the moment is no good for anybody. I felt like I'd stepped into a void when I left cricket. It had been my life. Now, nothing.

I'd gone from being told what to do, what to wear, where to be, what to eat, everything laid out in front of me, to being in the house all the time, getting under everyone's feet. I had nothing coming in money-wise, just bits and bobs. It felt like I'd lost everything. What was I?

Instead of training every day, I was drinking every day, because I had nothing else to do. I'd wake up feeling ill, go for a game of golf and by the third pint I'd be feeling good about myself again.

Then I'd get up feeling even worse the next day and do it again – and again, and again. It became a vicious circle. I'd drink to get to sleep, drink to get myself happy but, in fact, I was just was making things worse. Alcohol was the worst thing in the world I could do. It's a dangerous road to go down, and so it proved. Me and Hayley weren't doing great at the time. I can't imagine me being a great person to live with full stop, but those two years after I packed up it was hard for her — hard for us.

It wasn't a case of wanting to be doing something different or being somewhere else — I love my wife and I love my family — but I was on a road to self-destruction.

At the same time, I'd got hooked on sleeping tablets towards the end of my career and trying to come off them was a nightmare. I was only going to go on them for a little bit but in the end, I was popping them every night for three years. If I didn't have them, I didn't sleep and if I didn't sleep I was in a mess. I tried to come off sleeping tablets when I finished cricket because I thought cricket was my problem.

But I hadn't realised how dependent I was. It took me a long time, six months, to get off them. It was tough, two good days, two bad days. Add into the mix the pressure of not having a job and it wasn't a very good time at all.

Finishing as a cricketer is like carrying heavy shopping out of the supermarket and not knowing where your car is.

All the time your shoulders are getting heavier and heavier and you've no idea where you should be going. The longer it goes on, the more the pressure. In the county game, players don't earn massive amounts of money but at 35, when they're finished, they've still got their wives, still got their kids, still got their mortgage. Those shopping bags are getting heavier. You can see why it gets too much for people. Something has to give. It's like coming out the army into civvy street.

In the normal world, someone my age is at the peak of their career but, for me, that career has gone.

The divorce rates, the suicide rates, the propensity to suffer mental health issues, that's all part of what happens when a cricketer comes to the end. I totally understand that. If someone was in my shoes who'd not had the career I had and the money I earned, I can see why they might go under. We've been fortunate that we've had money put aside, but that money won't last forever. The less it gets, the bigger the strain on us as a family.

At the same time, I'm spending more and more time in my own head, and that's a dangerous place. I'm scared of hours of emptiness. I hate emptiness. I get itchy feet. Hayley goes mad. I can't sit still. I'm not a big TV man. If I find something I like I'll watch the whole thing on a boxset until six o'clock in the morning. I'm a bit OCD like that. I have demons, I know that! But I hate being in the house.

I think that goes back to touring, spending so much time in places I didn't want to be. I feel like I want to get out. I've got to be doing something. I don't like sitting by myself. That's when I start thinking negatively. I'm scarred by touring, being in hotel rooms on my own. Even though there are other people nearby, you are still by yourself. It's a team environment but once the dressing room door closes, it's very much you and your thoughts. I need to do something for my own sanity more than anything else.

I'd love to go back into Durham in some capacity, working

with the Academy, the kids. I'd like to take what I know into the cricketing environment, but you've got to have badges, qualifications, and I'm not a massive fan of that.

There'll be forms to fill in, and I wouldn't be able to do it. Why it has to be like that, I don't know. Trying to improve people doesn't come out of textbooks, it comes from experience.

Qualifications aren't everything. When Graeme Fowler was running the academy at Durham University, he said himself how frustrating it was having an asset like me on his doorstep and not being able to use it.

I applied to be an England selector the last time the position came up. I got an automated email to say I wasn't successful. The same email that Joe Bloggs, 3rd XI captain, would have received if he'd applied. I was disappointed, but at the same time couldn't stop laughing at how ridiculous it was.

I told Michael Vaughan and he was spewing. He went public with it, saying it was a disgrace. I then got a letter off England managing director Paul Downton saying sorry.

After another 5-0 thrashing in Australia, and the whole Pietersen saga, I believed England needed someone who'd just come out the game.

I hear Ian Botham talking about picking such and such out of county cricket to play for England. David Gower does the same. But they never see county cricket, so how can they judge?

Others forget what it's like to play. I sat at the back of the commentary box once listening to Atherton having a go at KP. 'Hang on,' I thought. 'You two blokes averaged late 30s and you're having a go at a bloke whose average is in the 50s?' But that's how TV is and that's how you earn a crust. You have to be critical to keep your job.

I do stints for Sky but if I ever felt I had to be critical just to make money, I'd move on. I'm always aware of other players who went from the game to the commentary box and started knocking people. I never liked that, and I don't want to be one of them. It's not always easy, but I believe you can be honest without putting the boot in.

The commentary box appeals to some people because it replicates the dressing room. But I find it hard sometimes. It can be a little bit selfish, a dog eat dog world where some people are trying to reach for the top, trying to get themselves a contract or on to the next level, and will do so by any which way. I had that in the dressing room and I hated it.

As much as I'd love to be part of the Test match team and sit in the box commentating on England's successes, I'm quite happy to do what I do. I think I give something different, not just a different accent, a different place, but someone who has been through everything. I don't think there's a topic where I've not got first-hand experience – suffering on tour, winning Ashes, losing Ashes, terrorist attacks, playing with greats and helping young players come through. Not to mention being the best bowler in the world and *that* first ball in Brisbane – you can't get higher and lower than that! There's not many situations I haven't been through, not many people who've done it my way. I hope that's what they see in me.

I can see what the BBC radio guys see in me – I've got the face for it! I love radio, it's relaxed and you can paint the picture, help the listener visualise what's going on. I also like it because you can be imaginative in how you fill the time when nothing is happening, whereas on the TV discussion tends more often than not to fall into how badly someone is playing and who can replace them. I don't like to sit around, talking about ending somebody's career. I never minded listening to the commentators as a player. I couldn't care less if they said bad things about me because I was quite thick-skinned and strong-minded and, also, , if somebody like Michael Holding had a relevant point, then all information was gratefully received.

The problem English cricket has is that top-class talent and knowledge is too often lost to the media. It's much better paid for a lot of ex-players to go into TV than back into cricket. Nasser's another who would be a great fit for a leading role with England but, instead, he's spent his retirement in the commentary box.

Media work comes and goes, there aren't many cricket jobs, academically I wasn't the best and I'm probably dyslexic – finding something to do has become tough.

Don't get me wrong, we live in a nice house with nice things. It's just that, at present, I'm living a slightly aimless life, not working consistently and spending too much time in the pub.

Time is starting to weigh on my shoulders. I need to find the right challenge, whether that's cricket or otherwise. I need something that's going to get the juices flowing so that the second chapter of my life is as good as the first.

Managing Ashington FC has been a bonus because it's allowed me some focus. I was always watching games on a Saturday and enjoyed being in and around the club, so when the opportunity to manage arose, I thought, 'Why not?' It was always going to be a publicity nightmare, but people who know me knew why I was doing it – I've been around the Northern League for most of my life with one family member or another. The others? I don't care what they think. I've enjoyed moulding the team. There's been some good characters at Ashington, complex characters, and I can see my former cricketing teammates in them – the jokers, the more serious ones, the know-alls, and the idiots.

I'm more of a relaxed character than someone who shouts and bawls and screams. The minute someone shouted, bawled, or screamed in any dressing room I was in, I was looking at the wall. I'd rather talk things through, try to work things out. Referees, I'll admit, can be an exception. I was handed a 12-match ban after I made my feelings known to a ref who should've sent one of their players off. It was a fuss over nothing. He made it sound much worse than it was and I had it reduced on appeal. That's the thing with referees at that level, you can't say anything to them or they'll have you.

Football gave me the chance to stay in the dressing room environment. Do I miss playing cricket? Not one bit. My body tells me that every day. But I miss the dressing room, the people and the characters I played alongside.

Every time I meet them, which tends to be once in a blue moon, I greet them with warm affection and then they're gone again. I miss them a lot. Players leave the dressing room and struggle to get back to normal life. And I'm one of them.

Getting back to normal life is hard. When the PCA asked me to get involved as an ambassador and talk about the transition, I was keen. I went round the counties and my message to the players was clear – "You've got to think about life after cricket." My plan wasn't great. Financially I was secure but the void was massive.

To go overnight from the routine and order of a cricketing

life to not having any drive or focus makes a person vulnerable. The PCA has been brilliant in helping people take the necessary steps. I know what it's like to be in a rut and that's the dangerous bit. All of a sudden alcohol becomes involved and you can't see the woods for the trees.

If I'm honest, I feel like that's where I am right now. I've stood still for a few years and need to get back into something in some shape or form. Cricket, and all the mementos that went with it, the pictures on the walls, the caps, the stumps, were great, but I'm through the other end now. I need to find something else to motivate me and get me going again.

When I do, I'll be away, happy and content. But at the moment I still feel there's a void in my life that I need to fill. It's time to get back to doing something in the cricketing world. Football has given me a release, but if a cricket job came up − coaching the kids or whatever − I'd have to give that the full-time attention it deserved.

Missing the dressing room is a common theme among ex-players, but the upside for me is it's given me time to be around the kids. Taking them to school, picking them up from school, the things that so many people find hectic, hard work, I like. It was something for 20 years I couldn't do, and for that I owe Hayley everything.

My kids could not have had a better mother, not for one minute could I fault her. She has been unbelievable to these four children and that's all I could ask for. At the same time, she's not just been my wife for the best part of 20 years, she's been my best friend, and sometimes my only friend.

From the point we first met, we spent a hell of a lot of time with each other every day and every night. Cricket meant nothing at that point – I'd played one game for Durham. She was working at the council, I was an apprentice bricklayer. I keep joking that she's only with me for me my money and she'll remind me that I was carrying bricks when she first met me, while she had a good job and a car.

When the cricket started properly, Hayley never said she didn't want me to go away, or that I should be doing other things. Instead she took on the responsibility of raising the family. Emily, Abbie and Isabel seemed to appear in no time, and then Charlie as well. We had to get there with a boy eventually! The minute Charlie was born I had the snip. It's not fun. It's the second injection that gets you because, by then, you know how much the first one hurt. Oh no, another one?

The thing I love about my children is they're so close. On Charlie's birthday, every time he got a present off one of his sisters he was giving them a hug. I was quite choked up about it. I was looking at Hayley and thinking how well she's done to bring these four up.

She deserves a gold medal for what she did for them while I was playing cricket. Putting up with me was bad enough, but to bring four kids up as well is amazing. I spent so much of that time concentrating on cricket, being selfish in a way. But as a sportsman you have to be selfish. You have to make sacrifices.

The kids are great. Relationship-wise we're great. It's 'dad' some of the time, 'Big Steve' most of the time – that's what the little two call me.

But I still feel a disconnect with my children, and I feel awful for that. I'm close to them, but I'll probably be closer to my grandchildren than any of my own.

I hope when they read this that they understand why I'm not

so touchy-feely with them. I've tried to let them be what they want to be as much as I possibly can. To come in and be the intense parent when you're only there a quarter of the time is unfair. It upsets me to have that detachment, but it's the way I wanted it because I'd rather me be upset than my kids.

I'd rather take that backward step and see them grow up, not from a distance, but their way and Hayley's way, and their grandparents' way, than get in the way of that myself. Their mam has always been the person who's their friend, who's going to shape them, and she's done an amazing job.

I'm not saying I wasn't a very good dad, but I just wasn't there to be the dad that everybody else has, and that makes me sad sometimes.

On the other hand, my kids have been brought up in such a way I probably didn't need to be there because their mother has been so strong that she's been a mum and dad to all of them. They're used to that, which means their routines are all around mum and not with dad. I'd rather they were content than try to muscle in on everything they have with Hayley.

That relationship is an unbreakable thing.

I could console myself that I was putting money in the bank, and the kids have got the security of a little leg-up in life when they need it. That's what I'd think when I was back at home and they said they'd rather do something else than be with me.

The lads all used to laugh at me about having a family really young, but when I get to 40 my kids will be either grown up or teenagers, whereas a lot of them have got it all to come.

The flipside of that is they'll see their children growing up. I could have seen mine more, but the question is do you be selfish and drag them away from familiar surroundings, sticking them in hotels around England and the world, so they're missing school and normal life?

Or do you let them get on with what they're doing while you're getting on with what you're doing and try to pinch some time with them in between? All you can do is hope that by the end of it, everyone understands it's been worthwhile. It has its upsides and its downsides.

The upside is we have the life we have. Emily has been to Australia five times. She's had a real travelling life. Some of the trips she probably can't remember going on, others will have left a big mark on her.

The downside is that, as a cricketer, family life takes a backward step. You get used to that being the way and even now, in retirement, I'm selfish. I still think of my time as my own. I'm used to doing what I do. It's very difficult when you've been one type of person for so long to try to be something different or change what you do. Not that I think of myself as a cricketer anymore. Kids have a habit of pulling me up short on that one. To the youngsters at Ashington Cricket Club, I'm just a fat old man. "I think he used to play cricket, although not by the look of him!"

When it comes to the demons I've had and what I've had to go through, no way would I change it for what we've got for the children and with the children.

I live in an area that can be heart-breaking. There's no jobs, it's very, very difficult. When we had the pits and the aluminium plant, there were jobs here. But there's nothing now.

They're spending money on the main street, but in the last

few years it's just been betting shop, charity shop, fish shop.

Sometimes I think the football club and the cricket club are all that keep any continuity with the past going. But things are changing. There's talk of a new train line going from Ashington to Newcastle and that will make a lot of difference. The county council is moving here as well. The north-east has been left behind too long and hopefully we can be at the heart of the revival.

I look at my brothers and my sister and I'm so proud of them because of what they've achieved for themselves. They've all got nice houses, they're all married, they've all got great kids, and they've all worked tirelessly hard to get themselves in a position to work and make themselves better. If I hadn't had this great family I don't know what might have happened. I'm just thankful I wasn't in that situation.

The family was always huge for me, I always had that big support network. I know that in Ashington there's always somebody here, and if you've got that you've got a great chance of coming out the other side of any problem. Wickets, games, awards, money, honours, none of that matters because to come through what I've been through, and to still have a fantastic wife, a fantastic family and a great support network means the world to me.

If anything happened to Hayley, I don't know where my life would be, emotionally or otherwise. I know the pin number to my bank card and that's about it. She literally does everything.

It's scary what's out there that I haven't got a clue how to do – bills, anything to do with money, everything. I've got a blue card in my pocket with four numbers that I put into a machine, the Queen's face appears and I go to the pub.

Insurance, mortgage, investments, ISAs, I don't know anything. Basically, she's brought up five kids. At the same time she runs her own business, Northumberland Tartan, with business partner Heidi. I sit in a room on one side of the house, reading or watching TV, while in the other, Hayley has her office. There is a mannequin in there that they use to make alterations and I have occasionally had to wear a kilt to see how it fits – it's not a pretty sight!

People ask, "Would you rather have not played cricket and not gone through some of the stuff you have?" and I say, "No." I was a 15-year-old lad who left school with no education. I was going nowhere and I dread to think what might possibly have been. This was a life I chose and, even though it broke me a few times, it never beat me.

Because I didn't crumble and crack, people think I didn't suffer as much as some other people. I would say exactly the opposite. I've suffered as much as other people, I just didn't let on to the extent, and that's why I'm telling this story.

It sounds stupid but other people suffering probably made my own battle easier. I'd spent so long telling myself that my head was not going to beat me that when other people began going under it gave me even more determination. That's why I kept it as quiet as I could right until the end.

When people talk about mental health, they mention Marcus Trescothick, Michael Yardy and Jonathan Trott. My name is never in there even though, arguably, my problems came before anyone else. I had to keep it quiet. My firm belief was that if I 'came out' it would have been the end of my England career.

I had to keep it away from everything. I didn't want it to be headline news. I was happy for it to be portrayed as simply struggles away from home rather than something more deep-seated and serious. I couldn't do anything else because my world would have ended if I'd said to my critics, "Shut up, you don't know the full story." That's why, as far as everyone else was concerned, it had to be homesickness. "Homesick? Well, that's OK. He'll have good days and bad days. Depression? That's it, he's gone."

To say that jacking in cricket would have helped is a total misnomer. I'd have had mental health issues whatever I did with my life. The demons are there if you're a factory worker, a bricklayer, or a banker. It's down to a chemical imbalance in the brain. I still get episodes of depression now. I'll shut the door for four days and that will be that.

Hayley knows exactly when they're coming. I just get more and more down. It used to cause issues because she didn't know why I was like I was. It's still not always easy, although now she just shouts at me, "Are you taking your tablets?" Because a couple of times I've tried to come off them. It hasn't worked, it's been a nightmare, and now I'm happy to be on them forever.

If I have a depressive episode at home, I just try to get through it as best as I can. I try not to show it in front of the kids. They're aware of my problems but we don't really talk about it. They just say, "You're even more miserable than you normally are!" Emily knows all about it because she's the eldest and has seen it in the papers. I always say to my children, for many reasons, "When you Google my name, forget the first two pages!"

It's never easy when depression strikes around the family. At least when I was away they didn't have to see it, but it's unpredictable and can overwhelm me at any time.

One year, before I headed to the subcontinent, we went to

Disneyland Paris because we wanted to make a big song and dance of the kids before I went away. I was sitting there in McDonald's, with my three kids and Hayley, having breakfast, and I was crying my eyes out. Hayley asked why I was crying and I didn't have the faintest idea.

All I knew was I felt ill, I was shaking, I was all over the place. There I was, wanting to have four great days away before going on tour, with Mickey Mouse, Minnie Mouse, my kids having a great time, and I was overcome with emotion and didn't know why. Hayley's having to tell them to go and play because I've got tears running down my face.

People assume if you've got happiness and success in your life, it will be different. But depression doesn't work like that. Once it gets you, you've got it. That's what I'd be more frustrated about than anything else. Good days, bad days – it was out of my control. I hoped it might change eventually, with medication and time, but it never really has. These feelings are, after all, deep-rooted. I've had these emotions from a young age. I've just learned to cope with them better and do what I can to stay positive. I try not to drink as much, and try not to let myself get bored as much.

I play golf at Newbiggin and Longhurst a lot, I sometimes go to Ben's gym for a coffee and then wait for the kids to come home. By that time, my day has been filled.

Throughout everything, both my career and my retirement, I've remained true to myself.

I've never hidden from the decisions I've made in life, and when I've been regretful, I've owned up.

In life I've messed up, but I'd like to think I've paid my dues. I never tried to hide who I was. I never tried to be a different person. I never tried to seem educated or baffle people with science. I was a not very bright lad from the north-east who worked hard to play cricket, worked hard to have a life that I wanted, and sometimes took a backwards step because of things I did or said – not going on a tour, going for a drink when I shouldn't and turning up pissed the next morning (or the next afternoon) – but that was the way I was.

Every time I went on the field I tried my hardest to be the best I could be. If I was good enough, great. If I wasn't good enough, it would never be for the want of trying. The low points never beat me, be they on the field, like making a fool of myself in front of thousands of people with the Brisbane ball, or off it, such as the chronic anxiety I experienced in South Africa in 2004.

Overcoming adversity was one of my strengths throughout my career. I'd come out the other side and that day would be gone. It was the next day that mattered. No point looking back.

If I was good one day, I didn't try to be better the next. I just tried to be the best I possibly could be and hoped that would get me to the point where I wanted to be.

And in an 18-year professional career, it worked, because I had more good days than bad days.

That's why, despite all the trials and tribulations, the negative experiences, I wouldn't swap any of it. I loved playing cricket for England. I loved playing cricket for Durham.

When people read this book, I think they'll say, "I knew he had problems, but I didn't think he was as bad as that." I've been lucky that there have always been good people around me at vital times to help me through my issues, and I would like to thank them all.

I can't say there haven't been some dark times where I thought it'd be easier if I wasn't here. It has, after all, been a long and difficult journey to this point.

One that, as a kid in Ashington, skipping school, football mad, I could never have dreamed of embarking on. And that's what I'm proud of, that it didn't beat me.

I still had a career, still got through it. I saw doctors all over the world, went to the Priory, sat with some of my best mates at ridiculous o'clock, all the time not knowing what the hell was going on inside my head.

But no matter what I was going through, no matter how bad it got, I knew underneath I was never going to let it win. Ever.

The negative side of my personality was the Steve Harmison who was so strong-minded that sometimes he said things he shouldn't have. The positive side was that was the Steve Harmison who was never going to let depression beat him. That is my most crowning glory.

Not 226 Test wickets for England, not an 18-year professional career, that I got through the whole lot without caving in, came out the other end, and put two fingers up to it.

That I'm here to tell the tale.